Also by Louis Rukeyser

How to Make Money in Wall Street

WHAT'S AHEAD for the ECONOMY

Revised and Updated

BY Louis Rukeyser

A TOUCHSTONE BOOK
Published by Simon & Schuster, Inc.
NEW YORK

For BEVERLEY, SUSAN and STACY
in the hope that what's ahead for them
will be beautiful

Copyright © 1983 by Louis Rukeyser
All rights reserved
including the right of reproduction
in whole or in part in any form
First Touchstone Edition, 1985
Published by Simon & Schuster, Inc.
Simon & Schuster Building
Rockefeller Center
1230 Avenue of the Americas
New York, New York 10020
TOUCHSTONE and colophon are registered trademarks of Simon & Schuster, Inc.
Designed by Irving Perkins Associates
Manufactured in the United States of America
10 9 8 7 6 5 4 3 2 1 Pbk.
Library of Congress Cataloging in Publication Data
Rukeyser, Louis.
   What's ahead for the economy.
   (A Touchstone book)
   Includes index.
   1. United States—Economic policy—1981-
I. Title.
HC106.8.R84   1985   338.973   85-2463
ISBN 0-671-55790-4 Pbk.

Contents

discover not just that Government spending should be cut, but that it realistically can be cut—deeply. Along the way: "Yeah—but Where Would You Cut?" . . . World Without End, Amend? . . . A Change in the Wind.

IV: TAKE THE MONEY AND SLOW DOWN 103

Consider Monetary Policy—what it is, what it can and cannot do, and how it might serve us better. Signposts: "Too Clever by Half" . . . Does Money Make the World Go Round? . . . A Policy, Not a Panacea . . . A Golden Rule? . . . A Modest Proposal . . . Get a Horse?

V: YOU CAN BANK ON IT 129

Banking and Credit is one of the most swiftly changing areas in the nation's economy. What do the current changes mean for the typical American? How can we improve the financial health of the system and its customers? A Saving Grace . . . But Will My Money Be Safe? . . . Was It Smart to Be Thrift-y? . . . Are We Borrowing Trouble? . . . An Oscar for Mr. Carter . . . Adjust Society.

VI: LABORING UNDER SOME DELUSIONS 148

Labor is both a victim and a cause of our American economic malaise. Why it's time to separate myth from reality in one of the most emotional areas of U.S. economic life. Who Leads American Labor? . . . Labor's Future: Dilemmas and Possibilities . . . "Unemployment, Unemployment, Unemployment" . . . How to Do the Job.

VII: GIVING US THE BUSINESS 169

Business faces massive problems, self-inflicted and otherwise, but there *are* ways to implement the key advance that would benefit us all: greatly improving U.S. productivity over the next decade.

Capital Formation: The One That Produces Economic
Touchdowns . . . Productivity Growth Is Everybody's
Business . . . "Neo" Nonsense . . . Why Businessmen
Don't Sell the System.

VIII: SEE YOU LATER, REGULATOR   195

Regulations and Restrictions—where things are seldom what they
seem. We discover some ways in which U.S. industry itself hides
behind an overregulated economy, we cast a critical eye on big-
business bailouts and we question whether those who profess to
speak for "the consumer" truly do so. On the Care and Feeding
of Dinosaurs . . . The Bigger They Are, the Softer They Fall?
. . . Success and Failure: The Twin Engines of Genuine
Prosperity . . . The Proper Role for Government . . . Who Really
Wins from Regulation? . . . How to Get Out of This Mess . . . A
Rare Kind of Vice.

IX: GETTING UP THE ENERGY   215

Energy—we point the way to solutions more valid than passing
preoccupations with allegedly permanent crises or gluts.
Doomsday Will Be a Little Late This Year . . . OPEC of
Trouble . . . The Real Answer on Energy . . . What the
Government Could Try . . . Of Men and Caribou.

X: MY BOUNTY LIES OVER THE OCEAN   230

On Foreign Policy: How we Americans are nothing if not fair—
having hobbled our domestic economic policy with an array of ill-
conceived governmental interventions, we have been more than
willing to do the same to our foreign economic policy as well.
Who are the players, what are the policies and where are the
possibilities? A Policy, Not a Retreat . . . Folly Number
One: "Please Kick" . . . Too Good a Friend at Chase
Manhattan? . . . Folly Number Two: Put Up a Wall . . . How
to Deal with Friends—and Enemies.

The Individual's role is crucial, for in the end a better American economy must be the product of the nation's people, not its political leaders. What are the specific steps that ordinary citizens can take to safeguard their own financial future, while at the same time trying to help the country's? You Can Be a Capitalist, Too . . . The Intelligent Economic Consumer . . . What More We Can Do.

Finally, the challenge is to produce a freer and more prosperous American economy. Happy surprise: The gloomsters are wrong; the mood of the people is changing, and we do have a chance. Our grandchildren will not forgive us if we fail to seize it. Why I'm Still an Optimist . . . It's Up to Us Now.

The Still-Possible Dream

One of the more engaging characteristics of the American spirit is the capacity to argue endlessly over precisely what that spirit is. It is a debate that often strikes foreigners, even those with a passing fondness for us and our peculiar ways, as quaint and juvenile: What makes us think we're so special? A Frenchman, after all, is usually French because historically his family happens to have been French. There is nothing overtly ideological about being Norwegian. A South Indian, speaking Malayalam and gazing across the palmy beaches of Kerala, is merely doing what generations of his ancestors have done; it was no more a conscious choice for him than for the cows he will not kill. My wife comes from the Isle of Man, a lovely droplet in the Irish Sea; I once innocently asked my father-in-law how long his family had lived there. He looked at me with astonishment before replying: "Always." It is not an answer that you are likely to encounter frequently in Denver or Minneapolis.

We are an invented nation, and this unusual fact pervades everything from our architecture to, inescapably, our economics. To deny this is to miss the point of America, its strengths and its failings alike. Travelers occasionally feel that the patriotism of any country other than their own is somehow bizarre, as anyone knows who has ever stood self-consciously in a foreign movie theater for an unfamiliar national anthem or watched strangely uniformed troops parade with a different step. But Americans often act like alien tourists in their own land, searching feverishly for an understanding of their own national character. And, given the notorious brevity of the U.S. attention span, our perception of ourselves varies rapidly and dramatically; in the course of a single

11

generation, the national self-image may swing from complacent infallibility to shamed embarrassment. (When I spoke on college campuses a dozen or so years ago, I found such wallowing in presumed national guilt that the biggest debate was between those who were sure we were the most immoral people in 4,000 years and those who thought we were only the worst in 2,000.) Even now, many Americans continue to react against what they see as a jingoistic tradition of proudly separate national identity. Their effort is as vain as it is misguided. For America in the end is absolutely inseparable from its essential ideas of itself; these ideas, after all, are why we are here.

But are we entitled to the dream when reality so often mocks it? No, say the angry revisionists; it was violence that really was as American as apple pie, the slaves did not come here as eager applicants for capitalist prosperity, we demeaned our women and oppressed our minorities and built a nation that was a sham. Yet I wonder—especially after more than a decade as a newsman abroad, watching how scores of other societies all over the globe organize themselves and offer or deny opportunities to their people. America may not have been as good as we once were taught, but it certainly is not as bad as we have come to think. A friend of my foreign-correspondent days once oversimplified the world like this: "There's only one thing you have to know about a country— are people trying to get in or get out?" The original ideas of America, even when imperfectly realized, as they surely are today, remain demonstrably more alive and powerful than their numerous detractors assert. And it may be that the time has come, in this chronically troubled American economy, to consult these underlying ideas again more respectfully.

Much has been made in recent years of the discomforting gap between promise and performance. This does not, as cynics suggest, necessarily invalidate the worthiness of the dream that lured our ancestors and whetted our parents' ambitions. On the contrary, it emphasizes what I would contend lies at its heart: a sense of striving. Without a clearer sense of what the American spirit truly entails, and requires, we will continue to flounder, both internationally and in improving the lives of our own people. That we have floundered so conspicuously for the last generation is attributable in significant measure to our fading national sense of self.

Our salvation, politically and economically, may lie in our ability to recapture and rekindle that sense of America's essence.

What that sense should be is, of course, a subject for endless argumentation. (Breathes there a politician with soul so dead who never to himself has said, "Thomas Jefferson would have been on my side"?) We pick our ancient facts to suit our present prejudices, but the feeling in this corner is that there is at bottom an identifiable American philosophical tradition that goes far beyond conventional Fourth of July oratory—and that could be amazingly helpful to us in sorting out the perplexing economic problems of the Twenty-first Century. It is a tradition rooted in two main ideas: the right of freedom and the chance to live better.

Now, it does not take the most acute analyst in the Western world to note that these two ideas may occasionally appear to be in conflict. Indeed, that seeming conflict has frequently led not to rational compromise but to economic chaos and malaise. Right from the start, then, we must understand that the words of the sentence are not interchangeable: we are not talking about "the *chance* of freedom and the *right* to live better." America is not, and never successfully has been, about the forcible redistribution of wealth; it is, most decisively, about the creation of wealth. The hordes of immigrants were not drawn to America by the misapprehension that this country's millionaires would soon be dissolving their estates and passing out the proceeds to all comers. What lured our ancestors here was the chance to build a better, freer life *through their own efforts*. Even when we turned, amid what we perceived as dire necessity, to a more interventionist, redistributionist role for the Federal Government, we did so reluctantly and with almost palpable distaste. Franklin Delano Roosevelt spoke scathingly of the dangers of a permanent "dole," and warned that temporary relief measures could turn into an undesirable narcotic. His predecessor, Jefferson, had sounded even more like Adam Smith in his first Inaugural Address: "A wise and frugal government . . . shall restrain men from injuring one another, . . . shall leave them otherwise free to regulate their own pursuits of industry and improvement, and shall not take from the mouth of labor the bread it has earned." There was considerably less ambiguity about the American dream then.

But most Americans, plainly, are neither historians nor ideologues. They perceive injustice around them, and lately many have been made painfully aware that the system has failed to deliver to them personally the economic promises they thought it had made. When inflation wipes out virtually all the gains the typical American family achieves through higher earnings during an entire decade, as it did in the Nineteen Seventies, that family does not need a Ph.D. or an econometric printout to know that something is disastrously awry. Our aspirations, by most world measures, are impractically high; but that does not assuage the disappointment. "The chance to live better" was never supposed to be qualified by the phrase "up to a point." The alibis about new "limits to growth," about adjusting to a changed world order in which people might be expected cheerfully to live worse, not only turned out to be factually invalid, as we shall see later in this book, but were never in tune with the driving engine of American history.

The ideas that vitalize the American dream, and provide the hope that it may be rescued from inexorable descent into historical nightmare, are not limited to the borders of the fifty states. Many of the economic concepts that so brilliantly matched the political notions of American independence were set forth the same year, 1776, by that astute Scot Adam Smith. It is an uncomfortable irony that, just as America in recent decades was losing faith (and losing steam), other nations grasped the falling flag and claimed it for their own. Today it is America that too often appears to be crouching in fear, irritation and envy, as others practice the lessons we once taught. As we move to meet this zestful new challenge from abroad, we would do well to seek not external barriers but internal strengths. My years of foreign residence occurred during a period of maximum military and economic strength for the U.S., and I listened then to legions of American diplomats and business executives preaching the advantages of open trade and the free flow of capital. We will be hypocrites indeed if we reverse our ideals the moment the flow turns against us. More important, we will be losers.

Just as the average American is conscious of slowing economic growth and pernicious inflation, so is he or she conscious that we have not solved the problems that preoccupied us during our change of course from the Nineteen Thirties to the Nineteen Eighties. If we had conquered poverty and brought the "underclass'' meaningfully into the mainstream of national prosperity, many Americans would count it time well spent. But there is growing evidence that our concern with "compassion" and "fairness" has misfired, and not only in the direction of those whose earnings paid the taxes. What American, whatever his or her initial biases, can fail to be concerned by the knowledge that, as George Gilder has observed, "the War on Poverty managed to triple black unemployment during the very decade of the Nineteen Seventies when a higher proportion of Americans got jobs than ever before in peacetime and some 12 million immigrants, many of whom did not even know English, found or created work in the very urban areas where black unemployment soared." Clearly, we must be doing something wrong.

If Americans are confused and distrustful today about all proposed remedies for the U.S. economy, it is scarcely a skepticism unearned. Economists are the failed priests of our generation. Two decades ago, we were told they could cure anything from hardcore unemployment to nasal catarrh through their supernatural ability to "fine-tune" the financial affairs of 200 million people. (P.S. They couldn't.) As computers became the nation's electronic scriptures, we heard of new econometric marvels, of precisely programmed economic "models" whose imposing mathematical equations could foretell with breathtaking precision the exact effect of any policy change whatsoever. (The computer people themselves had a prescient answer to that one: "Garbage in, garbage out.") With increasing desperation, citizens clutched at each new theology that promised instant answers: "Keynesianism," "monetarism," "supply-sidism," "neo-conservatism," "neo-liberalism"—everything, it seemed, except neo-arithmetic. The disillusionments came nearly as rapidly as the initial promises were offered.

America is by nature an optimistic society, but we are living through the pessimists' heyday. That will change only if our dream of America revives, if we can speak of it again without embarrassment or derision. Based on the recent past, economic frustration is the new American destiny. It's my contention, however, that we have lost our way, but not our chance. If we are to remedy our errors and restore the dream—this time for every one of our citizens—then we cannot look for scapegoats or magical new theories; we must look fearlessly in the mirror. We can, realistically, once more infuse the average American's existence with both the right of freedom and the chance to live better, and we can do it without a perpetual hollow snort of disappointment. But this transformation will not be accomplished just by voting for a different politician, or rushing lemminglike behind some painless new economic nostrum. It will take uncharacteristic patience, perseverance and hard work in each of the ten different critical areas to be covered in this book: education, the budget and taxes, monetary policy, banking and credit, labor, business, regulations and restrictions, energy, foreign economic policy and the individual. The alternative is awfully clear (and clearly awful): more of the frustrating same, or worse, collapse into the kind of ultimate cataclysm the doomsters have long declared inevitable. This country, uniquely, was built on ideas, and we will either return to the best of them or join history's junkheap. The clock is ticking, but the choice, happily, is still ours.

Shall we begin?

I

The Education
of Henry American

It would be nice to believe that the final conquest of inflation, the exuberant rebirth of economic growth and the blissful reincarnation of the American dream could all be accomplished overnight, miraculously and with somebody else paying the bill. We are regularly encouraged to believe this by politicians playing on our characteristic national desire for instant solutions and instant satisfaction—for a happy ending before the final commercial. But the bad guys inevitably return the following week; the lovely campaign promises prove as elusive as the video vision of erotic triumph through use of the right deodorant. Much has been made of our economic role as consumers, but far too little of our role as mindless consumers of economic pap. And so, of the ten areas in which action is needed to restore and revitalize the American economy, the first and most important is public education—to remedy, insofar as possible, our perennial state of economic illiteracy, to which the events of recent years have contributed so significantly, and to rally an understandably confused electorate behind what would be a sensible, nonpartisan program for economic action.

The need for this kind of economic education in our country is immense—and that need slashes right across party lines, regional lines, economic lines and racial lines. It makes mincemeat of partisan pretense, and presents our modern Presidents with their greatest unmet challenge. This country desperately needs wise, informed, courageous and consistent economic leadership; and the sad fact is that we haven't been getting anything resembling an adequate supply of it in recent decades from either political party.

If Ronald Reagan has been the nation's latest economic disappointment, with his devastating deficits and fantasy-filled forecasts occasionally turning Credibility Gap into Credibility Canyon, he is not exactly unique in our recent Presidential history. There's nothing partisan about this: Jimmy Carter was a whirling dervish of economic policies, carrying on a four-year sequence of nonstop debates with himself—in which, incidentally, both sides lost. And, back on the Republican side of the fence, don't forget that it was Richard Nixon of whom it was said that if Nixon had been captain of the *Titanic,* he would have told the passengers that they were just stopping briefly to take on ice.

So let's put aside the placards and be frank: in this respect, as an economic educator of the American people, it's been a long, long time since we have been able to point with pride to any of the men in the White House. And the ultimate joke has been on us.

Each recent incumbent has cleverly tried to figure out not how he could talk straight to the American people about authentic economic causes and effects but something quite different: how much economic truth it was *politically* safe to tell us on any given day. And the results of this shabby mind-set—what I call "Gallup Poll cynicism"—have been entirely and sadly predictable: repeatedly we have tried short-term politically concocted so-called solutions to what are in reality long-term fundamental economic problems. It shouldn't surprise anyone that these alleged panaceas never seem to work as originally advertised.

One reason Presidents behave this way is the perennial, and ludicrous, tendency to ascribe all the nation's ills (and not a few of its successes) to whoever happens to be occupying the Oval Office at the moment. This myth of simultaneity impels our Chief Executives both to overpromise and to underperform. And it provides us with a handy scapegoat, even when the incumbent President is not responsible. A recent example was the immediate impulse to blame the severe cyclical slump of 1981–82 entirely on the supposed failure of Ronald Reagan's new economic program. One might have been forgiven for concluding that until the arrival of the hated "Reaganomics," the modern U.S. economy had enjoyed unbroken decades of glorious prosperity. That the reality was distinctly the reverse—that Reagan had, in fact, inherited an economy of stagnant growth, failing productivity and prolonged inflation—became an inconvenient and forgettable truth. This was perhaps understandable for those politicians who were anxious to return as quickly as possible to the policies that had produced this dismal morass in the first place. But we civilians had no such excuse.

The inflation problem that underlies the ills of America's Eighties got off and running as long ago as the mid-Sixties, and I think it's worth briefly recalling this historical background before going on to current remedies, because our memories are so notoriously short in this country. Indeed, the shortness of the American memory span is among the phenomena of the Western world; I once calculated it as 20.9 seconds.*

Our national inclination is to believe that whatever is occurring at any given moment in the economy—inflation, unemployment, punishing interest rates—is something that, if it has not always been with us, now certainly always will be. I am occasionally approached by well-meaning people who wonder why I continue to "dwell so much on inflation." † Others will tell me that "we've always had inflation," or that "we've got to have inflation, you know, if we want to grow in the modern world." This is, as it happens, absolute nonsense. We have had many periods in our economic history in which we had vigorous growth without an inflation problem; in some of them, prices actually fell. To recall a period in which we were essentially untroubled by inflation, you don't have to be an elephant (financial or political); you need cast your mind no further back than the eight-year period 1958–65. Those years were, overall, years of excellent economic progress in the U.S., and they produced almost no inflation: the average annual increase in the Consumer Price Index was less than 1.5 per-

* Just over two-thirds the length of an average commercial.
† When the problem recedes, as it normally does, in the wake of recession, the tendency is to consider it gone forever. A television network correspondent reported with surprise in the spring of 1983 that many Americans still said they were worried about inflation—apparently not having got the word, he informed us, that that problem had been licked.

cent. (If you really want to make your mouth water, consider that in the twenty years starting in 1948, a period of explosive growth in American living standards, the annual consumer price increases never topped 3 percent in peacetime—and were below 2 percent in fully thirteen of those years. It can be done.)

This was not, then, a time lost in the mists of ancient history. The most recent period of extended price stability ended less than two decades ago. We may well ask what was so different about the eight years from 1958 to 1965, in which we had impressive growth and just over 1 percent inflation, as compared with our more recent period of sluggish or no growth and up to 20 percent inflation. (It is, incidentally, a difference we might usefully recall the next time the moralistic finger-pointers of this world try to establish one more Government bureaucracy to deal with the wrong problem.) Were businessmen from 1958 to 1965 all saints? Were they not trying to maximize their profits at every opportunity? That's not the way I remember it. Well, then, did the other side carry the can? Were workers from 1958 to 1965 not trying to squeeze every penny they could out of the boss, every chance they got? Nonsense, again: same kinds of human beings then as today. Okay, if business didn't behave essentially differently, and labor didn't behave essentially differently, who did behave differently in those better economic years? The answer is obvious, and instructive: the Government behaved differently.

In those better economic times the Government did not go on, year after year, finding new excuses, new alibis, new economic theories to explain why—whatever its hopes for the future (and sometime in the future, of course, you can be sure that all politicians plan to be wondrously responsible)—in the here and now it couldn't possibly be expected to live anywhere within its means. This unprecedented series of rationales for continuing fiscal irresponsibility has managed, predictably, to produce an unbroken series of deficits in every year but one since 1960. (The sole exception was 1969, when the Government eked out a $3.2 billion surplus, much to its own surprise; it had, with characteristic foresight, predicted a deficit in that year.)

The production of the deficits was the first act in an endlessly repeated two-act drama whose denouement invariably involved a "surprisingly" high rate of inflation. For, having found good and sufficient reason to spend vastly more than they had any prospect of taking in, the politicians of the day sought next to cover up their mischief. This effort led to Act II. Theoretically, at least, deficits don't have to be inflationary; it's the method of financing them that becomes the villain. You could, if you wished, pay for huge deficits solely by selling vastly more Government securities; that, however, sends interest rates into the ionosphere and is clearly and immediately destructive of private savings and investment. (The horrors of the early Nineteen Eighties again dramatized some of the dangers of this course, both politically and economically.) And so the tendency has been for the Government, having produced a scary deficit, to seek to cover up its mischief by encouraging the monetary authorities at the Federal Reserve Board to create ton after ton of ever more worthless confetti paper money. That eventually and inevitably does mean more inflation. More money is around, but not more goods; we have paid ourselves more than we earned. This vicious circle of fiscal profligacy followed by monetary self-deception is the actual, and relatively simple, explanation of how inflation was set loose in this country—and how it has been perpetuated.

For years, though, we were misled by attempts at the highest political level not to deal with the basic causes of inflation and national debilitation, but to deal melodramatically and spuriously with the symptoms. The inflation that has bedeviled us since the Nineteen Sixties, and remains the root cause of the problems of the Nineteen Eighties, did not (as has so often been implied) begin with some greedy businessman in Pittsburgh or Houston, or with some grasping labor union in Detroit. The inflation whose threat to resurface remains the greatest menace to American prosperity in the next decade began with the politicians in Washington, D.C.

How is it, then, that these home truths have so often fallen by the wayside? How could a succession of Presidents, armed with a succession of apparently diverse economic advisers, have repeated so many of the same basic errors? Why, in short, have we been so miseducated and misled?

Plainly, the economics profession itself must shoulder some of the responsibility for the endless deficits and their horrific consequences. Economists, right and left, were always ready with explanations of why, in the special circumstances of that particular year, a deficit would be totally harmless, if not downright good for us. In other words, there was always a coterie on hand to tell the reigning politicians whatever it was their spendthrift hearts most yearned to hear. (One economist who was honest about this was the Nobel laureate Milton Friedman, who, when asked in 1977 why he thought he had been invited to give economic advice to the new government of Israel, replied with characteristic candor that he had no special message to carry to Jerusalem and that there were plenty of qualified economists already on hand in that country. But the new Israeli government was committed to steering the nation toward more free enterprise, and it knew that Friedman would counsel precisely that, so it was inviting him to give the advice it was anxious to hear. Friedman's honesty ought to have earned him another prize—for he had put his finger on the actual relationship between politicians and economists, not just in Israel but in the U.S. and elsewhere.)

Politicians traditionally seek the advice of economists who will give them the opinion they seek. If a politician wanted to hear that greater freedom would mean greater growth, he could summon Milton Friedman. If he wanted to hear that the time had come to impose wage and price controls, he could press the button for John Kenneth Galbraith. There is always someone of reasonable eminence associated with each economic policy option, and he is not likely to reverse himself in your hour of need. Moreover, Presidents are well aware of how eager practically everybody is to give them advice, and smart Presidents know how to exploit this yen. In 1963, while en route from London to New Delhi, I was granted fifteen minutes with John F. Kennedy to get his private views on Asian policy. Kennedy, after amiable recollections of a previous meeting four years earlier—which I took as a tribute to his 3-by-5 filing system—began by asking me what I thought of the new British Labour Party leader, Harold Wilson. I replied briefly and then said that, while I was flattered that the President would seek my opinions on any question, I knew his time was extremely limited, and I was actually there to get his views. Kennedy smiled and said: "You caught me, huh? You'd be surprised how seldom that happens!"

To understand how Presidents use their advisers, official and volunteer, is to understand how empty is most of the perennial speculation about a President's economic counselors. The real question is usually not what he is hearing but what he wants to hear, for this in the end is apt to wind up being the same thing. Indeed, there are entire intellectual factories standing by waiting to tell a Chief Executive that his political biases are economically correct. (For Democratic support, consult the catalogue of the Brookings Institution; for Republican bolstering, phone the American Enterprise Institute.) The way Ronald Reagan ate up, and then spit out, his more extreme "supply-side" advisers was entirely in keeping with this tradition.

What explains this ready availability of theoretical economic support for virtually anything a politician might want to undertake? Is it because, as the popular mythology has it, economists never agree on anything anyhow—that, in the words of the old joke, if you stretched every economist in the world from end to end, they still wouldn't reach a conclusion? Not really; indeed, when they stick to their economic lasts, the mass of reputable economists is in agreement far more often than the public suspects. Most favor free trade, for example, and most were aware that we would get more badly needed energy if we had fewer Government controls. It is only when they put on their semipolitical hats and start talking about the "practical realities" that they start giving advice from all over the spectrum. Prejudices and priorities outside the purely economic realm begin to take over.

This again is not a partisan question: Paul Samuelson's interventionist energy recommendations seemed quite frankly based as much on his political analysis as on any pretense of economics, while Arthur Burns (whose resemblance to Samuelson was otherwise remote) operated for years on the confident assumption that he was the shrewdest political analyst in the District of Columbia. Nor is it an especially new development. When Franklin Roosevelt first ran for President in 1932, he denounced Herbert Hoover as a spendthrift; when Roosevelt's own view of what the country required in the form of Federal spending changed spectacularly, so did the bulk of the economic advice he was receiving.* When John

* Roosevelt frequently invited Bernard M. Baruch to the White House for widely publicized visits. Baruch commented: "Even though he doesn't take my advice, he continues to bring me to the White House. Maybe this is to create the impression he is seeking objective counsel."

Kennedy wanted to believe that an "activist" President could "fine-tune" the economy, there was no shortage of economists eager to tell him that he was absolutely right. And when Richard Nixon and Gerald Ford wanted to go the other way, they were careful not to call at the same stores.

Government economists tend to tell their bosses what they want to hear, then, both out of normal human ambition and from a desire to show "sophistication" by adjusting their counsel to take account of "practical politics." Even when an economist regards himself as of unassailable integrity, it doesn't take a Ph.D. to recognize that a certain flexibility on principle, a willingness to adjust to what is perceived as political necessity, will do wonders for one's longevity as a Presidential adviser (with the accompanying national celebrity). The word "advice" is often misleading when it comes to the mutually self-serving world of politicians and economists.

So let's go back to the place where, as Harry Truman put it, the buck stops. And so we'll know how to judge what we are hearing from our leaders of the Eighties, let's briefly review the contributions of some of their distinguished predecessors in helping to transform a period of price stability and husky expansion into the mess that became the American economy of more recent years.

At the helm when things started to go badly awry was Lyndon B. Johnson. Johnson, who once genially contended that he was both "liberal" and "conservative," may have had some personal difficulty making hard economic choices. In any event, he assumed that the American people couldn't (or at least wouldn't) take the truth about the consequences of all the varied and ambitious policies he was pursuing. Thus he tried, in effect, to sneak the Vietnam war into the Federal budget—to pile a huge new military spending effort in Southeast Asia on top of a huge new domestic welfare spending effort ("The Great Society") without even beginning honestly to confront the authentic financial costs of that kind of enormous double endeavor. As a result, the Government wound up letting the Federal Reserve Board finance the conflict by printing too much money. The current inflation unquestionably did start during the Johnson Presidency. This once-controversial assertion is now moving toward bipartisan political acceptance. Charles L. Schultze, who was President Johnson's budget director and later served as chief Carter economic adviser, acknowledged to me in an interview that "we tried to finance the Vietnam war and the Great Society programs without a tax increase, and clearly that started us on our course of inflation." Schultze is that Washington rarity, an honest man.

Richard Nixon, who inherited a bad economic situation, promptly proceeded to make it very much worse by changing economic course with every shift in the political winds. Nixon has become so controversial for other reasons that most Americans seem to have forgotten entirely what he did in the economic area. Yet his influence there, in my judgment, ultimately should be seen as having been far more significant, and far more enduring, than in the more melodramatic events that led to his downfall.

Early in 1971, I had a private forty-minute interview in the Oval Office with Richard Nixon, accompanied by the chairman of his Council of Economic Advisers, Paul McCracken. (I was seated in a chair that, it subsequently was revealed, contained a "bug," or electronic recording device. So far, however, our conversation has —astoundingly—failed to make the headlines.) We covered the entire range of economic policy, current and future, but three specific points seem especially relevant now.

(1) Pointing out that Nixon had spoken trenchantly of the dangers of inflation, I said I deeply shared this concern but wondered whether he really believed he could win an election on the issue. He started a bit, smiled (I had his full attention at this point; we were no longer lost in the realm of theory) and declared that it had never been done by any politician at any level. I asked him whether his own belief was not that people bellyached about prices but were more inclined to vote on the basis of employment. He confessed that it was. (Nixon had long felt that Kennedy beat him in 1960 only because President Eisenhower failed to stimulate the economy.) Here was evidence, first, that Nixon distrusted his own rhetoric about the degree of popular concern over inflation, and, second, that his inclination would be to step hard on the economic accelerator before the 1972 election. This he indeed did—and, not at all coincidentally, the nation arrived by 1974 at double-digit inflation.

(2) I observed that some of the Nixon Administration's economic forecasts seemed extraordinarily optimistic, and asked him

whether he genuinely believed the targets were attainable. His reply was cynical, but honest: it didn't matter whether the targets were actually reached or not; the only important thing was the trend, as perceived by the voters at election time. In 1962, he recalled, unemployment had been higher than it was in 1971, but the ruling Democrats had done well in the Congressional elections anyhow, because voters felt President Kennedy was getting a handle on the problem. The public's perception of the economy's direction was what counted—not the keeping of specific promises.

(3) I asked Nixon whether he thought the state of the economy could be turned into a positive Republican issue in 1972. He replied that it was extremely difficult for a modern Republican President to utilize the economy as a positive election issue. What he could more realistically hope to do, he said, was to "neutralize" it. And this, objectively, is what appears to have occurred in 1972. There is scant evidence that the economic issue helped to bury George McGovern, but on the other hand it clearly didn't hurt Nixon, either. What concerned Nixon as a political tactician was the knowledge that folklore is often as important as fact when it comes to voting. And part of our modern American folklore is a widespread belief that Democratic Presidents get us into wars and Republican Presidents wreck the economy. Neither cliché will withstand rigorous intellectual examination, but any connection between rigorous intellectual examination and voting is usually coincidental. Nixon appeared far more concerned with the short-term considerations of political tactics than with the long-term task of economic healing, and he did not stand alone among our recent Presidents in this respect.

Interestingly, most Americans, even now, whether they admired Nixon or detested him, recall him as having been a crusty old conservative kind of fellow. They must have listened to his campaign speeches and then gone to sleep. (An understandable phenomenon.) Oh, he talked like a Tory all right: Nixon's the fellow who gave in 1968 the speeches that Jimmy Carter picked up and reread in 1976. (Jimmy got a blurred carbon, which accounts for the delivery.) In 1968 Nixon was the candidate who told us he was going to "balance the Federal budget so we can all balance our family budgets." Sounds good, doesn't it? And familiar? But what we actually got from Nixon in this area was five years of budgets that ultimately contained more red ink than the country had seen in the previous twenty-three years put together.

A conservative? Nixon was the President who emerged from the Oval Office in early 1971 to announce that we were all Keynesians now; that he too had become a disciple of the Englishman whose economic teachings have been interpreted (or, more precisely, misinterpreted) to justify our modern course of nonstop deficits. Later that same year, Nixon took what was perhaps the single most popular—and foolhardy—economic act of his Presidency, plunging the country into a highly damaging round of wage and price controls. In fact, when we detach ourselves from the partisan assertions of both sides and look back on Nixon's authentic economic policies while in office, as opposed to what he said they would be or the public perception of them, we see that those policies in reality consisted of a series of the most startling reversals since Christine Jorgensen.

Next on our list of economic heroes came Gerald Ford, who turned out to be a highly uncertain beacon for a nation at sea. Indeed, unlike an earlier Republican President, Ford too often seemed to walk stickily and carry a big soft.

Ford came to the White House with a reputation for having spent a quarter century in the U.S. Congress without having made a single enemy. While indicating commendable affability, this was not a reputation that suggested a piercing mind likely to provide brilliant illumination on the nation's ongoing economic problems. And, in truth, while Ford earned considerable good will for his honorable character and healing leadership after the trauma of Watergate—and while he and key members of his economic team are still actively preaching conservative economic doctrine in books and speeches—his Administration's actual economic policies were considerably less clear-cut. There was a repeated conflict between Ford's rhetoric and his actions on such issues as the budget, taxes and energy.

It was during the Ford Administration that I began to believe that the three vainest hopes of mankind were perpetual motion, something for nothing and expecting our political leaders to educate us about economics. On the country's most pressing issue, inflation, the new President quickly entered comic-book history in 1974 by declaring the nemesis "Public Enemy Number One" and launching a major war against it—fought entirely with "WIN" buttons. The very name (standing for "Whip Inflation Now") suggested incorrectly that the problem could be conquered without extended, painful effort; its Madison Avenue conceptual origins pandered to an attention span as short as the TV campaign time for a new soft drink. When the product did not immediately sell, when the nation's attention turned instead to the symptoms of recession, even the buttons were shelved. And inflation, while it eased notably, as it usually does during a cyclical downturn in the economy, stubbornly and predictably refused to surrender.

Nor did Ford's capacity for thoughtful economic education improve during his term of office. Toward its end he went around assuring anyone who would listen that the economy was approaching utopia: "Everything that should be going up is going up, and everything that should be going down is going down." Not only was this a factual misstatement (many of the nation's economic trends still badly needed reversing), but it set Ford up to look silly the minute a single unfavorable statistic appeared—as it inevitably did.

It was not known, for example, whether Ford's unalloyed delight in the economic statistics extended as far as the matter of deficits, where in two years he managed to beat the previously staggering totals for Nixon's five. The $66.4 billion shortfall in 1976 set an all-time record, surpassing the worst of World War II or subsequent Carter totals, and stood until 1982. Nor did Ford win educational Brownie points for deciding to sign a spectacularly ill-conceived 1976 tax bill, which in the seductive (if misleading) name of "reform" contained a number of provisions—including an *increase* in the required holding period for capital gains—that in reality further hampered such fundamental U.S. needs as the provision of more investment capital for economic growth. Encouraging such growth was the only plausible route to more jobs (as Ford's senior economic advisers privately acknowledged), but the public had never been made to understand that this was true—and a Presidential campaign was deemed a bad time to start.

So then we got Jimmy Carter—and if Ford too often had seemed overcautious and indecisive on economic issues, he turned out to be a model of clarity and precision when compared to his opponent and successor. Carter managed to go through four years of the

Presidency without ever showing enough consistent educational candlepower to save a rowboat. You may think he was ineffectual, but you have to admit he never once knew where he was going. Yet he was undeniably sincere in his confusion. Late in Carter's Presidency, a member of his senior staff said to me somewhat belligerently: "Lou, I think he's doing the best he can." "That's what worries me," I replied.

The fuzzy Georgia peach gave early hints that he did not intend to be preoccupied with any hobgoblin of consistency; during the 1976 campaign, he offered sharply varying positions on issues ranging from curbing the bureaucracy to revising tax policy to restraining Federal spending. One of my favorite examples of Carter bafflegab came when, having skillfully and persistently exploited the anti-Washington mood of the country to achieve his party's nomination, he confronted a hostile audience of Washington career officials—the very folks he had been lambasting elsewhere. But, he assured them, they had nothing to fear: "A reduction in the bureaucracy does not necessarily mean a reduction in the total number of people employed." Ponder that one for a while, and this whole problem of political economics may come into clearer focus. Even if it does spoil your breakfast.

Much of this, perhaps, can be written off as confusing the electorate more than miseducating it. There traditionally has been, in an election season, a certain allowance for meaningless campaign rhetoric—what we might term "the baloney factor." More troublesome, though, as a hint of what lay ahead, were the Carter statements that played on mass neuroses without any consideration of the ultimate damage they could do to the mass economy. In the first Presidential debate, for example, the former Georgia Governor complained about "those rich corporations" that "don't pay their tax." Such talk is undeniably rousing emotionally, as its perennial reappearances dramatize, but it is also highly dangerous —because it feeds the mistaken belief that we can have all the Government spending we want, if only we can get somebody else to foot the bill. There's no way a corporation, "rich" or otherwise, can pay a penny of tax itself; the tax ostensibly paid by the corporation in the end must fall on people: customers, stockholders or employees. But to explain that would be to educate the public, instead of inflaming it.

Similarly empty of genuine economic content, as the nation came to see, was Carter's pledge to support what he called "the right of the people to have an adequate income." The heart may applaud such demagogic oratory, but the mind boggles. Forgetting the problem of defining "adequate"—no small task in a society where yesterday's luxuries quickly become today's necessities—who is to be responsible for providing this "right," and is there to be any commensurate "responsibility" on the part of the recipients? (If not, who is the slave to whom?) Are we talking here about some massive new Government intervention in the economy; are we talking about some form of negative income tax, enabling us to dismantle the welfare bureaucracy; or are we just talking nonsense?

The foggy days in Washington town became endemic during Carter's stay. Inheriting a declining inflation rate (the increase in consumer prices had dwindled from 12.2 percent in 1974 to 4.8 percent in 1976), he had a chance, proceeding with only moderate care, to emerge as a national economic hero. Instead, Carter immediately called, almost incredibly, for a further "stimulus package" including sharply increased public spending. The results were dishearteningly predictable: the "stimulus" proved effective only in helping to rekindle inflation, whose rate nearly tripled by 1979 —and stayed in double digits for two years.

Carter's misreading of the country's basic economic requirements combined with repeated rhetorical overkill: he would talk of "national austerity" while failing to make any meaningful cuts in Government spending, or even to endorse reasonable restraint by the monetary authorities; he would trumpet the "moral equivalent of war" on energy, and then seek punitive taxes on those who produced it; he would flunk the test of national leadership, and then blame his failure on the electorate's "malaise." No wonder the nation despaired. Through it all, economic miseducation flourished; Carter peppered us with statements that were, to put it charitably, factually misleading—as when he informed us that inflation had inexorably "increased to an average of 8 percent" in the three years before he took office, so what did we expect? In reality, the rate was in a steady downtrend during those three years, subsiding below 5 percent in 1976—when he had wrongly told us we needed more "stimulus." Only some members of the media were fooled for long; listening to Carter's "austere" words and neglecting his persistently inflationary tune, they decided that he had to be a "fiscal conservative." Sure he was—if you regard Fidel Castro as a moderate. More perceptive was my friend the Dutch financial expert Adriaan J. Schrikker, who inelegantly but accurately predicted in 1978: "As long as Jimmy Carter is talking his head off about fighting inflation on one side and on the other side is printing money, he's got no hope in hell."

So if Ronald Reagan sometimes came to think, as he clearly did in the extended winter of his economic discontent, that public trust in the Presidency is not all it might be, he shouldn't have been so surprised. We haven't exactly been playing with a Super Bowl lineup of economic educators at 1600 Pennsylvania Avenue.

THE DREADFUL CONGRESSIONAL DISEASE

To be sure, our Presidents, whoever they may be, cannot in fairness be expected to do all this country's economic educating all by themselves. We cannot reasonably expect superhuman achievements from our fellow human beings. And this is not just because of the most obvious handicap that faces any President when the thought of doing some serious, consistent economic educating crosses his brow for a millisecond or two—that handicap being, of course, the United States Congress: an institution whose members, overwhelmingly, tend to suffer from the same acute physical disease. Practically every Congressman I've known has been afflicted with some variety of this ailment, in which, metaphorically at least, the first finger of his right hand was about one quarter normal size—from having been held wet in the wind for so many years.

Quite simply, expecting that group of habitual followers to change the behavior of an entire career, and suddenly begin providing the nation with something resembling genuine economic leadership, is like expecting an armadillo to learn how to play the harmonica. It is wholly beyond the capacities of that animal to learn how to play that instrument. The Senate showed what kind of beast it really is when its members heroically voted without dissent in 1981 not to touch the Social Security system, at a time when every respectable economist (and thinking citizen) in the country was aware that failure to make alterations in the system was to assure its collapse. So much for economic leadership in the upper house. The House of Representatives, not to be outdone in the pusillanimity sweepstakes, the following year saw its once-proud Ways and Means Committee abandon any pretense of coming up with responsible tax legislation—choosing instead immediately to go to conference with a tax bill from the Senate, which under the Constitution cannot originate tax legislation. Why bother with ethical (or Constitutional) details when there is an election on the horizon? So far from providing any identifiable economic education in its own right, the national legislature seems perennially concerned only to validate the dour insight of that Nineteenth Century French observer Alexis de Tocqueville, who concluded: "The American republic will endure until the politicians find they can bribe the people with their own money."

YOU CALL THAT NEWS?

But it's not just our weak-backboned (or small-fingered) legislators who are to blame, either. No, lump together the failures of all our politicians in this critical area of economic education, and that failure, immense though it is, is more than matched in my judgment by the failure in this very same area of most of our U.S. news media—and, even more fundamentally, by the failure in this area of our U.S. educational system itself. So let us look at each of these areas, starting with the field in which I have spent my own professional lifetime since the age of sixteen, journalism. In recent years, finding myself on occasion the subject as well as the author of journalism, I have developed what may be a useful double-edged perspective on "the media." I have often remarked to agitated businessmen that what actually is true of journalism is true of a number of other professions (notably including Wall Street) as well: outsiders tend always to overrate the malice and underrate the incompetence. It's very hard to get things straight, and only a minority in any occupation is capable of accomplishing it. The task of sensible news executives should be to expand and fortify that minority in the field of economic journalism.

The first problem in economic journalism is simply to get enough attention paid to it. There I think we could fairly conclude that there has been some improvement, but still an embarrassingly long way to go. Some personal recollections may be apropos in this connection. While I had a lifelong interest in the subject (my father was a pioneering economic journalist, and my own college specialty had been "public aspects of business"), it became my journalistic preoccupation relatively late in my career. I had been a newspaper political correspondent in the Fifties and then, for more than a decade, a foreign correspondent based in Europe and Asia, culminating in service as Paris correspondent and London bureau chief for ABC News. During all those years, I was led ineluctably to the conclusion that economics was the worst-covered subject in the business. How in the world could you intelligently cover what was going on in countries like Britain and India if you didn't understand the economics of those countries? If you didn't understand the economics, you didn't understand anything. Yet time and again I found myself not so much beating my colleagues in this area as having it wholly to myself: first in a field of one. (I remember, on my first trip to Vietnam in 1963, hearing Defense Secretary Robert S. McNamara ask an assembled group of media superstars what they could tell him about the impact of the war on the economy of the country; not one appeared to have a clue. "I'm afraid we haven't done our homework on that one," confessed David Halberstam of the *New York Times*.) As domestic and international financial problems multiplied in the late Sixties, I began to get, in spite of myself, an unsought reputation as an economic expert. Far from being jealous, my colleagues seemed actively relieved. ABC's political editor, the late Bill Lawrence, joyfully threw me all the economic questions on our annual year-end speaking tours, customarily prefacing them with the words "If there's anything I don't know anything about, it's economics." I could not shake the feeling that he was not apologizing, but bragging.

It surprises me to this day that, as recently as 1968, when I created the job of economic editor of ABC News, I was the very first national economic commentator on U.S. network television. More astoundingly, when I left ABC five years later, I was still the only one around. Similarly, although my "Wall $treet Week" program has been a weekly half-hour fixture on public television since

1970, the successful major competition one might have expected for such a widely acknowledged breakthrough has failed to appear. This leaves me less relieved than perplexed: there should be fifty good careers emerging in this badly undercovered area of economic television. And so, when in recent years kind colleagues have honored me for my achievements, I have naturally been appreciative (recognition from one's peers being especially sweet), but I have not always been the perfect guest. When asked to say a few words, I have operated on what may have been the dangerous assumption that they did not issue me the invitation solely to massage their egos. (I have told them frankly that I was going to assume that that job was well taken care of in their newsrooms—or, if not there, in their bedrooms.) And I have asserted unequivocally my continuing belief that economic coverage remains the Number One failing of our profession.

This, I think, is particularly true of commercial television, which, while it has belatedly added a few working specialists, seems to have taken as its special mission to tell us almost everything about the moon and almost nothing about our money. Too often, network TV still tends to cover the subject of business and the economic system, if at all, in only one of two ways: either totally superficially, as when it throws out a raw statistic and leaves it lying there essentially uncooked (provoking, ideally, a flash emotional response, though scarcely adding to our understanding), or else in an occasional mood of crusading exposé. I have nothing against good exposés—they are an important part of journalism—but the present situation is as if journalists covered Washington only in terms of its scandals, and gave no coverage to the ongoing business of government. Balance and insight take knowledge and work; playing on prejudices through reflexive hostility toward institutions like "big business" or "the oil companies" is a considerably less demanding occupation.

The media's real job is not to look down at business (or up at it), but *at* it. And even when bias or intellectual laziness are not the operative handicaps, television coverage of economics is inhibited by the search for exciting pictures. This works not just in the obvious cases, such as avoiding subjects that seem "complicated" or not immediately visual (and thereby disregarding the counsel of the late Edward R. Murrow, who observed that one of the most interesting pictures you could get was of a person thinking). It means that the emotional set is always on the side of the most immediately apparent, dramatically exploitable effects of any economic event. Hence, for example, unemployment is marvelously visual, with its human impact on an individual family. The benefits of a decreasing inflation rate, on the other hand, seem vaguely theoretical and harder to present, even though in truth they may extend to a far wider segment of the population—and ultimately help the poor far more than the continuance of every hotly debated welfare program. The point is certainly not that you should stop covering the tragedies of unemployment; it is that, to be responsible, you have to take yourself beyond the visual clichés of Hollywood protest movies.*

Nor, I believe, are most newspapers doing the job they should be doing in helping the average citizen better to understand the way this economic system really works, as opposed to the knee-jerk clichés on which the politicians thrive. While newspapers, like television, have belatedly expanded their attention to economic questions, too many newspaper business sections still consist of a sea of agate type surrounded by rewritten press releases (assuming, of course, that they are rewritten). When it comes to solid economic analysis and commentary, which the public needs and in fact craves when presented with flair, hundreds of papers go no further than columns that purport, more or less, to tell the reader how to buy a rug (the print equivalent of television's ubiquitous "consumer reporters"), or limit themselves to investment questions and answers (the questions being far easier than the answers in recent years), or else, worst of all, present the views of phonies who pretend to be able to tell you precisely why the stock market did what it did today, and precisely what it is going to do tomor-

---

* Interestingly, the people have long been ahead of most TV news executives and producers in this respect, not only in the public's always "surprising" interest in the economic programming that is done, but in being attuned to the fundamental issues—rather than what others may assume are the typical person's concerns. At the worst of the mid-Seventies recession, for example, and despite media preoccupation with its symptoms, such as unemployment, pollsters repeatedly found that the average American continued to list inflation as his or her biggest personal economic worry. Indeed, and not insignificantly, they got this as the first answer from one third of those officially listed as unemployed.

row. (I suppose we could call those fellows philanthropists—that is, if they had ever managed to be right.)

What is needed, in contrast, is considerably more (and considerably more insightful) coverage of the nation's economic scene: reporting, analysis and commentary of the highest order, adequately and prominently displayed by publishers and producers. We need more bright young journalists educated and trained, able and willing to operate on that broad frontier where politics and economics meet—and confuse each other. It is a lonely frontier, largely neglected by the big-name Washington reporters, who traditionally have acted as if they believed they were the high-policy types, concerned with the excitement at the top and with those whose job it was to set goals and ideals for the nation; the economic technicians, they appeared to believe, could come in later to cover the press conferences the White House man disdained, and clear up the piddling details. The trouble with that, as we have seen so excruciatingly over the last two decades, is that if we don't get the economics straight, nothing else counts; the loftiest of intentions turn to gravel. Yet this frontier where politics and economics meet has been neglected, too, by the purely financial types and their insular colleagues in academe.

What we need is more journalists with the ability, and the exposure, to audit our Presidents with some subtlety (as when they glibly tell us that we're going to "whip" high prices with a shiny new button, or that if it weren't for OPEC we wouldn't have inflation in the U.S.)—and not just to push the appropriate emotional switches and decide for us, preferably within a fortnight or two of its inception, whether a complex and often self-contradictory program like "Reaganomics" is to be regarded as the success of the ages or the biggest flop since the Edsel. One way to accomplish this, I suspect, would be to get away from the journalistic preoccupation with putting a label on everything and everybody: a shorthand that provides a convenient substitute for the more difficult process known as thinking. The idea presumably is that if you know the right label for a fellow or a program, whether he or it is (say) "liberal" or "conservative," then you know how you feel without having to do any further research. If the journalist wants to do you the ultimate service, he may add the prefix "ultra" (as in "ultraconservative," for example), and then you can truly rest easy, without having to devote any further time or examination to the actual ideas being presented.

The labels never really made much intellectual sense. A businessman who was genuinely "conservative," in the sense of resisting change, would not be a successful businessman for long. And as the financial disaster that befell New York City in the last decade so vividly demonstrated, there was nothing enduringly "liberal" about overspending tax money in the name of humanity and progress. In this area, too, intelligent voters have gotten well ahead of many of those who serve them the news. The citizenry shows repeatedly that it is less interested in the ideological brand on a program than in a realistic assessment of how it is likely to work. In the political arena, this already has been reflected in a nationwide flight from labels and readily identifiable ideological positions. In the economic realm, however, overlabeling remains pervasive. An ideologue (and media favorite) like John Kenneth Galbraith could always capture attention and put down those who differed with him by suggesting that their economic views belonged to an earlier century. Such talk was undeniably fun, and could stir the partisan juices something fierce, but it also happened to be intellectual baloney. First, because the ideas of economic freedom and market competition that were being dismissed as "old-fashioned" are, in fact, among the newest of historical concepts. The scant two centuries since that platinum year when both the Declaration of Independence and Adam Smith's *Wealth of Nations* were written represent a strikingly short period in a long history of letting Government do it. Second, because many of the notions that are being presented today as radically "modern" are, in reality, out of another century themselves. This was brought home to me in a way that should be of special interest to my fellow journalists when I visited Emporia, Kansas—home of the *Emporia Gazette,* which under the editorship of the late William Allen White brought small-town journalism to national attention. While going through the White memorabilia at this Fourth Estate shrine, I read a copy of his editorial "What's the Matter with Kansas?", which he credited with creating his reputation. It was widely quoted in the Presidential election of—get this—1896. In it, White trenchantly criticized many of the ideas that are being presented as brand-new today, nearly a century later: mindless consumerism (he observed that simply parroting that "the rights of the user are paramount to the rights of the owner" was an excellent way to discourage investment), good-heartedness as a political substitute for IQ (he spoke derisively of those who boasted that they were "just ordinary clodhoppers, but they know more in a minute about finance than [the veteran statesman and former Treasury Secretary] John Sherman") and redistribution of existing wealth rather than the creation of new wealth (he blasted those who would "legislate the thriftless man into ease" and who believed that "what we need is not the respect of our fellow men, but the chance to get something for nothing"). And some of the "fallacies of populism" he quoted William Jennings Bryan as espousing would need no rewrite to qualify as the up-to-the-minute, never-before-thought-of ultramodern "new ideas" of the Nineteen Eighties.

So maybe U.S. journalism and its customers would profit if we all gave a rest to labels—and were a little less sure that ideas are born whenever we first hear them. We may not solve all our problems by so doing, but at least we will restore a smidgen of integrity to the English language. And perhaps, too, a new resistance to facile labeling would assist journalists in penetrating something even more insidious, which is promulgated by politicians of both parties (and all kinds of labels): the notion that this nation's economy is essentially a question of class war, with the Government needed to run things and distribute the arms more fairly. The truth is that this has been one of the major destructive bipartisan fallacies of recent decades—and we in the news business have failed to audit it properly. Journalists, in fact, often nurture this fallacy because it makes it easy to translate all issues into simple confrontations: who gets helped and who gets hurt, who's for it and who's against it, do the rich get richer or the poor get poorer? As the record of the last generation reminds us, though, this simplistic approach to economic issues is not just repugnant but downright false. The years in which the poorest of our citizens truly were assisted, in which millions left the poverty rolls for productive private employment, were also years in which the middle class of America progressed spectacularly, in which the average American family could see its own standard of living improving tangibly year after year. And—wonder of wonders—these also happened to be years of booming business profits and a soaring stock market.

Then we embarked, in a flurry of misconceived Nineteen Sixties "activism," on what turned out to be an extended ideological war against business, profits and economic success. Often whooped on by gullible journalists infatuated with trendy concepts of "social justice," this war became a remarkable success: we managed to damage our industrial base, lay waste to the investment markets, cripple American productivity and come disastrously close to exterminating the golden goose that had made all this high-minded experimentation possible. Yes, it sure worked: we, "soaked the rich" and made their stocks and bonds a joke. But can even the most enthusiastic journalistic supporter of this crusade tell us now that we helped anybody else?

The operative lesson, I suggest, is that we should go easier on the confrontational clichés of shallow economic journalism. The record suggests that it is the politicians, not the people, who gain from the prevalent media instinct for melodramatic polarization. In reality, it would seem, the mass of private citizens have far more in common than in opposition—and it is in their common interest that the Government not get away with escalating its own sense of self-importance at the economy's expense. Our enemy, in short, is less likely than we have been told to be each other, however much it may serve the politicians' interests to believe that it is. Journalists have to go beyond the contrasting quotes of two opposing Congressmen if they hope to uncover more substantial economic truths. The ultimate point is not that journalists should be out to sell a case (even the one I have just made), but that we clearly need much better informed, more critical examinations of what Washington happens to be saying on any particular day about the economy—and why.

It may be that this job will never be done properly by the Washington press corps, which has its own self-interest in making the politicians' role in our economy seem more vital than it is. That's the Washington correspondents' story, after all. To acknowledge that the Government's capacity for fostering a healthy U.S. economy is decidedly limited, and that Washington might do well to develop an unaccustomed modesty in this area, could mean less time on the air or fewer excursions onto Page One. Most news organizations now locate a disproportionate number of their personnel in Washington, possibly because everybody else seems to be doing it; by the simple weight of gravity, this tends to mean a disproportionate amount of TV air time or newspaper space. (One of the most serious professional charges that can be leveled against a foreign correspondent is that he has developed "localitis," meaning that he has been too long in Afghanistan and is no longer able to put it in a rational perspective for the average American. By that standard, the worst case of mass "localitis" in the business can be found not overseas but in Washington, D.C.) Similarly, the endless ritualistic coverage given by the commercial television networks to the national political conventions contrasts ever more embarrassingly with the broadcasters' failure to dig more than a quarter inch deep into the problems of the U.S. economy.

One problem, of course, is that most bright young journalists want to do the kinds of things I used to do, working as a political correspondent and a foreign correspondent: the jobs that historically have paid the most money, carried the most glamour and been the traditional paths to top positions in news and news management. (I once told a meeting of the American Society of Newspaper Editors that if they really wanted to lure more good people into this ever more important area, one way would be to show their new interest in the most sincere fashion—by paying their economic specialists a lot more money. They delightedly took the point, if not the suggestion.) Some of this is changing, but all too slowly. Yet the requirement for better economic journalism is inescapable, and I suspect it will be increasingly recognized as such. As the millions who regularly watch "Wall $treet Week" may have helped to demonstrate, the public has an enormous appetite— widely unsuspected by the conventional professionals—for clear and understandable economic news. The task of supplying it is one of the most exciting and demanding facing any ambitious young journalist; to the extent this challenge is met, the nation's need for better economic education will be served.

WHY EDUCATORS FLUNK

If the journalists too often simply follow the politicians, and if the politicians too often trail after what they perceive to be the public's passing whims, then the quality of the nation's fundamental economic education becomes critical. The evidence there is not inspiring. In our educational system today, the evidence points to a general loosening of intellectual rigor, a specific and distressing lack of grounding in economic fundamentals and a disturbing growth of "Marxist" teachers at a moment in history when Marxism can be seen by anyone who ventures 300 yards beyond the classroom to be an unarguable worldwide flop.

First, consider some findings of recent studies about the intellectual caliber of the present U.S. population: One in five U.S. adults lacks the reading and writing abilities needed to handle the minimal demands of daily living. That's 23 million people. Another 30 million are rated only marginally capable of being productive workers. The number of functional illiterates grows annually by nearly a million school dropouts, plus immigrants often unable to read and write either English or their own language. There is a direct correlation between illiteracy and unemployment—and illiteracy and crime. The U.S. spends $6.6 billion annually to keep 750,000 illiterates in jail. Pollster George Gallup reports that "the spread of illiteracy in this country is a scandal as serious as the spread of crime." Meanwhile, even those who stay in the educational system come out increasingly unprepared. Half the freshmen at the University of Missouri at St. Louis now have to be placed in a remedial course; 42 percent of Ohio State's first-year students must be assigned to remedial English or math, at an annual cost of $10 to $12 million. Two thirds of our institutions of alleged higher learning have been driven to providing such basic instruction. At the University of California at Berkeley, which claims to pick only from the top one eighth of high school graduates, nearly half of each incoming class goes straight into a remedial composition course. Publishers of college textbooks find it necessary to use more pictures and simpler language, a process known in the trade as "dumbing down." The Army, apparently concluding that anything above the comic-book level is hopelessly hard for today's recruits, uses five pages of pictures to show a soldier how to open the hood on a truck. Thousands of U.S. companies, in desperation, have set up their own remedial courses in basic subjects. Yet remember: while, according to a nationwide survey by the Adult Performance Level Project at the University of Texas, 20 percent of adult Americans cannot interpret a bus schedule or address a letter, there is one thing they can do. They can vote.

Who's to blame? The easy answer is that we need still more

Government spending, that any attempt to curtail Federal aid to education will exacerbate the dilemma. But a growing number of concerned Americans, including many who differ strongly on other issues, have come to think that the basic problem resides in attitude—in an abandonment of the concept of personal responsibility in favor of a belief that someone else should take care of us. The causes are several. Ironically, this lapse into weakness traces in part to an earlier misconception of maturity and strength. Amid the self-indulgence of the Sixties, many students were encouraged to write their own curriculum and to believe that anything old and "established" could be assumed to be contemptibly wrong. Education as a tool for a better life became secondary to the fashionable pursuit of "relevance." Parents and teachers alike too often let the inmates run the asylum, creating an environment that historian Barbara Tuchman called "without rules, without authority, without respect for authority," and moving her to inquire: "How are these people ever going to acquire the habits and the knowledge that can run the country, or run the businesses, or produce the works of art?" These are the failings not of underfinancing—the traditional complaint of the professional educators—but of overpermissiveness. Many students themselves eventually came to recognize the folly of an ideological flight from educational utility; in the last decade, for example, there has been a dramatic increase in the proportion of college students electing such old-fashioned career-oriented courses as business administration. Yet the loss of intellectual rigor in the nation's classrooms remains scandalous, and economically perilous.

The omnipresent television tube must take part of the blame. Consider the findings of the National Assessment of Educational Progress, a federally supported research organization, which reported that teenagers in the Nineteen Seventies became "less likely to try to interpret what they read and more likely to simply make unexplained value judgments about it" and that "17-year-olds' papers became somewhat more like 13-year-olds' papers . . . shallow and superficial opinions at the expense of reasoned and disciplined thought." At least some of the responsibility seemed to lie with the instant satisfactions and instant answers provided by video games and TV sitcoms. These apparently convince many students that they will "emerge from school into an electronic world that will require little reading and less writing." Observing that "nothing could be further from the truth . . . in a world over-loaded with information," the report concluded somberly that "a society in which the habits of disciplined reading, analysis, inter-pretation and discourse are not sufficiently cultivated has much to fear." Those should be chilling words for any American.

The problem is nationwide, even though the acute symptoms of functional illiteracy are most visible among the poor (40 percent of adults with incomes under $5,000 a year are deemed functionally incompetent) and minorities (56 percent of Hispanics and 44 per-cent of blacks, compared with 16 percent of whites). But it was the militant Jesse Jackson who, before losing his way in the routine demagoguery of Presidential politics, best put his finger on the only ultimate solution—not just for those who clearly cannot perform productively but for the middle-class white kids whose lazy minds appear to rely on the possibility that adult life will turn out to be a rerun of "Laverne & Shirley." The real responsibility, Jackson declared, lies at home: "Parents are the foundation of the school system. The school system can do without teachers. Many of them survive with poor ones. They can do without superintendents. But no school system can get by without parents. If parents don't make kids, there won't be any schools. If parents don't pay taxes, there won't be any teachers. If parents do not assume the primary responsibility for monitoring and disciplining their children, there won't be any results." Surely, he is right. We can shut off the television, produce wiser teachers and elect more challenging leaders, but if we do not accept our own responsibilities as parents systematically to nurture educational excellence in the home, we will be flunking the course ourselves.

If the frightening state of U.S. education has become a matter of legitimate national concern, how are we doing in the specific area of economic education? Superficially, it would appear, we are doing better. The National Survey of Economic Education 1981, undertaken by specialists in the field under the auspices of Phillips Petroleum, found that economics was approaching the status of a mainstream course of study in America's junior and senior high schools. Once reserved for older college-bound students, the sub-ject now reached a broad range in all grades. For most teachers, though, teaching economics was a secondary responsibility—and economics tended to be a subsidiary subject, usually taught as part of another discipline, such as government or mathematics, rather than as an independent course. According to the teachers, there was a marked difference between the focus in public school economic instruction on the "practical"—such as "consumer issues" and "consumerism," decision making and "how-to" skills—and the greater concentration in private and parochial schools on helping students understand some of the more "theoretical" topics.

The quality of such instruction is of course debatable (professional economists who analyzed the survey were disturbed at the lack of attention given to what they regarded as some of the fundamental concepts of their field); what seems less arguable is the need for more and better economic education. Repeated surveys show that many in the nation's putative intellectual elite are themselves abysmally ignorant on the most basic questions of economics. When the Gallup Poll asked college students for their "best guess" about how much profit a large national corporation made on each dollar of sales, the average answer was 45 cents. At my own alma mater, Princeton, the answer was 49 cents. (By some accounts, a similar poll of the faculty delivered a higher number.) The students in the national sample added that a "fair" share would be 25 cents for the corporation's profit. In reality, as Gallup noted, the correct answer is that the median share of profits for the companies in question is less than 5 cents for each dollar of sales. Is it any wonder that demagogues find it easy to designate large corporations as scapegoats when such fundamental misinformation is already widespread?

The apparent surge of Marxist sentiment on U.S. campuses provides an unsettling footnote to this discussion. It is ironic (if not downright ludicrous) that at a time when Marxist economies have demonstrably been outstripped by market-oriented economies, not just among the great powers but all over the world, an increasing number of U.S. college professors seem to have found it intellectually fashionable to preach Marxism. There could scarcely be a more damning indictment of the campuses' detachment from economic reality; it's as if the ivory tower had become a distant spaceship.

The exact velocity of this flight from common sense is difficult to quantify. *Business Week* reported in 1980 that "there is no precise measure of Marxist influence on American campuses, but it has clearly grown enormously over the last decade." Estimating that radical campus caucuses had more than 10,000 members and supported more than a dozen Marxist journals, the magazine quoted Professor John H. Coatsworth, a University of Chicago historian, as saying: "As a set of theories that explain social and economic developments, Marxism is more strongly adhered to now than at any other time in U.S. academic history." Two years later, *U.S. News & World Report* took note of this phenomenon, observing that many of the professors had been "radicalized" as students or young instructors in the turbulent Sixties and that they viewed their role now as "providing an intellectual base for launching a nonviolent assault on the American capitalism they blame for inflation, unemployment and a host of other troubles at home and around the world." As Professor Frances Fox Piven of Boston University, a Marxist and a vice president of the American Political Science Association, saw it, "There is a growing acceptance of the critical approach taken by Marxists and other radical leftists as a useful means of advancing our knowledge of society and its problems." (Piven is among the resources available to the Institute for Policy Studies in Washington, which has been described as the most important Marxist transmission belt in the U.S.—and which, according to the *Washington Post,* was asked by fifty-two mostly Democratic members of Congress in 1982 to finance a series of studies ranging from defense to housing.) The Marxists have not been shy in advancing their claims to be heard across the vast range of national policy; Professor Samuel Bowles of the University of Massachusetts at Amherst, son of former U.S. diplomat Chester Bowles, declaimed in *Schooling in Capitalist America,* co-authored with Herbert Gintis: "We venture to suggest that all of the glaring inadequacies in political democracy in the United States are attributable to the private ownership of the means of production and the lack of a real economic democracy." You betcha.

How in the real world has this happened? One leading campus Marxist, Professor Bertell Ollman of New York University's Center for Marxist Studies, declares proudly that "a Marxist cultural revolution is taking place in American universities," and two other advocates chortle that "there are hundreds, perhaps thousands, of openly socialist professors, [helping] their students to understand the bourgeois culture that oppresses them." An academic critic of this movement, Arnold Beichman of the University of Massachusetts at Boston, concludes that Marxist studies have in fact become "one of the biggest growth industries on U.S. campuses today" and wonders how "such a discredited theory . . . found a respectable home." One possible reason cited by Beichman in the *Wall Street Journal:* "Marxism today has enormous power and influence over mainstream intellectuals because it makes possible for them to be ritualistically anti-Soviet and pro-Communist left at the same time. When the USSR does something terrible—like the seizure of Poland and the destruction of a free labor union like Solidarity—the Marxist can announce his solidarity with the Polish working-class but then in his pro-Communist persona demand NATO's disarmament. . . . For Marxism, the jury is always out; it never returns a verdict and so it never makes a mistake. Marxism's partners—Moscow, Peking, Havana, and all the others—are always defined out of existence by Marxists, who never suspend judgment on democracy." The double standard, he finds, is pervasive. While the practical failures of Marxism wherever it has actually been tried are endlessly explained away, Marxists and their sympathizers promote the notion that capitalism cannot take care of the poor—ignoring the happier reality that the number of persons with incomes below the poverty line in the U.S. is now about 5 percent, as compared with about 40 percent in 1929.

How much should we care about this campus ferment? Not very much, perhaps, if it were only a sign of vigorous academic give and take, of intellectual broadening. Maybe a tad more if, as Beichman suggests, "This campus Marxism isn't being taught as intellectual history, which would be proper and no different from teaching Machiavelli, Hume or Rousseau. It is being taught as a moral code, a form of secular salvation, an incontrovertible analysis of failing democracy, and cruel and collapsing capitalism." Even if one regards the faculty Marxist fad as a containable phenomenon, it underlines the extent to which, if Americans' faith in their own remarkable system cannot be restored, others are standing by with considerably worse.

Interestingly, this preoccupation with old, unworking systems of thought like Marxism occurred at a time when our leaders in Washington were, at least theoretically, trying out a lot of "new" ideas—freeing up the economy, moving away from traditional stat-ist control. One might conclude that the campus and the capital had somehow zanily switched roles. Such observers as Philip N. Marcus, executive director of the Institute for Economic Affairs, a nonprofit organization aimed at bringing the business and aca-demic communities together, find this unamazing: "We are in the midst of a 'revolution' in economic theory, and currently witness-ing a deliberate break in Washington. . . . It is not surprising that economic education lags behind the innovations in theoretical eco-nomics and practical policy making." But others at a forum orga-nized by the institute were less sanguine. Leslie Lenkowsky, a foundation program officer experienced in economic education, declared glumly that, while "few areas of education have grown as rapidly in recent years as the teaching of economics," the faculty tilt is so far leftward that "instruction in the subject might, ironi-cally, lessen support for our economic system." Irving Kristol, doyen of the "neo-conservatives," was convinced that "there can-not be 'economic education' that is non-ideological. And we ought to face this fact candidly." Meanwhile, Alan Reynolds, chief econ-omist at Polyconomics, Inc., seemed the least anguished. "There has been a very real revolution in the whole approach and tone of economics," he contended—and he didn't mean Marxism, but its opposite: the increasing turn away from advocacy of governmental solutions. Observing (correctly) that "the 'old' economics is mainly the quaint economics of the Thirties, while the 'new' eco-nomics is largely a sophisticated revival of the insights of the Eigh-teenth Century," Reynolds thought the academic trend he perceived toward "a healthy respect for the efficiency of markets . . . would be even more apparent except that a few surviving old economists still get a lot of media attention, no matter how often their theories clash with reality. Their own younger students do not believe them, however, so the old ideas will virtually disappear within a generation."

So you pays your money—endlessly!—and you takes your choice. My own view is that the truth is somewhere in between: the glass is both half full and half empty. The growing (if far from predominant) craze for faculty Marxism is a genuine phenomenon, and one that might usefully be studied by those asked to contribute to the support of these institutions: not with an eye toward repressing dissent, but with the intention of assuring that the private-enterprise side of the story gets full attention. We have nothing to fear from such a vigorous debate (the facts, and the force, are with us), and my personal preference is for defeating these intellectual ostriches in open discussion. Plainly, though, this presupposes that students be exposed to enough basic economic education to be able to audit the charlatans and separate sense from sententiousness.

HOW NOT TO USE THE "BULLY PULPIT"

Since, as we have seen, the failures of our society in solid economic education are widespread, is it fair to pay so much attention to what our recent Presidents have or have not done? My answer is an emphatic affirmative: it is essential that we demand more intellectual clarity and consistent performance from those who purport to lead us. While it is patently unreasonable to present this as a one-person task, the President does occupy what Theodore Roosevelt called a "bully pulpit," and he more than any other individual can make a critically important start in the economic education of America. The power of the Presidency in this area is immense, not just in shaping public opinion to his own way of looking at issues but in deciding which issues we are to look at on any particular day. The President must avoid the temptation (to which all his recent predecessors routinely have succumbed) to talk passingly popular, polls-oriented political balderdash about the U.S. economy. As we decry the mindless Marxism of the campus, we should decry the equally escapist balancing acts of fearful politicians.

It means, for example, that a President cannot try to substitute good intentions, or soaring rhetoric, or magical new theory, for the hard numbers of a sound and credible economic program. And it means that he cannot indulge in that all too familiar Presidential exercise of always seeking private scapegoats for public failures—whether those scapegoats are sought, as Jimmy Carter sought them, among oilmen in Houston, or à la Ronald Reagan, among investors in the U.S. stock and bond markets. Reagan, whose supply of vitriol is limited, stopped short of utter idiocy in this department after a few mild sallies in 1981 accusing the financial markets of undermining his program. (He may have won the heart of every losing investor in America when he asserted that he had "never found Wall Street a source of economic wisdom." One assumes that he was not immediately thinking of his own Secretary of the Treasury, Donald T. Regan, who when appointed was chairman of Merrill Lynch.) But the President's relative restraint did not inhibit his acolytes. The most bizarre was the Senate majority leader, Howard H. Baker, Jr., who seemed to have developed the interesting theory that Wall Street was in a sinister conspiracy to lose its own money. Apparently acting under the delusion that the millions of investors all over the world who had more than $5 trillion at risk in the U.S. financial markets were, in fact, just a sort of errant Senate page boy, securities analyst Baker warned Wall Street that it had better watch out if it knew what was good for it. Declaring that "it's time indeed that the financial markets realize that they're playing a dangerous game," the Tennessee Bernard Baruch threatened that if those dastardly markets did not perform as he wanted them to within "days," then Congress might retaliate by passing laws imposing controls, higher taxes and a lot of other things that had never worked in the past. One might have thought that Wall Street was a mean man hiding in a cave, who adored high interest rates, a crumbling stock market and a bond market whose appearance would have had to improve considerably to qualify as a good-looking corpse. (The stock market, not surprisingly, promptly produced not the comeback Baker had demanded but its worst single week of the year, as terrified investors figured that things must be even worse than they had thought if a U.S. Senator had to be out there touting stocks.) But Baker may, however inadvertently, have made his own small contribution to the economic education of the nation by demonstrating, for anyone still in doubt, that neither political party had a monopoly on fatuity.

What I am suggesting is that, instead of applauding our Presidents when they stroke our particular prejudices, or even when they go halfway toward reducing the hogwash content of Washington chatter about the economy, we must demand that they go all the way, all the time—giving national economic education the Number One priority it so urgently requires. It is not the insight of the century that they would prefer a more ambiguous posture; any politician at any level can convince himself that his compromises with principle are excusable because things would be so much worse if he were not there. I think we ought to serve notice on the President, and on every one of our noble statesmen in Congress, too, that we are going to be holding them to a much higher standard of consistent integrity and performance than we have been used to receiving from Washington where the U.S. economy was concerned. We have to recognize that the hour is now late: that our country's economic problems have by now reached the critical flash stage where we can no longer tolerate even a modicum of what the Washington apologists love to call "politics as usual" about the economy. This means that we have got to make up our own minds not to do what they all want us to—which is, of course, to get real partisan about this, choose up sides and then be afraid to say anything critical of our guy when he goes astray (and later be surprised and disappointed, two or three years down the pike, that he hasn't made a significant difference, either). It means we shouldn't just sit back and say, "Oh, give him a chance," when one of the candidates we happen to favor gets elected: that we have to be watching them, and pushing them, every day that they are in office—making them aware that we are now going to be insisting throughout on less political malarkey and more economic sense, and that we have become fed up to our eyebrows with Washington's nonstop amateur night with all our money. We can no longer afford the conventional alibis for nonfeasance; this country's economic problems have by now reached the point where the traditional Washington talk about the alleged "political realities," which always seem to stop us from taking adequate action to heal our economic ailments, must now finally and permanently be put aside—and put aside by both parties, and at both ends of Pennsylvania Avenue.

There is no secret about why the typical politician resists this kind of counsel. It is dangerous to educate (you might get somebody mad, you might lose a vote), while it is far more tempting to ply the traditional route and play on fear, on class war, on envy of one's neighbor, on that near-universal neurosis known as paranoia. But there is, in the end, something unsavory about this. I get just a mite peeved when some of the same politicians who have

gone on cheerfully miseducating the American public about economics, and done it so successfully in political terms over the
years, then turn around and say to me (as a good many have done,
when the doors were closed and the cameras weren't running)
something like this: "Okay, Lou, of course you're right that we
haven't done everything we could be doing to solve the economy's
problems. But come on, now, Lou, you're a sophisticated fellow,
you know why we couldn't do all those things—because unfortunately, you see, the public just wouldn't understand them." Well,
I humbly submit that we don't need any more favors like that from
our friends in Washington. What we do need, in my judgment, is
absolutely clear: we need more one-term politicians. We need
more men and women who are willing to tell us the truth, do
whatever seems right and necessary and sufficient, and then let the
political chips fall where they may.

And in that connection, it might be useful to close this section
on economic education with a story about a fellow who reluctantly
dropped out of the political game a while back: John B. Connally.
Connally followed me to the rostrum once at a meeting in Green-
ville, South Carolina—the state that ultimately dashed his own
Presidential hopes, as it happens—and when he got there, he said:
"If I had any sense at all, I'd just say 'Amen' and sit down."
(Then he gave a good-sized speech.) In the course of his own
oration, he remarked at one point: "I'll tell you something else
that might surprise you that I agree with Mr. Rukeyser about. I
think he's right on target when he calls for more one-term politicians." Well, I looked up with renewed interest because I recalled
that he had had three terms as Governor of Texas, and I hadn't
been aware that this was part of his political philosophy. Connally
went on to propose a Constitutional amendment limiting the terms
of President, Senator and Representative, and whatever you may
think of that particular method for producing rotation in office,
what he next said seems to me to be undeniably cogent. At the end
of that limited period, Connally declared, let's have a brass band
out at the airport, let's have a ticker-tape parade and let's have
some speechmaking. And let's say, "Welcome home, sir or
madam, and thank you for your brief period of public service. Now
you come home and live among us—with the laws you passed and
the regulations you promulgated."

In the happy thought that this alone could do wonders to improve the U.S. economy over the next decade, let's turn now from
education to action—and to the nine other areas in which we might
grasp a more prosperous future.

II

Tax and Tax . . .

The economic area that perennially grabs most of Washington's attention, if only a small part of its IQ, is the budget and taxes. The twin subjects focus a politician's mind wonderfully, and for what are likely to seem to him or her the most impeccable of reasons: the former can win votes and the latter can lose them. The power is so immense that the temptation to play endlessly with both sides of the equation proves irresistible to each succeeding crop of subcommittee chairmen. But political potency should not be confused with economic efficacy. Despite all the self-serving oratory that reaches a crescendo around election time, the ability of a government to create prosperity is demonstrably nil, no matter how pure its intentions or compassionate its oratory. Politicians are at best kibitzers on the sidelines of a nation's economy, not engineers of its prosperity. Yet the humility that would be appropriate to such a role is not conspicuous in the nation's capital. This would be merely annoying if it were not for a more unpleasant reality: while governments cannot create prosperity, they are marvelously equipped to destroy it. Even a cursory examination of recent American economic history leaves one in awe at the ability of succeeding governments, each presumably composed of well-intentioned and at least middling intelligent citizens, to lay waste to a basically healthy economy.

Happily, though, the situation is far from hopeless. As Adam Smith observed, a nation can stand a lot of ruin. So in search of a more positive role for government in this area, let us first focus specifically on tax policy.

THE AMAZING INVISIBLE TAX CUT

In order to think sensibly about taxes, we must disentangle ourselves from partisanship and paranoia alike, and try to discover what could truly work and improve our own lives and those of our fellow private citizens. If the American people are not thoroughly confused by now, it is a tribute either to their innate common sense or to their capacity to ignore their putative leaders. Take that phased series of tax cuts passed in 1981 (which many Congressmen have been trying to do since the day it was enacted). Though the original proposal had been substantially watered down, the prevailing view in political, academic and media circles quickly became that we had gone too far: that it had been irresponsible to slash taxes so deeply. This view was advanced not only by the Reagan Administration's traditional critics, but by many of his own team leaders. Panicked by the explosion of interest rates and deficit projections, they eventually enlisted even the President in a brief, ill-advised policy reversal in 1982. In the middle of the country's worst postwar recession, a bill was enacted aimed at boosting tax receipts by $100 billion over three years, in large part by reducing a variety of existing incentives for investors and savers. The Commander-in-Chief seemed determined to shoot himself in the foot. And the Republican Senate, which in 1981 took pride in passing what it gleefully called the biggest tax cut in history, apparently took equal pride in 1982 in originating what was arguably the biggest tax increase in history. We were of course assured that these tax increases were "different," that they were "reforms" that would not delay or cut back the (politically vital) completion of scheduled cuts in individual tax rates. It was, in short, the same old story: the Reagan White House, having discovered that it was politically difficult to cut spending as much as it had hoped, decided that the easy solution was to try to reduce deficits through higher taxes. Never mind that this strategy never had worked; indeed, the tax increases similarly billed as "reform" in 1969 and 1976 had managed to help produce the worst string of deficits in the nation's history. And certainly never mind that once you penetrate the Washington fog it becomes apparent that any new transfer of private wealth to Government coffers is a tax increase, whether you have the honesty to call it that or whether you attempt to disguise your actions with such euphemisms as "tax reform" or "loophole closing" or "revenue enhancement." In the words of the immortal *New Yorker* cartoon: "I say it's spinach, and I say the hell with it."

So let me not disguise my own apparently highly unstylish view on taxes, which is that the much-vaunted cuts of 1981 not only stopped well short of being excessive but were in fact invisible. Taxes went up—not down—in 1981. What our legislators actually produced, amid so much misguided disputation, was only a reduction in the tax *increases* that otherwise would have landed on the populace in the early Eighties. Legislation already in place provided enormously larger revenue burdens, of which major increases in Social Security taxes and the impact of inflation in pushing taxpayers into higher brackets (with lower buying power) were only the most conspicuous. Congressman Jack Kemp, chief architect of those allegedly excessive tax cuts, later observed that "in effect, taxes went up by $37 billion in 1981." While the original Kemp-Roth tax proposal had called for an immediate 30 percent across-the-board marginal tax rate cut, what eventually transpired amounted to a 23 percent reduction over four years—and virtually nothing in that critical first year, as the economy teetered into recession. The eventual Congressional dispensation for 1981 was described as a 5 percent cut starting October 1; in the real world, that translates into a somewhat less than exorbitant 1.25 percent reduction in our scheduled 1981 taxes.

Nor did it stop there. In 1982, by which time we were being told on all sides that the tax cuts had gone much too far, taxes actually took a greater share of the gross national product than they did in 1980. And even if the entire series of planned "reductions" had been allowed to play itself out without any further moves to counter it with "revenue enhancement," we would have entered not some brave new world of super-low taxation but only the same level that had prevailed in this country as recently as 1978. An overly generous "governmental giveaway," indeed! What sheep we were to accept the notion that some imaginary "huge" tax cuts were the villains in our economic scenario.

Once again in 1983 rhetoric fought reality. Economically, it was becoming apparent that the impact of the 1982 tax increases had been somewhere between counterproductive and suicidal; they had not even accomplished—by so much as a nickel—their supposed objective of reducing the deficit. The projected shortfalls were larger than before the bill was conceived. No one should have been surprised: if raising taxes were truly the way to eliminate deficits, we would have had the biggest surpluses in U.S. history right through the Nineteen Seventies. Instead, we produced the most horrendous string of budget deficits on record, as the gargantuan tax increases (1) crippled savings, investment and production growth, and (2) encouraged greedy legislators to spend all these bountiful new revenues—and more. The worst of these tax increases was the most dishonest: the hidden tax known as "bracket creep," in which inflation pushed workers into higher tax brackets without any genuine economic elevation. Ordinary workers found their earnings taxed at rates originally intended for the affluent.* Congress, the chief beneficiary of this governmental con game, gleefully took advantage of these "inflation dividends," and then some. From 1970 to 1980, unlegislated increases in personal income-tax revenues totaled 176 percent. Why, then, couldn't the Government balance the budget during that decade of windfall tax increases? The answer is that Congress, characteristically, used this bonanza as one more excuse to avoid cutting spending; Federal outlays from 1970 to 1980 bounded ahead by 194 percent—even faster than revenues. Scant wonder, then, that in 1983 so many politicians resisted the implementation of the final stage of the 1981 tax cuts, because—for the first time—these finally had a chance to deliver a year of authentic net reductions. Despite the obfuscating campaign to convince ordinary citizens that the Reagan tax cuts were by then a proven failure, the uncomfortable truth was that they had barely begun.

Perhaps too much had been made of such trendy new slogans as "supply-side economics." The name was a response to the long-prevailing academic preoccupation with the economy's "demand" side—that is, with putting money into, or taking money out of, people's pockets. Supply siders emphasize that, as Kemp put it to

---

* The remedy for this form of larceny is full implementation of tax indexing, discussed in Chapter XI.

a 1982 conference sponsored by the Federal Reserve Bank of Atlanta, "people are spenders and consumers, but they are also producers, savers, investors and entrepreneurs. Instead of using both monetary and fiscal policy to pump up demand, or choke it off . . . monetary policy should be used to stabilize the dollar, and fiscal incentives used at the same time to encourage individual and business production, saving and risk-taking." Leaving aside for the moment the question of how best to stabilize the dollar, this meant in practice that supply siders advocated substantial cuts in "marginal" rates of income tax—that is, the top rates paid on the last dollars earned—so as to encourage more work, savings and investment. If the tax system were less confiscatory, the argument went, individuals would have the incentive to become more productive (with themselves and with their cash), and the overall economy would benefit. At its best, then, what was presented as newly minted theory was merely a restatement of some of the basic principles of classical economics. At its worst, in my judgment, some extreme "supply siders" fostered the notion that massive tax cuts could cure all the nation's economic woes rapidly, painlessly and without any significant attention to reducing Government spending.

Consequently, those who identified themselves as "supply siders" tended to be on the defensive when nirvana did not arrive in the wake of the 1981 tax legislation—but deepening recession did. While critics maintained that the tax-cut theory had been discredited, a more fundamental problem was that the original legislation had been oversold both as a cure-all and in the extent to which it actually reduced the nation's tax burden. "Supply siders," whose own occasional addiction to hyperbole had proved self-defeating, insisted with some justice that the White House itself had contributed to the nation's confusion by leaving the impression that the cuts went deeper than they genuinely did. For example, when I pressed economist Arthur Laffer about that ever-changing mix known as "Reaganomics," Laffer—though still an official Presidential economic adviser—bubbled over with at least as much criticism as praise for the incumbent Administration. (Laffer, the ebullient professor who has been called "the guru of the tax revolt," popularized the theory of growth incentives through tax reductions—the Laffer Curve—that underlay the President's original tax program.) Laffer challenged the conventional wisdom that the reductions had been too lavish, and argued instead that Reagan's real error had been in doling out the goodies in such small portions. The first stage of the three-year tax reductions was doomed to be ineffectual, Laffer told me, because people naturally wait for the full impact before swinging into positive economic action. It's true, he maintained, for "price cuts or tax cuts": if they're on the horizon but not yet here, people will hold back until they arrive. His contention, in other words, was not that the tax cuts were too large but that they should have come in one massive, stimulative dose. One need not rely exclusively on the tax-cut method of economic salvation to recognize that the dribbles with which such reductions actually did descend—in mid-1982, they amounted to $4.20 a week for a couple with two children and a weekly income of $400—suggested that this view had considerable merit. (It's not a bad idea to try a policy before repudiating it.)

Meanwhile, despite all the fashionable talk about supposedly excessive tax cuts, Congress went right on letting taxes rise—both indirectly, through the impact of inflation on the Government's revenues, and directly, through the staggering and continuing boosts in Social Security taxes and all the other goodies perennially emerging from Capitol Hill. By 1983 Reagan was trying to refurbish his image as a tax cutter, but he had weakened his credibility—and his case—by advocating the increases of 1982. In that year, how quickly even the President seemed to have forgotten why he carried forty-four states in 1980—forgotten, indeed, his own comments in 1981 ("Even the extended tax rate cuts which I am recommending still leave too high a tax burden on the American people") and earlier in 1982 ("Raising taxes is no way to balance the budget"). One would think it would have given his tax-boosting allies, such as Senate Finance Chairman Robert Dole, at least a modicum of discomfort that this about-face drew effusive applause from all the wrong people: from those who consistently endorsed the free-spending, high-taxing policies that got us into this economic mess. (One of Lyndon Johnson's former economic advisers told me that he was happily surprised to find Dole acting so "responsibly.") My own view is that while tax reductions clearly cannot do the entire job in curing the nation's economic ills, they are a vitally important part of the solution. Given the runaway increases in Federal taxes in recent years (increases largely unlegislated but produced by the Government's own inflation), given the tremendous burden those taxes have placed on the American economy, given the enormous drag they have represented on every attempt to renew healthy economic growth in this country, I think it would have been irresponsible not to move to reduce the revenue load in 1981. We need, not a retreat, but a sturdy advance into further (and more authentic) tax reductions in the years ahead.

A little history may be helpful in targeting exactly where we are on taxes, and how we might move to a more attractive terrain. Congress passed the income-tax amendment in 1909, and when it was being debated in state legislatures, assurances were given that it would never exceed 4 or 5 percent, and would affect only a relatively few rich people at that. Indeed, the first law passed under this amendment, in 1913, called for a 1 percent tax on incomes over $3,000 ($4,000 for couples), a level exceeded by only 3 percent of the country's wage-earners. (A tax of up to 7 percent was levied on ultrahigh incomes, from $20,000 to over $500,000.) So lofty were the entry levels that among those freed from any tax whatsoever were 81 percent of America's lawyers and 79 percent of its bankers. Since then, as you may be aware, there have been some changes made.

While most of these changes have been in a predictable direction, two aspects of our tax history seem particularly relevant to the current situation: the recent immense expansion of the tax load on the average wage-earner, and the consequences (almost altogether joyful) of those rare occasions when Congress brought itself genuinely to reverse the trend.

First, consider the typical American worker. While tax rates went up during both world wars, soaring to a theoretical high (which few paid) of 94 percent in World War II, even after those years of severe inflation the average family was only beginning to be touched by the tax code. In 1947 four out of five families earned less than $5,000 annually; the effective tax rate was about 8.4 percent. A worker making $5,000, married with two children, paid around $420 in income tax plus $30 in Social Security taxes. He faced a marginal tax rate (i.e., the tax on any additional dollars of income) of less than 20 percent. Very few people were in high

marginal tax brackets. The situation today is dramatically different: four out of five U.S. families have incomes over $11,000, and
half are over $23,000. The average worker is not only "facing taxes
intended originally for the rich," David Boaz of the Cato Institute
in Washington wrote in the *Wall Street Journal,* but he pays as
much Social Security taxes in two weeks as anyone paid in a year
in the first two decades of that system (1937–56); "in recent years
Federal tax liabilities have risen twice as fast as income for an
average worker." To Boaz this was evidence that "the politicians
and special interests in Washington will never decide that taxes are
too high."

The fact is that the conventional Congressional talk about "fairness" and "making the rich pay their share" is essentially a diversion from the demands being made on ordinary taxpayers. Since
there simply isn't enough money in the hands of the truly affluent,
even if we confiscated it, the average guy is now paying through
the nose (on a scale uncontemplated even a few years ago) to
support the Government's headlong spending. Between 1965 and
1975 the average tax rates for the median-income earner increased
more than 35 percent; in the next five years, those rates went up
an additional 22 percent, mainly due to inflation-induced "bracket
creep" (in which your tax rates go up, but your living standard
goes down). The marginal tax rate faced by the median-income
family of four in 1980 was 24 percent. Paul Craig Roberts, then
Assistant Secretary of the Treasury for Economic Policy, testified
in 1981 that, when you took into account Social Security and state
tax increases, the marginal tax rate facing the average American
family was 40 to 44 percent. On average, this amounted to about
$10,690 per household. "Does anyone seriously think," inquired
Thomas M. Humbert of the Heritage Foundation in 1982, "that
adding to this burden would create a more healthy economy?"

Apparently, somebody did. Never mind that the 10 percent personal tax reductions in mid-1982 would at best scarcely more than
offset the $13 billion increase in Social Security taxes mandated
that year and the $28 billion caused by the inexorable "bracket
creep." Never mind that, according to the Congressional Budget
Office (scarcely a bastion of "supply-side" theorists), tax levies
were already scheduled to rise from $605 billion in 1981 to $923.3
billion in 1986. Never mind that, as noted, the fully implemented

Reagan tax cuts would do no more than return the nation to the level of taxation in 1978. Congress—and the White House—seemingly couldn't wait to get back to their bad old ways of boosting someone else's taxes rather than buckling down and cutting their own spending. (Perhaps the silliest alibi of all was the claim that such tax increases were necessary to mollify Wall Street and bring about lower interest rates. Jack W. Lavery, chief economist for Secretary Regan's old firm, Merrill Lynch, quickly noted with alarm that Washington was threatening to take back nearly three quarters of the tax cut for business by 1986—and that as a result of these and other actions, individuals would lose close to half their promised cuts as early as 1983. What was truly needed "and as yet is by no means in evidence," Lavery declared, was "a credible and broad-based restraint on Government spending." And Moody's Investors Service, the bond-rating firm, was equally unambiguous: "Efforts to balance the budget via higher income taxes could have a devastating effect throughout the economy. The expected drop in interest rates could well be meaningless in the long run if the economy's underpinnings continue to deteriorate—as we would expect them to do under greater tax burdens." In short, the real message of the financial markets on taxes was the same as that of the average discouraged and overburdened worker: enough already.) So much for the "Reagan revolution" on taxes.

As the average working stiff finds himself subjected to tax rates designed for somebody else entirely, he reacts predictably. (By 1982 the marginal tax rate for a typical American family earning $20,000 had climbed to 28 percent; for those in the $40,000 range —hardly the J. P. Morgan category in modern America—rates had reached 44 percent.) Tax avoidance becomes a national preoccupation. As recently as 1970, when I hosted a series of TV specials on taxes for ABC, the Internal Revenue Service boasted about the fantastic compliance record of Americans in voluntarily paying their taxes. There was a striking contrast in those days between the U.S. and practically every other nation in the world: here, unlike France and Italy, a good citizen voluntarily paid his taxes; respectable members of the community did not brag about the tricks by which they had evaded the revenue authorities. Now both the financial situation and the moral attitude are clearly different. The traditional view that hard and honest work brings its legitimate rewards is being rapidly eroded. At a time when U.S. productivity and work standards decline perilously, an "underground economy" flourishes. Now it is not just the wealthy who must think of the tax man with every decision. Tens of billions of dollars, much of it earned by people whose life styles are many miles from any historical definition of affluence, are funneled into tax shelters. And millions of Americans just plain cheat. As the dream of getting ahead, of living better than one's parents, disappears into the ever-expanding maw of the IRS, people who would once docilely, if not happily, have paid their taxes now find it easy to rationalize their evasion. The "cash" economy grows; if it's "off the books," nobody's to know, right? No one does know to what extent this attitude is distorting the modern U.S. economy, and rendering official statistics from production to unemployment suspicious. But we have a hint: the IRS, which for years grudgingly refused to admit the extent of "noncompliance" in the belief that such recognition would itself contribute to the system's breakdown, estimated in 1982 that fully $97 billion due in taxes was not reported. The apparent belief in Washington that the way to close such enormous gaps is to come down even harder on those who do pay their taxes is characteristically loony.

All well and good, the moralists tell us: of course everybody wants to pay lower taxes, but given the present level of Government spending it would be irresponsible to offer larger cuts in taxes. As it happens, this proposition is historically false even if one allows that highly questionable "given" to slip by. It is based on a single controlling fallacy, which is that the amount of income earned in this country is static and therefore that higher tax rates automatically mean higher tax revenues. In the immortal words of Sportin' Life, "It ain't necessarily so." Consider our actual experiences on the two previous occasions when the U.S. instituted major tax reductions: the 1922, 1924 and 1926 cuts devised by Treasury Secretary Andrew Mellon and the 1964 cuts proposed by President John F. Kennedy.

Hostility toward those who earn high incomes is not a recent phenomenon; in 1921, top-bracket income was taxed at a rate of 73 percent. The predictable result was that people avoided making much cash income that would be taxed at that level. This turned out to be bad not for them but for the poorer members of our

society, who lost in two ways: (1) there was less saving and investing by upper-income groups, and thus fewer new tools were financed and growth in worker productivity and earnings was
slowed; (2) since there was little taxable high-bracket income, 72
percent of all income taxes were collected from people earning less
than $100,000 annually. But lo and behold, look what happened
when the theoretical rates of 60 to 73 percent on incomes over
$100,000 were reduced, by 1926, to 25 percent. With the new in-
centive of being able to keep 75 cents rather than 27 cents of each
new dollar earned, top-bracket taxpayers went enthusiastically to
work earning taxable income. They paid 86 percent more taxes in
1926 than they had in 1924. This amounted to fully 51 percent of
the total tax collected. From little more than a quarter of the nation's tax load in 1921, the highest earners were carrying more than
half by 1926—though the rates on their income were spectacularly
lower. Meanwhile, the average worker's earnings climbed by 12
percent and the Consumer Price Index fell by 2 percent. There
could scarcely be a more telling indictment of the philosophy of
class war in tax collections.

Unfortunately, however, we failed to learn from this salutary
experience, and when a combination of such unrelated factors as
disastrous trade and monetary policies plunged the U.S. into a
Great Depression, we were ready to respond to demagogic attempts to blame it on the rich. And so tax rates were raised sharply
again in 1932, with the levy on $100,000-plus incomes jumping from
25 to 56 percent. And, what do you know, the biggest declines in
reported income occurred in the highest tax brackets. The affluent
may or may not have been less worthy than the rest of us, but they
proved no more suicidal.

Similarly, in 1963, our counterproductive desire to squeeze
those more fortunate than the average had taken the tax rates even
higher; incomes over a mere $50,000 were now taxed at rates rang-
ing from 59 to 91 percent. The Kennedy cuts lowered these levels
to 50 to 70 percent. Did the rich get richer and the poor get poorer?
Not on your life. The result was entirely in keeping with the previous pattern: the cuts produced more revenue from those whose
rates were lowered. Even adjusted for inflation, tax receipts from
those with incomes over $50,000 increased by 34 percent in 1965
over 1963.

When a machine operates the same way every time, when a turn of the wheel in a specific direction produces a predictable result and the reverse action produces a reverse result, it may be time to put aside our instant prejudices about other people's taxes and, as Al Smith would have it, look at the record. Nor are the reasons for these results obscure. As James Gwartney and Richard Stroup noted in a study published by the Federal Reserve Bank of Atlanta, "Tax rates—particularly marginal tax rates—influence the reward structure confronted by individual taxpayers, and thereby exert an impact on the allocation of labor and capital resources. . . . When taxes are levied on an economic activity, the quantity of that activity undertaken will decline." Consequently, Gwartney and Stroup concluded, the projected 1981–84 rate reductions seemed likely to increase the relative share of tax revenues derived from high-income earners: "Far from shifting the tax burden toward the poor, the Reagan program will shift the tax burden toward the rich."

Yale Brozen, professor of business economics at the University of Chicago's Graduate School of Business, put it this way in an article for *National Review:* "In attempting to redistribute income from the rich to the poor, a high tax rate on the rich will, paradoxical as it may seem, result in less of the tax burden being borne by them, because they will seek shelter in investments that yield capital gains rather than current income—high-growth stocks that don't pay much in dividends—or they will put their money in tax-exempt securities, vacation homes, etc. Reducing tax rates on our upper-bracket taxpayers increases the revenues collected from them and increases the share of the tax burden they bear." Brozen concocted a "law" for this: "Whenever the government attempts to redistribute income from the rich to the poor, it creates more poor people, impoverishes the nation, and decreases the portion of the tax burden borne by the rich." And Robert D. Hershey, Jr., of the *New York Times,* challenging the polemical assertions that "bigger tax cuts for the wealthy shift more of the burden to the less well off," reminded readers: "Unappealing though it is to some, tax cuts have to be given to people who actually pay taxes. The rich are also better able to save money from their tax cuts and put it to productive use." In sum, disinterested observers from varying points on the political spectrum uniformly have concluded, when they did their homework, that reducing high marginal tax rates is not a sop to high earners but a way to get them to pay more taxes. The problem is not that we moved in this direction in the Nineteen Eighties but that we did so so halfheartedly.

Part of the difficulty, I would contend, is that we are too loosely using that emotive phrase "the rich." In terms of what it once conveyed in this country, the phrase has lost all meaning. Who are "the rich" in America today? They are not, I submit, those who through their own industry, ingenuity or good fortune earn a high income. That, as every statistical study reiterates, is a rapidly changing group—and, as we have seen, we are currently taxing at rates designed for "the rich" millions of American families who would justifiably seek to have you committed if you tried to describe them or their standard of living as "rich." ("Did you ever think you would be making this much," I used to ask my college classmates, "and not be living better?") No, I think we err seriously when we confuse the permanently rich with the temporarily successful. The true rich are a definable group in our country: they are the lucky few who are born to families of great inherited wealth, and who have the option of living in leisured luxury even if they never work a day in their lives. (Ironically, some of the offspring of this tiny coterie routinely go into public life, where they often spend their careers living in mansions and voting for legislation that will require you and me to pay more taxes. They are considered very liberal fellows.) But this definition of the authentic rich in our country does not describe in the slightest the typical American earning a high income today—be that person a corporate executive or brain surgeon or entrepreneur. When we are urged to denounce our top achievers as "the rich," we are attacking not entrenched wealth but ambition and success. We are attacking, in short, the dream we should be nurturing.

So ingrained is the politics of envy, however, that we are inclined to grasp endlessly at the straw of "fairness." And so, recently, we have seen a seemingly wonderful new development on the tax front, drawing smiles from such diverse folks as Ralph Nader and Ronald Reagan, Bill Bradley and Jesse Helms, Art Laffer and organized labor. It's the flat (or at least flatter) tax movement. In spite of such august backing, I hope it doesn't appear churlish of me to question the absolute magnificence of such a universally applauded idea.

It's not that I don't share the yearning for a tax system that is at least a little less ridiculous than our current mind-boggling code. It's just that I think the chances of our moving now to a truly simple, low and flat tax on U.S. incomes are roughly equivalent to our chances of moving the entire population of Cuba to the Falkland Islands.* Furthermore, when so many politicians spend so much time gabbing about something that is positively not going to happen, the thought stirs in my suspicious little mind that they are merely trying to divert our attention from what actually is going to happen to our taxes.

First, let's recognize that talk about a simplified tax code and a flatter tax-rate structure is popular for precisely the same specious reasons that earlier demagoguery about "tax reform" used to be so appealing: each of us, in hailing such high-minded suggestions, privately believes that it will translate into "I'll pay less and the other guy will pay more." A moment's contemplation should reveal that such a widespread ambition cannot be arithmetically realized. In fact, the flatter tax proposals do not truly approach the genuine problem of unreported, hidden "underground" income that (according to the IRS estimate) annually costs the Government nearly one quarter the amount actually taken in from individuals and corporations. Instead, these proposals play on the suspicion that the "rich" habitually evade taxes they should be paying. On that point, which is pervasive in much of the continuing rhetoric about taxes, the actual evidence may be surprising. According to the nonpartisan Tax Foundation, in 1980, the top 10 percent of U.S. earners paid more than half (51.8 percent) of all the taxes going to Uncle Sam. The top 25 percent paid more than three quarters (77.5 percent) and the top 50 percent paid nearly all (94 percent). And this situation prevailed even before the start of the 1981 tax bill's incentives to earn and report higher incomes. Contrary to popular assumptions, most wealthy people paid relatively high taxes, and the average tax paid rose significantly with income. While we all might like to believe that if only the Bunker Hunts of this world could be squeezed harder the rest of us could

* A true flat tax has two main components: (1) the rate levied is the same on all incomes; (2) all tax deductions are eliminated, except for the cost (strictly defined) of earning the income.

get off dramatically easier, the realities simply don't bear this out. Income subject to the maximum 50 percent tax rate comprises just 3.2 percent of the Federal income-tax base and generates 8.3 percent of collections. We're talking about 1,431,000 returns, or 1.9 percent of the total filed. There is scarcely a limitless assemblage of fat cats crouching out there just waiting to be declawed.

Okay, some say, but why shouldn't these affluent fellows pay even more? (Self-righteousness about other people's incomes comes cheap.) Let's investigate that. In 1979, the Tax Foundation reports, $29 billion in income was subject to tax rates of at least 50 percent (which is now the maximum); it yielded $18.2 billion in taxes. And what would have happened if you had taxed all this income at 100 percent—in other words, confiscated it? Why, you would have raised a grand total of $10.8 billion more, which (based on total 1979 Federal spending of $439.2 billion) would have run the Government for precisely eight days. And you could get away with doing it only once, because never again would there be any salaries paid at this level. The point is that the only *substantial* way to raise taxes on reported income is to raise taxes on the ordinary citizen. Anything else is a deliberate mirage. As we have repeatedly seen, "closing loopholes" is about as sincere as "tax reform": the other fellow's "loophole" is always your own legitimate incentive, and the chances of otherwise convincing, say, the nation's charities, or its realtors, are akin to those of paying off the national debt by 1990.* Milton Friedman, who has honestly advocated a truly low and flat tax for decades, was quick to recognize the insincerity of its most recent proponents; the chances of our actually getting what he had suggested, he acknowledged, were "zero." He was surely right. Congressmen are not going to sacrifice permanently either the power to make cuts and increases, or that extremely lucrative source of campaign contributions: seekers

---

* Unsurprisingly, the various so-called flat tax proposals recently floated in Congress and by the Reagan Administration uniformly contained exceptions (certain privileged deductions would be retained) and avoided genuine flatness (the top rate in some cases would be more than double the bottom rate). While superficially appealing to the nation's yearning for greater simplicity, such proposals would have a predictable outcome: the spenders would soon be back seeking to raise the top rate, and both sides would seek new legislated deductions on grounds that they were at least as legitimate as those already permitted.

after new, favorable exceptions to the tax code. All the rest of the "flat tax" talk, however alluring in its first presentation to a nation aching for relief, may feed our paranoia—but will ultimately leave us flat.

A more useful tax program for the Eighties might be one that combined positive inducements for savings and investment with a more radical reduction in personal income-tax rates. As we have seen, such incentives truly do work, both in providing a goad to extra effort and production in the economy, and in raising the Government's actual cash receipts. History suggests that a top rate no higher than 25 percent is advisable. At that level, more Americans might be tempted to say, "The heck with all this complicated tax planning; let's just say it's three dollars for me and one dollar for Uncle Sam, and let's get on with business." Clearly, this is not the reaction even with a top rate lowered to 50 percent, especially when that level is topped off with state and local levies. Tax shelters, created by Congress in its infinite assurance that it knows better than the markets where investments should be made, still beckon alluringly. (Ironically, when Congress moved in 1982 to hit vindictively at the pension plans of high earners, and reduce allowable contributions, it thereby assured that money that then went into the socially useful stock and bond markets would henceforth be diverted to unproductive shelters.) If Americans were able to choose investments on their merits, as opposed to their tax consequences, the ultimate impact on productivity and revenues alike could be explosive. Congress ought to lower the barriers and get out of the way.

Having done so, Congress ought to do two other things. It ought to deliver on the promise of tax indexing (see Chapter XI), and it ought to resolve to ease up on its endless tinkering with the tax code. As things stand, private decision makers don't know from one year to the next what the rules are going to be in such fundamental areas as pensions, depreciation and capital gains. This uncertainty inhibits adventuresomeness and makes a shambles of any serious attempt at long-range planning. No wonder the short-term money market booms and any prospect further off than the next quarter seems foolishly theoretical. The typical business executive wants what all of us want: he wants everything. But what he will settle for is knowing the rules of the game. Tell him what they are and stick to them for a while, and he will be able to make sensible decisions on which investments are worthwhile. But allow the tax code to be a perennial Tinker Toy for the power-mad kids in the Capital, and you create not just a free-for-all for lobbyists (and a paradise for accountants) but a private economy that is understandably scared of its shadow. A little more modesty in Washington could make things a lot less taxing for us all.

HOW—AND WHY—TO BALANCE THE BUDGET

It once was said that God must love poor people because He made so many of them. Could the same be true of Americans and budget deficits? Not if you look at the polls. Though we haven't seen anything but red ink since 1970, and though the flood has become a veritable Red Sea in the Eighties, poll after poll taken over the decades has shown that the average citizen thinks budget deficits are simply dreadful. A Roper Poll in 1981 found Americans declaring themselves "conservative" on deficit spending by an astounding 9-to-1 margin, higher than those who so described themselves on homosexuality, interracial dating, marijuana smoking or a bunch of other "social issues" about which the population is supposed to be so exercised. Could this be the same electorate that the politicians allegedly have been trying to please? Never doubt it for a minute. This is why even the freest-spending legislator often can be found, in his biennial appeals to his constituents for one more renewal of his contract, piously aligning himself with the cause of fiscal responsibility. It is always somebody else's fault, of course: big businesses don't pay their taxes, or the Pentagon is too greedy, or the Government is spending too much in some other part of the country, or whatever. It's certainly not the fault of good old Congressman Joe, who is merely trying to get us the benefits we need right here in our community.

Before we look at how we could actually reduce the overall burden of Government spending, it might be useful to put those hated—but seemingly ineradicable—budget deficits into a more meaningful perspective. This seems especially necessary since I have just suggested significant further reductions in income taxes, a step that the conventional wisdom believes would deepen the already-intolerable deficits (even though, as we have seen, the historical reality is that such reductions quickly increase government revenues).

The proposition here is that we can and must deal with these deficits, but that it is essential first to recognize that deficits differ importantly in their causes, cures and impacts. Interestingly, the idea that deficits are not all alike is subscribed to in less polemical moments by virtually all economists and national leaders. John F. Kennedy concluded that strikingly different results were produced, depending on whether the deficits arose from wasteful spending increases (which he purported to oppose) or from tax cuts (which he advocated). Arguing that the choice confronting him was not between budget surplus and deficit, Kennedy said the choice was "between two kinds of deficits—a chronic deficit of inertia, as the unwanted result of inadequate revenues and a restricted economy, or a temporary deficit of transition, resulting from a tax cut designed to boost the economy, increase tax revenue and achieve a budget surplus. . . . The first type of deficit is a sign of waste and weakness, the second reflects an investment in the future." And, as it turned out, the Kennedy cuts were so successful in encouraging more production and revenue that only the most incredible Goverment-spending binge in American history was able to shove the budget into chronic deficit.

Two decades later, the Administration in power was supposed to be "conservative Republican" instead of "liberal Democrat," but it reached an amazingly similar conclusion in its quieter moments—before the born-again taxers took control. The 1982 Annual Report of Ronald Reagan's Council of Economic Advisers, while expressing a strong commitment to reducing future projected deficits, went out of its way to warn against panicking when a deficit appeared during a recession. "The impact of a specific deficit will vary," it noted, "depending on the conditions that lead to it." The Reaganites added that since borrowing requirements of businesses and consumers tend to decline during a recession, "at such a time a given deficit can be financed with less pressure on interest rates than during a period of growth." This was sound analysis. The later decision to seek to lower interest rates by increasing taxes represented a serious misreading of the financial markets, whose concern was less with the immediate deficit than with the absence of any visible long-term restraint on spending. Investors understandably feared an eventual rebirth of double-digit inflation and the abandonment of any pretense of credible monetary policy.

The skepticism of the public toward any attempt to discriminate among deficits is understandable: the rationales seem to keep changing, but the deficits keep coming. And so does inflation. Interestingly, most of the theoretical blame for the predominant red ink of the last half-century goes to an economist who may have been profoundly misread: the Englishman John Maynard Keynes. Keynes, with his emphasis on the Government's role in stimulating demand in a depressed economy, has become the intellectual alibi for two generations of big spenders. Yet Keynes never advocated that deficits should continue during times of prosperity. During an upswing in the economic cycle, the idea was to run a surplus and even the accounts. In an essay written in 1919, Keynes was scathing about politicians who chose inflation as an easy way out. Observing that "Lenin is said to have declared that the best way to destroy the capitalist system was to debauch the currency," Keynes declared: "Lenin was certainly right. There is no subtler, no surer means of overturning the existing basis of society than to debauch the currency. The process engages all the hidden forces of economic law on the side of destruction, and does it in a manner which not one man in a million is able to diagnose. . . . Governments, being many of them at this moment reckless in their methods as well as weak, seek to direct on to a class known as 'profiteers' the popular indignation against the more obvious consequences of their [own] vicious methods. These 'profiteers' are, broadly speaking, the entrepreneurial class of capitalists, that is to say, the active and constructive element in the whole capitalist society. . . . By directing hatred against this class, therefore, the governments are carrying a step further the fatal process which the subtle mind of Lenin had consciously conceived." Well, how about that? The original "Keynesian" not only argued against a high level of Government spending under normal circumstances, but correctly foresaw the kind of scapegoating that would lead extravagant politicians more than half a century later to blame their own inflation on "the big oil companies." No wonder *Forbes* magazine, recalling this essay in 1981, commented: "People like Teddy

Kennedy who regard inflation as-preferable to cuts in welfare spending would do well to wrap themselves in another robe than that of Keynes. A more powerful diatribe against vote-buying politicians who 'debauch the currency' is hard to imagine.''

But if not even the academically dominant school of Keynesianism in economics can justify our recent reckless budget course, does it then follow that deficits lead directly to inflation? The evidence on that is less clear-cut than is assumed by most ''liberal'' and ''conservative'' arguers alike. Not only does it make a difference how the deficit is incurred, it makes a crucial difference how it is financed (as we shall see in Chapter IV). If we don't grasp this, we will be thoroughly baffled by the experiences of such countries as Japan and West Germany, which regularly run deficits amounting to a significantly higher portion of their gross national product than does the U.S., but nonetheless have less inflation and more growth. Their secret, as Professor David I. Meiselman of Virginia Polytechnic Institute has observed, is that ''money has increased more slowly and smoothly in those two countries than in the U.S., and neither country taxes saving and investment as severely as we do.'' In contrast, Meiselman noted in the *Wall Street Journal,* high U.S. tax rates ''do not reduce prices and do not fight inflation'' but ''do reduce output, employment and economic growth.'' Not exactly the world's tastiest recipe for budget balancing—or anything else a hungry economy might desire.

A preoccupation with deficits can lead to other errors that, ironically, may eventually help perpetuate the very problems we are trying to eliminate. A conspicuous example is inflation itself. In theory, the Government wants very much to get rid of inflation, but in practice, given our present tax system, rising inflation is a big spender's best friend. For every 1 percent increase in the rate of inflation, the Government can count on an increase of more than 1.5 percent in its revenues. Rising inflation means rising tax receipts—and thus an excuse for even more spending. Over the last twenty years, while real growth has slowed in the U.S., inflation has accelerated the nominal growth in dollars. Uncle Sam has been the principal beneficiary; before the recent reversal, Federal receipts had mounted from 18.5 percent of the nation's output to 21 percent. In contrast, when inflation moderated more rapidly than expected in 1981–82, there was such a shortfall in projected

Government receipts that panic developed in Reagan Washington—resulting in the near-hysterical reversal on taxes already noted. At times like that, many a politician might wish for just a whiff more inflation to bail him out of his deficit problem.

Another danger in focusing too much attention on projected future budget deficits is that they are, to put it kindly, fiction. The record of succeeding Administrations and Congresses shows not only that they have been wildly off base in forecasting the deficits for future years, but that they often miss badly even on the year in progress. When Ronald Reagan was in the process of revising his 1982 deficit estimate from $43 billion to $99 billion*—a mild mid-course correction, by Washington's expansive standards—House Ways and Means Chairman Dan Rostenkowski piously warned, "This time we want solid figures, not phony estimates." Presumably it would have been considered a breach of Congressional courtesy to remind Rostenkowski that less than two years earlier he had given the nation a "balanced budget" for 1981—which, due to a slight miscalculation, actually came in nearly $60 billion in deficit. Nor are all the errors in the usual upward direction (as we found out again in 1984); in the mid-Seventies, technicians were baffled by a "spending shortfall" in which the Government, for a while, proved uncharacteristically unable to spend all its allotted funds. Hence a certain caution is necessary in dealing with terrifying estimates that are cited as the excuse for demonstrably bad policy.

Much of this alleged concern about what will happen in distant years is patently fraudulent. Consider the fascinating recent spectacle of the United States Congress, architect of forty-five budget deficits in the last half-century, accusing Ronald Reagan of fiscal irresponsibility—and claiming, if you please, that he was insufficiently concerned with balancing the budget. It was as if Karl Marx had suddenly put on an Adam Smith necktie. Unhappily, it did not take long for Congress to prove that the change was purely sartorial. In February 1982, the Administration was denounced for proposing a 15 percent increase in spending and only an 11 percent increase in revenues; three months later, our legislators showed where their hearts really were by projecting a spending increase closer to 19 percent. It's this sort of thing that leads critics like

* The actual final total was $110.7 billion.

Milton Friedman to say they are for any tax cut at any time for any reason, on the theory not only that it will let us spend more of our own money but that it will somehow inhibit Congress from spending even more. "The most effective way to hold down Goverment spending is to hold down Government revenue," Friedman has argued. Denouncing those he called "born-again budget balancers," the Nobel economist said in a *Human Events* interview: "They are talking as if their concern is to enact higher taxes in order to keep budget deficits down. Their real motive is to keep taxes up so that the Government can resume big spending programs as soon as the present public drive for lower taxes and spending passes." Paul McCracken, Nixon's chief economic adviser, similarly warned his conservative friends against joining the hue and cry for tax increases, asserting in the *Wall Street Journal:* "The strategy of holding off on any tax action until the budget is balanced is simply leading us down the road to yet higher levels of public spending and budgets chronically in the red."

Others are less convinced than Friedman that the size of the deficits can actually serve a healthy role in putting pressure on Congress to reduce spending. (Milton once told me he would rather see a $200 billion budget with a $100 billion deficit than a $400 billion budget that was balanced. He feels there is some outer limit to the dimensions of a deficit that will be tolerated, thus lower receipts will lead eventually to lower spending.) Rudolph G. Penner, director of fiscal policy studies at the American Enterprise Institute, says this argument gives the politicians too much credit: "Milton Friedman thinks Congress worries about deficits even though he doesn't. . . . Cutting taxes doesn't necessarily keep Congress from raising spending. In the past, Congress has raised spending both when it was cutting and when it was raising taxes." Penner also takes issue with the monetarist contention that, as David Meiselman put it, "there is little, if any, direct historical connection between budget deficits and inflation, or between deficits and money growth that causes inflation." Penner contends that "there is a clear relationship between the size of the deficit and money creation." * This is a debate to which we will return in

* Penner's beliefs will be put to the test in his new job as director of the nonpartisan Congressional Budget Office, to which he was appointed in the summer of 1983.

Chapter IV; my own view is that our budget deficits have in any event become terribly damaging, for reasons we can define and to a degree that we must now move with much greater force to contain.

There is, for starters, the severe psychological impact upon all of us of a Government that visibly fails to deliver on its promises. Every four years we hear solemn pledges of balanced budgets, yet once in office Presidents uniformly renege. (Ronald Reagan in 1980 originally promised a balanced budget by 1983—which, by no coincidence, happened to be precisely four years after 1979, the year Jimmy Carter first promised to balance the budget when he was the out-of-office candidate for President. Isn't tradition wonderful?) It is all very well for Washington's apologists to talk about the alleged difference between campaign oratory and "the real world," which for them translates into a chronic unwillingness to restrain Federal spending. But the impression of perennial default and disarray in the nation's capital cannot help but exert a negative influence on private decision making throughout the economy. ("Deficits are one of the things the average consumer thinks he understands and relates to," notes Jay Schmiedeskamp, chief economist for the Gallup Organization. "So all the talk of deficits undoubtedly is having a considerable effect on consumer attitudes.") When economic leadership in Washington deteriorates repeatedly into a Potomac version of the Marx Brothers' *Night at the Opera,* the spectators in the private sector understandably become significantly more wary about their own long-range commitments. Deficits are a continuing symbol of Washington's disingenuousness and incompetence in dealing with the economy, and as such are destructive to the national spirit as well as the national pocketbook.

Beyond this, the huge deficits of the Nineteen Eighties are whittling away the country's savings and hiking the cost of borrowing, thus impeding every effort to rehabilitate the shopworn U.S. industrial base. This makes it that much harder to resume U.S. productivity growth at a rate that will enable us to hold off our more aggressive world competitors. Businesses that want to invest in productivity-boosting plant and equipment must draw on the nation's savings pool. In 1982, according to estimates by Gary M. Wenglowski of Goldman, Sachs & Co., this pool totaled about

$199 billion (including personal savings of $130 billion, corporate savings and retained earnings of $33 billion, and state and local government surpluses of $36 billion). But the Federal deficit, Wenglowski figured, consumed about 70 percent of the total savings pool and, even with a prospective recovery in 1983, would still absorb 60 percent of the nation's total savings. This is an enormous increase, for as recently as 1981 the Government's red ink soaked up only 32 percent of the nation's savings, while during the capital investment boom of the Nineteen Sixties its share was a mere 5 percent.

When the Federal Government wants to borrow, moreover, it shoulders aside every other prospective borrower in the market—its credit rating, ironically, is tops. The reason is that Washington alone has the power to meet its obligations by waving a magic wand and printing more money. But since the total savings pool is limited, heavy Federal borrowing to finance enormous Federal deficits means that there is less money left for nongovernmental purposes. All other would-be borrowers must compete fiercely for what remains, and the result of that competition is an increase in the price of money: "real" interest rates (the difference between the nominal rate and the current rate of inflation) climb ominously. This adds to costs, slows investment and growth—and ultimately produces even wider deficits as the Government's receipts fall. Big Government deficits, in other words, rob the private economy of part of its future.

The present deficits are frightening not only because of their prodigious size but also because of the lack of any credible plan for eliminating them. As we have seen, long-term budget forecasting is a notably flawed art (an error of one percentage point in predicting unemployment can change the deficit by more than $25 billion). But the prospect of adding well over half a trillion dollars to the national debt between 1982 and 1985—more than in the previous thirty years combined—is unsettling even if it turns out to be inexact. Previous deficits were supposed to be self-correcting as the economy recovered; Charles L. Schultze, the chief Carter economic adviser, assured me in 1980 that it was only the recession that had kept the budget unbalanced that year, and that we could expect the deficit to be eliminated "as, if and when the economy moves up toward prosperity." A year later, the Reagan people were still insisting that we would see a balanced budget in 1984. But by 1982, when I pressed Murray Weidenbaum, then Reagan's chief economist, on when if ever we actually would achieve a balance, he was unable to name any specific year. Not long after, Treasury Secretary Donald T. Regan offered the interesting (if absurd) view that there was no demonstrable relationship between huge deficits and high inflation and interest rates. That was too much even for Reagan loyalist Alan Greenspan, who had been President Ford's chief economist and who told me on "Wall $treet Week": "The basic problem is that as the Government borrows more, both directly and indirectly in a number of guises, it invariably absorbs the excess savings in the system. What that does is require individuals and businessmen to go to their banks to get funds, because they're elbowed out of the [credit] market. That, in turn, pushes interest rates higher and, historically, [an] at least partially politicized Federal Reserve has created excess money that has led to inflation—and, invariably, both to inflation and high interest rates. I think the relationships are very clear and those who have difficulty finding them are using the wrong tools."

Greenspan's clarity and candor were a refreshing antidote to the usual Washington bilge. The issue plainly has moved beyond partisanship. Otto Eckstein, the former Lyndon Johnson economist who built Data Resources into the nation's largest economic consulting and forecasting firm, told me that while "whoever is in office tends to explain away the deficits," the new situation had serious qualitative differences: even if recovery arrived on schedule, the deficits would "run 4 or 5 percent of the gross national product" and "we've never tried that before." No wonder the financial markets have remained uneasy despite the Treasury's ringing assurances that all will soon be well. By the Reagan Administration's best-case scenario, deficits would reach a historic high of 4 percent of the nation's output in 1983 and then ease only gradually to 2 percent in 1985*; by contrast in past recoveries, *Business Week* noted dourly, "deficits dropped sharply to well below 1 percent." And not even the most unreconstructed "Keynesian"

* This forecast proved predictably—and wildly—overoptimistic. The actual 1983 deficit came in at a whopping 6.1 percent of GNP, by far the highest since the all-time record of 7.8 percent in 1946. The deficit's share of total U.S. output then eased to only 5.2 percent in 1984 and was heading up again in 1985.

can argue any longer that deficits do their long-claimed job of "stimulating" an anemic economy; Paul A. Samuelson, the first U.S. Nobel laureate in economic science (who in 1972 came on "Wall $treet Week" to defend the economics of George Mc-Govern), now concedes glumly that "deficits do not have the same expansionary kick they had back in the Forties, Fifties and Sixties." From virtually all points on the economic compass, the exhortation to our national leaders is unmistakably clear: Stop unbalancing the debate. Start balancing the budget.

The final reason for the politicians' putting our money where their mouths are takes us back to where we started: the psychological impact. Just as failure to balance the budget has been damaging, achieving the goal could be profoundly inspirational. The American people are understandably suspicious of all promises in this area; they have heard endless talk of balancing the budget, yet they have seen endless budget deficits. But think of the potential impact on inflationary expectations, in every sector of the economy, if we had a Government that actually kept its word. A Government that really did balance its expenditures and receipts could restore trust and optimism, and discourage the kind of "devil take the hindmost" attitude that not only seeks immediate, legislated (and ultimately self-defeating) protection against the crowd's inflation, but also makes long-term thrift and investment seem a sucker's game. Imagine the incredible shock of seeing a Government that set out to discipline itself and then achieved its goal. It appears so improbable now to the average American that he or she might react with wonder, confidence and vigor if it truly arrived. A balanced budget brought about by governmental responsibility and restraint could itself make a significant contribution to the needed resuscitation of the American spirit. Cynics, of course, doubt that this will ever be possible, but our politicians could do worse than listen to the relevant advice of Mark Twain. "Always do right," he advised. "This will gratify some people and astonish the rest."

. . . Spend and Spend

If raising taxes won't balance the budget, what will? Hint: look at what has been going up even faster than taxes. It is, of course, Federal spending. Everybody who has taken even the most cursory glance at what has been occurring in Washington will concede that the budget process is out of control; however, efforts to do something about it have been so puny or downright diversionary as to make King Canute look like Mr. Fix-It. The reason is not so baffling as it may at first appear: the politicians think you and I are pretty stupid. They think we will complain bitterly about the level of Government spending, all right, but we will defend to the death that portion that reaches our own coffers. Hence it is more important for one who wants to survive at the ballot box to continue the spending that most affects his or her own constituents. The consequences of such decisions, namely more inflation and worse economic times for everyone, are theoretical and down the road a piece, and can always be blamed on somebody else.

Is the cause hopeless, then? Are we doomed to hearing promises of fiscal responsibility at every election, but then confronting the ever-darkening prospect of varying degrees of irresponsibility in between? This need not be our permanent fate, either. But a reversal will require our thinking afresh about some of the most emotional issues in American life today. Where Government spending is concerned, we must recognize that it is the genuine, overriding issue—not just in keeping us from balancing the budget but, even more important, in keeping us from achieving that combination of individual freedom and higher living standards that could and should be our Twenty-first Century destiny. As the Government intrudes increasingly on our liberties by seizing an ever larger share of our earnings, the challenge to reverse that trend becomes critical. The proposition here is not just that Government spending should be cut, but (perhaps more controversially) that it realistically can be cut—deeply.

"YEAH—BUT WHERE WOULD YOU CUT?"

The budget deficits, as we have seen, are clearly evil, cutting into the national will and the national capacity for economic regeneration. In recent years net private investment has been only 6 percent of the country's gross national product, its total output of goods and services; let the deficit consistently take even another 2 percent of GNP and you reduce net private investment by fully a third of a rate that is already perilously anemic. What would be ahead for the economy then would not be pretty. The need in the Nineteen Eighties is not just to balance the budget. We must do better than that: we must begin at last to run some budget surpluses. That rare event would enable us to start paying off at least a portion of a national debt that has now run recklessly past a trillion dollars;* it would signal true grit in the fight against inflation and enable interest rates to move significantly downward. Achieving such a happy result would not take a miracle, despite present appearances, but it would take competence and will.

What it will not and should not take, despite much of the recent Washington oratory from both parties, is a succession of self-righteous tax increases. As we have seen, they just don't work. Raising taxes proved spectacularly counterproductive in the Nineteen Seventies. It succeeded not in bringing budgets into balance but in contributing to an economy short on incentives and growth, and long on inflation and frustration—individual, industrial and national. Surely the record by now is plain enough that it ought to

---

* Interest on that trillion-dollar national debt has become the third-largest item in the budget; in 1982 it totaled more than the entire Federal budget in 1963.

lead us to clear not just our heads but our vocabularies; an obvious candidate for expunction would be that dreadful Washington phrase "tax expenditures." Much mischief has been done to the economy under that misleading banner, which is designed to foster the nonsensical idea that a dollar spent by the Government is in no way different from a dollar not taken in taxes. Let's think on that for a moment. Congress, whose role in creating our present budget problem is second to none, officially enshrined the phrase in its Budget and Impoundment Act of 1974, defining so-called tax expenditures as "revenue losses attributable to provisions of Federal tax laws which allow a special exclusion, exemption, or deduction from gross income or which provide a special credit, a preferential rate of tax, or a deferral of tax liability."

There are three things wrong with this easy characterization. First, it tends to prejudge the desirability of provisions that often were designed only to determine what was indeed properly taxable income; there was no automatic connotation of a "loophole" in this process. Second, the phrase is a captive of the static-income philosophy: the notion that everybody earns and produces the same no matter what the taxes on that income and production may be. In reality, those "tax expenditures" may evaporate if you actually try to recapture them. (In this respect, they differ markedly from true Government expenditures, which once legislated move in only one direction.) Third, and most fundamentally, the phrase is based on the insulting and untenable belief that all income earned in America belongs to the Government—which, in its generosity, may decide to let us keep a little. This pernicious assumption encapsulates the arrogance of Washington; both American tradition and economic reality make a very different assumption, namely that the people produce the income and empower their paid public servants only to take a minimal portion for essential purposes agreed to by their employers, the electorate. When politicians act as if they are giving us a remarkable (and somehow shady) break in failing to apply unconscionable rates to every dollar we earn, the case for major new tax reductions becomes not just persuasive but downright urgent.

But having said all this—having said that, while not every provision of our hacked-together tax code should be regarded as chiseled in stone, the basic need is for still-greater tax reductions

to get the country going in this decade—let's not try to kid ourselves the other way, either. This is only half the job and, at least
superficially, the more attractive half. Let's not attempt to fool
ourselves that we will have solved the fundamental problems facing the American economy today unless and until we are ready to
take that much harder second step—and genuinely slash the Government's spending.

One reason the high taxers continue to get away with advocacy
of their discredited economic formulas today is that overzealous
"supply siders" promised too much as a result of the slim initial
Reagan tax cuts in 1981. One of their first mistakes, in my judgment, was not just overpromising but overmarketing: the phrase
"supply side" itself suggested some radical new theory about the
U.S. economy, to rival—and be compared with—such other dog-
mas as "Keynesianism, "monetarism," "neo-liberalism" and
anything else an ambitious young economist wanted to put forward
as brand-new and sexy. As we have seen, the best of these theories
often turn out to be nothing more than a return to some of the
abiding principles of classical economics, as opposed to the quirky
deviationist pretensions of the last half-century, by which we operated in the belief that an "activist" Government could repeal the
business cycle and make all things wonderful. In the real world,
supply and demand lives, and governments are most effective
when they treat it with respect. Jack Kemp was at his most perceptive when he observed, "If you tax something, you get less of it.
If you subsidize something, you get more of it. The problem with
the United States today is that we tax work, savings, thrift, production, capital, and we subsidize non-work, welfare and consumption." The recitation of a straightforward reality like that is
far more useful than pretending to have discovered a magic potion.

The American people not only are rightfully skeptical of all such
claims by now, but are almost totally uninterested in the label on a
specific program—which is usually the media's preoccupation.
What the typical voter wants to know is something quite different:
How is this actually going to work, how is it going to affect me?
The folk wisdom here may be deeper than the academic competition to invent a new and comprehensive theory, as if the role of
economists was to emulate television producers creating a flashy
new sitcom to bedazzle the next season's audience. Everybody

wants to be chic, but in economics that can often be a losing game. I have observed over the years that those fellows in Congress are extremely powerful: they can pass laws, change laws, repeal laws. But even their powers are limited. And one law they have never been able to repeal, despite repeated and frequently trendy efforts, is the old-fashioned law of arithmetic.

It was foolish to pretend that if we got what appeared to be the big tax cuts for which we yearned, we would not have to worry any longer about the sticky, difficult and unpleasant task of actually cutting significantly more deeply into Government spending. Tax cuts are indeed important; we need more, including some better-targeted to deal with our specific ongoing problems and deficiencies (see Chapter VII). But this is only half a policy in the budget-and-tax area.

The real tax we have to pay every year is not the one we beef about in April; that's only a fraction of the total. The real tax we pay is nothing other than the level of Government spending in the economy. Eventually, we have to pay every penny of that spending, whether we do so directly today in taxes or indirectly, but just as inexorably, tomorrow in the form of even worse and more drastic inflation. Hence the greatest economic failure of the Reagan years may eventually be seen to be the Administration's glaring failure to come through on its pledges to slice boldly into the Government's share of the economy. Too much was made in late 1981 of the confessions of Reagan's errant budget director, David Stockman, that there had been the customary element of guesswork in preparing this Administration's economic projections; too little was made of his late-blooming enthusiasm for tax increases as a substitute for the job to which he had been assigned. The President's message to Stockman should have been short and unsweet: Your task was to reduce the Federal Government's share of the U.S. gross national product from 23 percent to 19 percent— not to alibi your failure to do so, and certainly not to make proposals that would enlarge the Government's take even further. (By August 1982 Stockman was acknowledging that Federal spending was topping 24 percent of GNP that year, the highest level since 1946. In 1983 it moved even higher.)

The irony of Reagan's budget program was that he was being simultaneously overpraised and overcriticized for a policy that was considerably less remarkable than either group of partisans assumed. In my judgment, he never deserved more than two cheers for his actions in this area. He did a brilliant job of articulating the major problems facing the U.S. economy in this decade—including too much Government, too much taxes, too much regulation—but he seemed unwilling to risk taking more than half a step in the right direction. If your doctor diagnoses a serious malignancy, you want him to proceed with major surgery; snipping off a little bit at a time is irritating without being efficacious. And so it was with the initial Reagan budget program. Specifically: (1) Having vowed to eliminate chronic budget deficits, he set a far too leisurely timetable for achieving that goal, and then moved so ineffectually that even this modest schedule became patently unattainable. Reagan's deficits quickly headed for a total that would top the combined deficits of every President from Harry S. Truman through Jimmy Carter— and swamp the red-ink record of Franklin D. Roosevelt. (2) Even before announcing his first budget, Reagan erred by formally exempting seven major domestic spending programs from any cuts at all. When you added those programs to such items as defense, where increases were openly planned, it was evident that the "revolutionary" Reagan budget program in effect had protected close to three quarters of the entire Federal budget from any spending reductions whatsoever. This necessarily meant that all the much-ballyhooed cuts were to come from what the politicians deemed the "easy" one quarter of the Federal budget. The fact that some of these cuts may have been ill-chosen, or that they inflicted pain on certain individuals, is in no way an indication that they represented a serious attack on overall Federal spending. Clearly, they did not. And it doesn't take a financial genius to recognize that a truly balanced budget would require much more courage and much more vision: a re-examination not just of the "easy" one quarter but of the full four quarters of Federal spending. This can't be accomplished by looking furtively over your shoulder for the poll results every step of the way. (3) The original Reagan budget for 1983 has to be considered one of the most unusual fiscal documents of our times. It had, at least, one unique success: it united the U.S. Congress. Not one legislator from either party had anything good to say about it. When I immediately suggested that the Reagan economic team go back to the drawing board and come up with significantly more meaningful spending reductions, I was told that this was politically impossible: Jimmy Carter had recalled a budget once, and it had cost him in the polls. Even this late in the economic day, it seemed, the White House relapsed easily into "politics as usual" in dealing with the people's money. I think we should be thoroughly intolerant of this readiness to let the political advisers continue to dominate economic policy; otherwise, the Reagan Administration, for all its assumed heroics, will inevitably be seen in retrospect as having just muddled along—talking revolution while proposing popguns.

Lest anyone conclude that I am carping unduly, let me point out that two entirely different stories were told throughout the opening months of "Reaganomics": one on the front pages and the other on the financial pages. As is so often the case, the story being told in the tiny agate type on the financial pages turned out to be the real story, the one that would eventually find its way into big black headlines on Page One. On the front pages (and the television news), we got the old familiar knee-jerk stories: Democrats vs. Republicans, liberals vs. conservatives, the anguished howls of those whose particular oxen were being gored vs. the hearty applause of those who thought it was about time. Yet all the time we were reading and hearing about these supposedly massive budget cuts, this alleged hatchet job on the entire Federal budget, the stories on the inside pages were telling a totally different tale: a tale of deep and continuing skepticism in the nation's financial markets about the ability and commitment even of this Administration to get the U.S. budget under control.* This market jitteriness was scarcely assuaged when some Administration stalwarts began talking as if budget balancing were an outmoded goal: as if actually ever balancing the Federal budget wouldn't make that much difference, anyhow, when you got right down to it. (This, incidentally —and ludicrously—came from many of the same Republicans who had adamantly demanded a balanced budget right up to the time they had a chance to submit one.) The President's own rhetoric on

---

* This explained why, even as the inflation rate came down in 1982 and 1983, interest rates in the long-term bond market remained disconcertingly high. Lenders sought protection against the resurgence of inflation they feared the Government's policies would produce when the economy recovered.

controlling spending so regularly exceeded his dollars-and-cents proposals that I remarked at one point that he seemed to have hit the ground ambling.

A brief look at the history of governmental spending may help us understand how we arrived at our present situation. For the first 130 years peacetime U.S. governmental spending was minimal, restricted to essential public goods, defense, monetary management and officials' salaries. The Federal budget for 1900, measured in 1972 dollars, amounted to $2.8 billion or about $36 per citizen. In 1930 the Federal budget was still less than 4 percent of GNP. Since the Depression, the Government's share has been ratcheting upward in periodic spurts. We may disagree about trends going back to another century; we may regard the New Deal of Franklin Roosevelt as a noble turning point or the beginning of disaster. But our view of these earlier policies, whatever it may be, will not help us in attacking the immediate budget problems of the Nineteen Eighties. For while it is certainly true that many social programs (of which Social Security is the most conspicuous) do indeed trace to the anti-Depression efforts of the Nineteen Thirties, it was not until Lyndon Johnson's Great Society three decades later that the Federal budget was truly subjected to a social-spending explosion. The explosion then became a volcanic eruption under—of all people—Richard Nixon. Statisticians define social spending as payments to individuals; such payments normally took less than 25 percent of the Federal budget until the late Nineteen Sixties, but before Nixon left the White House the portion had soared to 40 percent. In 1964 all social programs, including Social Security, took $32 billion; in 1981 the figure was $317 billion. (Even adjusted for the inflation it helped to produce, that's a quadrupling of Federal expenditures in this area.) Meanwhile, when you sift emotion from fact in the area of military spending, you find that defense outlays in the past two decades have dropped sharply both as a fraction of gross national product and as a fraction of the Federal budget itself. In Kennedy's time the U.S. spent close to two dollars on defense for every dollar of social spending; the lines crossed in Nixon's first term, and the Kennedy proportion is now reversed. From the mid-Sixties to 1981 social spending increased three times as fast as defense spending. The point is not that all that social spending was necessarily bad (its "compassionate" proponents regularly trumpeted the reverse); the point is that any realistic look at where we might cut Federal spending must begin with a recognition of where the geometrical recent increases have occurred.

We must, at long last, begin some serious national rethinking of the out-of-control Government transfer payments that really underlie the U.S. budget problem. These are the open-ended programs in which Washington takes from one individual and gives to another—and then has the nerve to say that the spending was "uncontrollable." This is arrant nonsense. The only thing even arguably uncontrollable in the Federal budget is interest payments on the national debt (Uncle Sam has to pay his bills, even if he does so with paper of ever-diminishing value), and the way to control that item is, quite simply, to move the annual budget into the black. The rest of the budget spending is immediately controllable, though politically risky. When politicians say spending is "uncontrollable," what they mean is that Congress has passed a law mandating that the money is to be spent. The way to control such "uncontrollable" spending is evident: get Congress to pass another law saying that less money is to be spent.

This means we can't just throw up our hands about the continuing increases, even under Reagan's mythical "austerity," in the so-called entitlement programs that have been growing at 15 percent a year for more than a decade—far faster and longer than any other part of the budget. It means that Reagan's pious talk about the need for an untouchable "safety net" to protect the "truly needy" is, in the end, just as phony as was the guilt-instilling, budget-busting rhetoric of Jimmy Carter. This "safety net" is not, as is constantly implied, a refuge for the genuine poor (whose own programs such as Medicaid, legal services and food stamps felt the keenest budgetary ax); it is, in contrast, part of a no-win situation in which more than half the population eagerly puts its hands into a bankrupt Federal Treasury. Washington is quick to criticize what it considers "greed" when productive private citizens seek higher net returns from their contributions to constructive economic growth, but it feeds happily on the desire of the nonproductive to boost their share of other people's incomes. We're not talking about aid for the impoverished few here, we're talking about programs that benefit people of average and above-average incomes

—people who believe, however foolishly (and ultimately self-defeatingly), that the Government is spending so much on others that they would be darned fools not to get their share. This is an attitude that makes media heroes of purblind legislators who pretend that programs like Social Security can extend benefits into the skies without sending the economy into the dumper. Such hypocrisy is about as "humane" and meritorious as any other kind of highway robbery. As former Commerce Secretary Peter G. Peterson pointed out in the *New York Times Magazine,* "By far the greatest victory for the middle and upper classes . . . has been the creation of the so-called 'safety net for the needy'—an exemption from budget cuts for a set of programs constituting more than half of all Federal spending not earmarked for defense or for interest on the national debt. These safety-net programs—Social Security retirement and disability payments, Medicare, veterans' benefits, railroad retirement and Federal-employee pensions—have in common one characteristic: Poverty or financial need is *not* a test for receiving the benefits. For this reason, the programs end up subsidizing the middle class far more than the poor. . . . The 'safety net' is in fact a well-padded hammock for a collection of middle-class interest groups." If we're not willing to face the necessity to adjust that hammock to modern economic realities, we are just hanging around the budget tree whistling "Dixie."

Social Security thus has a key contribution to make, not only because it is the largest (and rapidly growing) entitlement program, but because it has become a symbol of demagoguery about the people's money. When Congress brought itself to address Social Security in 1983, the self-congratulation echoed from committee chambers to Presidential speeches, hailing a supposed triumph of bipartisan cooperation that had "saved" the system. The actual result was less miraculous. While the bill contained some modest benefit cutbacks, its "solutions" came overwhelmingly in a variety of tax increases. Moreover, in a dangerous break with the past, the bill provided for large infusions of general-treasury money into Social Security, thus eliminating whatever discipline had been imposed earlier by the tradition that the system be self-financing. Louisiana's Russell B. Long, the ranking Democrat on the Senate Finance Committee, calculated that this change could add $48 billion to the nation's budget deficits over the next seven years, and declared: "I refuse to vote for fiscal irresponsibility." His was a lonely voice, however, in the chorus of euphoria. Those who complacently accepted President Reagan's assurance that "a dark cloud has been lifted" from the endangered system might better have read a little history. In 1958 Representative Wilbur Mills pushed through a tax measure that he promised would "get the program back on a sound actuarial basis," and as recently as 1977 —when Congress passed another $227 billion tax increase—the venerable Claude Pepper assured us that this time we had surely strengthened the system "not just for the immediate future, but far into the next century." Hence the widely reported view that nearly all Congressmen thought the 1983 changes had saved Social Security from insolvency "for the next seventy-five years or more" might well be taken with a grain of salt—and Pepper.

A rational approach to Social Security would take more fundamental account of a future in which a relatively dwindling work force will be expected to pay ever more handsomely for a relatively exploding group of retirees. If we continue to place such heavy reliance on an apparently unending series of tax increases, we risk more than just budget pangs: we risk adding a bitter conflict between young and old to the strains already existing in our society. There are several specific possibilities for reining in excessive Social Security spending without defaulting on genuine commitments to those in or near retirement:

(1) An adjustment to the system for calculating annual cost-of-living increases is critical. Tying these boosts to changes in the Consumer Price Index (a method introduced a decade ago with the intent, ironically, of holding increases below those Congress otherwise would legislate) has not only overstated the average retiree's personal cost increases but has meant benefits kept rising faster than the salaries of workers who paid them. (Average wages rose 30 percent between 1979 and 1982; Social Security benefits rose 40 percent. Throughout the Nineteen Seventies, wages received by workers paying Social Security taxes ran three percentage points below benefits received by Social Security pensioners.) Possible solutions to this problem—each percentage point of which costs the 1984 budget an estimated $4 billion—include freezing or stretching out scheduled increases,* paying two or three

* A method employed in a token way by the 1983 provision delaying cost-of-living adjustments for six months.

points less than the CPI (whose overemphasis on housing costs tends to exaggerate inflation's impact on retirees) or, perhaps least inflammatory and simplest to explain, tying future benefits not to changes in prices but to the percentage increase in nationwide wage rates, minus productivity gains. The idea is to bankrupt neither the beneficiaries nor the system.

(2) Having moved thus to deal with the pressing immediate problem, we must begin to think more creatively about possible longer-term revisions in a system that otherwise will not be able to deliver on even a percentage of the promises it has been making with each weekly payroll deduction. It was constructive that the 1983 bill at least provided that the retirement age for receiving full benefits be raised gradually from sixty-five to sixty-seven in the next century. This was the first official recognition that there is nothing eternal, or necessarily eternally good, about the idea of everybody retiring at age sixty-five. That age, as it happens, was chosen originally by Bismarck in Nineteenth Century Germany, where few workers ever lived to see it; it was then selected during the Depression in the U.S., when jobs were scarce and healthy old age was a rarity. Times, happily, have changed: since Social Security began, the life expectancy of an American has become twelve years longer. A gradual stretch-out over the next generation, taking early retirement to sixty-five and normal retirement to sixty-eight, would not only recognize modern health realities but make a significant contribution toward keeping the system solvent in the Twenty-first Century.

(3) We should move toward expanding the degree of voluntarism in the system. A young worker starting out today should have the option of funding his or her own retirement plan. If the system is as lovely as advertised, it should be able to withstand this market test. In any event, the fragile link between contributions and benefits should be strengthened.

(4) If legislators balk at the suggestion of voluntarism, let us then quickly move to bring into the Social Security system as dues-paying members all the currently excluded Federal, state and local employees—starting with the 535 members of the Senate and House—so that they can share the blessings now being bestowed only on us private citizens. The 1983 bill provides for including new Federal workers in the system, but why exclude the majority

of those currently voting periodically to raise taxes on the rest of us? As things stand now, Congress is allowed to practice representation without taxation. Its concern for our painfully escalating Social Security tax burden may thus understandably be diminished.

(5) We should emphasize that Social Security was intended from the start to provide only a minimum prop for retirees, not a complete and adequate pension plan. Hence our leaders should urge the advisability, for every working citizen, of supplementing Social Security with a private savings and investment program. It should be explained candidly that this is the only route either to personal financial security or to avoiding excessive, repeated Social Security tax increases over the years. And such savings should be encouraged far more enthusiastically by the tax code.

Moving on to that array of other social-spending programs, it seems clear that we must find a better way of taking care of those who genuinely are in need in America—to keep both the budget and the society from cracking apart. I have for some time been urging the appointment of a major Presidential task force charged with sifting alternative means of meeting those needs. Such a task force on welfare and related issues would increase its chance of success if it began by explicitly recognizing what I believe to be two important national consensuses in this area: (1) Americans are a compassionate people (we do not require self-serving politicians, skilled at generosity with other people's money, to tell us that), and we do not want our luckless fellow citizens to starve. (2) The present system of providing benefits is an abomination—inefficient, prone to corruption, demeaning to the recipients, supportive of a vast unnecessary bureaucracy and failing in its basic intent to make people self-supporting. I believe we can find a better way to accomplish our humane objectives without distorting every single national budget in the process.

My own preference would be for some form of what has been called a "negative income tax." We probably wouldn't call it that; the American inclination rarely has been to call things by their right names. (Asked if we would ever have fascism in America, the wily Huey Long replied: "Oh, sure. But here we'll call it 'anti-fascism.' ") What I am talking about is a system that rigorously determines who is authentically in need and then delivers cash to that person at a level adequate to meet minimal human needs but low enough to encourage efforts to rise above this condition. We would then eliminate the vast middle-class bureaucracy that stands between those who pay and those who receive. We would eliminate the official who says, in his infinite wisdom, this dollar is for food and this dollar is for housing. We would eliminate the social worker who looks under the bed to see if there is a man in the house. And by so doing, we would save more than enough not only to pay for this minimal cash-support program but to free a huge amount of other, misdeployed national resources.

The reaction I have received over the years to this proposal has been interesting. Some people, of course, met it with reflex bias: it was, they contended, shockingly hardhearted even to think of altering the present benefits to the underprivileged in our midst. But the favorable comments did not come exclusively from irate taxpayers or workers weary of subsidizing the idle. "As a mother of two on welfare," a California woman wrote after reading one of my newspaper columns on the subject, "I applaud your solution." She warmly agreed that an almost mechanical income-support program, providing sustenance but encouraging work, would help the truly needy without fracturing their dignity and wasting the taxpayers' substance. And from the other side, a former welfare interviewer in New York concurred heartily that such a program would indeed make possible enormous financial savings, by eliminating most of the present social-welfare bureaucracy, that would more than cover the cost of the minimum-income program. But while he said I was "correct, 100 percent on the button," he also doubted that the existing welfare bureaucracy would permit such a change to be fairly debated.

The welfare bureaucracy is indeed a potent special interest in American life. It is the middle-class administrators rather than the poor who have the real vested interest here. Emotion thus becomes a substitute for analysis on either side. Those who are working at jobs they don't adore, under conditions they despise, understandably have little patience with welfare recipients who don't take work because they can't find anything they deem suitable. ("Degrading," as applied to some kinds of honest toil, is an inflammatory word to many who are paying the bills.) And those who are involuntarily on the dole, and would honestly prefer to be

working, understandably object bitterly to the notion that all recipients are frauds and loafers. The answer, it would seem, would be
to take the anger out and put sense in. Americans, by and large,
do not want their countrymen consigned to poverty, but most of
them (payer and payee alike) rightly regard the present transfer
system as an extravagant flop. The beginning of wisdom will be to
stop the name-calling and start the solution.

The overriding principle in this area, for economic and social
reasons alike, might be: it should never be more profitable for any
American not to go to work. That in itself would represent a radical
and healthy change. As things stand now, for example, overly
stringent "means" and "needs" tests based on income can be
counterproductive: actually discouraging welfare recipients from
taking work. If a member of a Los Angeles family of four, with
one member either unemployed or disabled, went to work in 1982
and raised his or her gross wages from zero to $1,300 a month, the
increase in net family spending income would be only $81. Rising
taxes and falling benefits would catch him in a cruel nutcracker.
No wonder Professor Arthur B. Laffer of the University of Southern California told me that "for an inner-city resident, it has never
been truer than today that it pays to be poor." Under these conditions, the surprise is not that many people prefer to drop out of
the working force but that so many still struggle to join and remain
in it. The extent to which well-intentioned Government spending
programs can impede the work ethic should never be underestimated. Sometimes it is obvious, as when welfare offers a package
more than double the minimum wage. Sometimes it is less so, as
when the benefits in Social Security disability pensions go up faster
than private wage rates. As these benefits did so over the last two
decades, the number of "disabled" workers grew from 2 million to
5 million. Professor Donald Parsons, conducting a study to find
out why so many men of prime working age (35 to 64) had dropped
out of the work force, found that the biggest reason was an increase in the pay for not working: a 10 percent increase in disability
pensions tended to increase the rate of nonparticipation in the
work force by 6 percent. We get what we pay for.

As we begin to see, anyone who seriously looks for ways to cut
the budget finds them in abundance. The old query "Yeah—but
where would you cut?"—asked always in the smug assurance that

it is unanswerable—turns out to have a plethora of useful replies.
When we *want* to find ways to cut spending, we can: even Jimmy
Carter managed briefly to piece together a theoretical balanced
budget, and when David Stockman found in 1981 that he had badly
overestimated his original spending cuts, he was able to come up
with many more within a week. Other areas for fruitful nibbling
seem endless: A more rational welfare system would eliminate the
scandal of illegal food-stamp abuse; with more than 22 million
Americans receiving $11.3 billion worth of the stamps in 1982,
criminals large and small were having a field day reselling them—
despite the combined efforts of the Agriculture Department, the
FBI and the Secret Service. The Government medical-care system
includes such extravagances as a Veterans Administration network
of 172 hospitals, distinctly underused, combined with plans to
build even more. Robert Nimmo, the VA's tough new chief, wondered: "Does it make any sense to spend $280 million for a replace-
ment VA hospital in Minneapolis where we've got 2,000 empty
beds already there and where you've got a declining veteran population?" Bureaucracies take on a life of their own; their bosses
build empires to show how many troops they command. The Department of Housing and Urban Development discovered it could
save $30 million a year just by ending a thirty-year practice of
paying duplicate interest for three days on public housing notes.
Ohio's Representative Delbert L. Latta reported that we could
save "billions" if we merely reduced housing subsidies on higher-
priced apartments. Tremendous budget bloat could be reduced by
moving away from automatic, inflation-feeding cost-of-living adjustments in the so-called uncontrollable entitlement programs.
The farm-subsidy program remains an expensive national sore: the
Government operates a cartel for dairy products and thus boosts
the price of milk to all consumers, including poor children in urban
slums; we boost the tax on cigarettes at one end (and spend tax
dollars warning of the dangers of smoking) at the same time we
blithely go on subsidizing the growing of tobacco at the other.
Food price supports take more than $6 billion a year. The Export-
Import Bank's direct lending to finance exports of such presumably "truly needy" corporations as Boeing swallows another $5
billion. Aid to college students runs $6.5 billion, largely subsidies
either direct or disguised as "guaranteed loans"; a sensible effort

to make such programs self-financing could save a substantial fraction of this. *Fortune* magazine estimated that a simple change in Government financing—issuing inflation-adjusted Treasury notes that pay a real interest rate instead of the present high-fixed-rate securities—could lop off $28 billion more. And all the above is even before you get down to squeezing out the prodigious waste and inefficiency in the Federal establishment. As the late Senate minority leader Everett M. Dirksen wryly commented, "A billion dollars here, a billion dollars there; after a while, it adds up to real money."

Nor should defense be excluded from this hard new look at the Federal budget. Anyone who, like myself, has spent two years in the U.S. Army knows that there is plenty of waste in the military, too. Not every new toy sought by every general or admiral has to be delivered in the next mail. But we would be unrealistic not to recognize (a) that military spending, as detailed earlier, has been relatively starved in recent years, and (b) that while no sensible person wants to spend one penny more than we have to do on defense, it could be fatal to spend one penny less. Some catch-up at this point is unavoidable. Real defense increases were held to 1.8 percent annually in the Carter years, and the social-spending eruption of the Seventies had been financed by both higher taxes and lower defense outlays. The customary arguments against such increased spending usually suggest that proponents are bellicose alarmists: "What do you expect—that the Russians are going to be invading Cleveland next week?" Unfortunately, as we have seen in recent years, the Russians do not have to be landing on the shores of Lake Erie for American interests to be badly injured by a perception of our relative military weakness. Such a perception has already damaged us from Angola to Afghanistan, from the Horn of Africa to Tehran; it is today helping to influence some of our alleged NATO allies toward a dangerous neutrality. Our military need a build-up, and the only valid discussion should be over how much and how fast. I think we can afford, in a national economic emergency, to reduce the Pentagon's projected real annual increases of 9.2 percent to 6 or 7 percent, saving perhaps $16 to $24 billion a year. Interestingly, this would not necessarily reduce our actual rate of preparedness; some of my friends in the defense industry have confessed privately that the original Reagan proposals might have put more dollars in the pipeline than they could immediately handle productively. Wolfgang H. Demisch of Morgan Stanley, an aerospace specialist with an unmatched record for tracking the U.S. defense industry, now believes that the answers may lie less in hardware than in brainpower. "I think that we're living in a very dangerous world," Demisch told me, "not because of the Russians but because there are thirty or so countries that by the end of this decade will have nuclear capability, and most of them don't like us. And under those circumstances, being able to blow up Moscow several times isn't worth much—but knowing what these guys are thinking, and hopefully being able to get there one step ahead of them, is worth a lot." Hence while Demisch is high on what are known in the trade as "smart weapons," he thinks the U.S. is going to find itself relying on more of the old-fashioned on-the-ground spying that tells more about the real intentions of specific human beings than a sophisticated spy satellite ever can. "The CIA is going to be the growth industry of the Eighties," Demisch believes. "If the CIA were a stock, I'd buy it." His analysis, suggesting that much of the future may belong not to the arms manufacturers but to the super-snoopers, also hints at a marvelous new career opportunity for this decade. (007, anyone?) So our safety cannot be measured in dollars alone. But it will, by any rational test, take more dollars, and our task is to make sure they are spent wisely and cost-consciously—not to abdicate the essential job of budget reduction elsewhere by creating a scapegoat of grandiose and greatly exaggerated outlays for the nation's defense. That way lies neither prosperity nor survival.

What we need for the budget, then, is basically a repair job on two decades of ostrichlike delusions: that we could sacrifice defense spending to social programs without leaving the nation vulnerable, that we could take endlessly from the productive and give to the nonproductive without fouling the machinery of production, that we could rely on inflation to bail out reckless Government spending because taxpayers wouldn't realize they were being boosted into higher tax brackets and paying even more, that we could pile up endless "entitlements" without ever fomenting a rebellion by the golden goose. If we want to build a happier and more prosperous America for ourselves and our children, we dare not wait another two decades to acknowledge our folly—and correct it.

WORLD WITHOUT END, AMEND?

A leading Congressman invited me in 1982 to testify in behalf of the proposed new Constitutional amendment purportedly requiring a balanced Federal budget. He was surprised when, after reflection, I told him that I felt unable to do so. He knew that in a number of forums over the years (and often when it was intellectually unfashionable) I had consistently stressed the importance of getting the budget back into balance. Why, then, would I not join President Reagan in enthusiastically supporting an amendment to require it? .

First, let me stress that the reason has nothing to do with any faltering of belief in the importance of doing—quickly—what we have failed to do in every year but one since 1960: balance the Federal budget (and indeed, at this point, push it comfortably into surplus). Despite the faddish talk about how deficits don't matter anymore, they clearly do: until they are controlled, the problems of inflation and high interest rates are likely to remain chronic. And while I am fascinated to see the incumbent President calling for a Constitutional amendment, I feel constrained to point out that, the way I read the existing Constitution, he doesn't need any such authorization to go ahead and do what he has so far conspicuously failed to do: actually submit a balanced budget. As noted, the Reagan target date has receded faster than low tide in the Pacific. Did the President need a Constitutional amendment to tell him that his own behavior was nuts?

Aside from my divining a faint whiff of hypocrisy at the White House and beneath the Capitol dome, five specific objections keep me from joining the many well-intentioned Americans who, sharing my concern over the trillion-dollar national debt and the perpetual-motion Federal deficits, now advocate a Constitutional amendment on the subject:

(1) We would be permitting the thieves to write the criminal code. Who but Congress is the author of all those previous red-ink billets-doux? Why, we might as well have let Willie Sutton write the laws to prevent bank robberies. Terming the proposed amendment "so fraught with loopholes that it imposes little restraint," Rudolph Penner of the American Enterprise Institute calculated that even a more meaningful amendment would simply encourage

Congress to find so many nonbudget ways of misallocating spending—such as regulations and Government-sponsored corporations
—that the amendment could work perfectly, but "even without
60-percent votes you could easily run a whole series of $100-billion
deficits." And former Senator Henry Bellmon of Oklahoma, who
was the ranking Budget Committee Republican before his retirement in 1980, acknowledged sadly that, although he had come to
Washington in 1969 as a supporter of such an amendment, his
experience had convinced him that what was now being proposed
"simply won't work." You doubt me? You think me unduly cynical about the capacity for duplicity along the Potomac? Okay,
here's a litmus test: Insert a clause in the amendment that if a
budget comes in with an unauthorized deficit, all those who voted
for the budget-busting spending must immediately resign. Do I
hear any "ayes"?

(2) The proposed budget each year is one of the nation's most
outstanding achievements, not in economics but in fiction writing.
Any resemblance between the original deficit projection and what
is actually produced eighteen months later is entirely coincidental.
What do we do then? Sue Tip O'Neill? The amendment that tried
unsuccessfully for Congressional passage in 1982 notably lacked
any credible enforcement machinery, saying only that "the Congress and the President shall ensure that actual outlays do not
exceed the outlays set forth in such statement." Indeed, the Senate Judiciary Committee went out of its way to state "the view of
the committee that the role of the Federal judiciary in reviewing
compliance with the proposed amendment will be sharply limited." Terrific. Once before, in the grip of high indignation and
moral fervor this nation decided to adopt a Constitutional amendment that in its actual operations turned out to be such a sham that
we eventually had to repeal it in embarrassment. We called that
experience Prohibition.

(3) We don't, in fact, always want a balanced budget—and using
the Constitution for such judgmental questions could be dangerous. Nobody wants to get the budget back into balance more than
I do, but I don't think you should realistically try to do it, say, in
the depths of a recession—when it is normal for relief outlays to
expand and tax receipts to diminish. Nor do I think it is peachy
keen, in the interests of economic growth or personal freedom, to

try to reach that goal in hard times by increasing even further the already burdensome tax load. What is indeed desirable is to balance the budget over the course of an economic cycle; what is worrisome is precisely that we have not done that in recent cycles, and show no signs of doing it in this one. Reservations about the elevation of a specific fiscal policy to a Constitutional command are by no means confined to big spenders worried about even the slightest knuckle-rap from the public. Barry Goldwater termed the resolution "impractical," and other conservatives have expressed deep reservations about the rush to amend the Constitution for this purpose. Senator Slade Gorton, Republican of Washington, put it this way: "I'm a strong partisan of balancing the budget as quickly as we can, but having made that decision in 1982 doesn't give me the feeling that I'm wise enough to make that decision for the year 2082, or 50 years from now, or for that matter even 10 or 12 years from now. . . . . To put an economic theory into the Constitution is too long a jump."

(4) If you could get a balanced-budget amendment, you wouldn't need one. The task is to elevate popular understanding of the damage that has been done to all of us in the name of misguided "compassion" and to audit more closely the actual effects of open-ended inflation-generating programs that have damaged both rich and (perhaps especially) poor. The point is that Congressmen don't vote for runaway spending because they are inherently evil; they do it because it's popular. (These fellows may not be as noble as they pretend, but they aren't Hollywood villains, either; they just want to be re-elected.) Make it popular, in contrast, to become fiscally responsible, truly to husband the taxpayer's money more diligently, and you won't need a Constitutional amendment to get these guys to behave. They'll be stampeding to pile up the surpluses, all by themselves.

(5) The budget-amendment talk is, then, essentially a diversion —and a diversion we can ill afford. Amending the Constitution is a difficult and slow process; the need to restrain spending is clear and immediate. A politician, contemplating at least four or five years for ratification and another few years for phasing in, can delightedly support a balanced-budget amendment in the sure belief that he will be long gone by then—having righteously ordered his successors to behave more responsibly than he ever did. Even

if a Constitutional amendment were otherwise completely desirable, we simply can't wait. And we shouldn't redirect even an
ounce of the limited available energy on this subject to arguments
about the indefinite future. The genuine, and urgent, job is to balance the budget during the recovery phase of this economic cycle
—and that's the job we ought to be getting on with now.

A CHANGE IN THE WIND

Finally, before leaving this critical area of the budget and taxes, let
us not be seduced into allowing our legitimate concern to be translated into despair. There is growing recognition that the pendulum
has swung too far toward mammoth government in the last half-
century: that, however humane our intentions, we erred in letting
the share of our economy taken by Federal expenditures leap from
3 percent to 25 percent. Not even the most devoted big-government fanatic could argue persuasively that life in America is eight
times better as a result. The signs are all around us that the average
citizen, while not anxious to dynamite everything that has been
done since then, is more interested now in returning to the idea of
living within our means, of getting the Government a little more
out of our lives and a little more out of our pocketbooks. We need
not a revolution but a new sense of restraint; it has been calculated
that a 2 percent annual decrease in real nondefense outlays, combined with a 3.5 percent economic growth rate, could solve most
of our budget problems within six years. This is well within the
bounds of possibility if we will relearn the lesson promulgated in
1817 by David Ricardo: taxes entail crowding out as much as government borrowing does. (Both take money that private citizens
otherwise could be using for economically productive purposes.)
Nor does that seem an empty hope. There has been a discernible
turnaround in American thought that preceded the Reagan Presidency. That turnaround was evident when tax-weary Californians
in 1978 electrified the nation (and shocked politicians as far away
as Washington, D.C.) by voting overwhelmingly to end their sentence with a proposition. It was evident later that year when a
Democratic Congress repudiated its own President's tax program
and voted to ignore the expense-account "three-martini lunch"

and actually lower the capital-gains tax. The legislators did not do so because they had had a spiritual conversion on the road to Washington; they did so because the message from their constituents had perceptibly changed. In recent years there has been, moreover, scant enthusiasm on either side of the Congressional aisle for launching the kind of hefty new Government social programs that seemed all but inevitable a decade ago (R.I.P., National Health Insurance). It is the spenders who seem outdated and who are fighting the rearguard action today, and that is not all bad.

The genuine course of national budget-and-tax policy will not necessarily be patent in the oratory of our leaders, as we all should have learned by now. I recall, between Jimmy Carter's election and his inauguration, being asked in a college auditorium by how many tens of billions the new President would be reducing the Pentagon budget. When I replied that the answer was zero—that he would, in fact, wind up increasing defense spending (as, however grudgingly, he did)—I was roundly booed and hissed. Had I not listened to the man's idealistic speeches? Similarly, on the other side, some of my friends in the Reagan Administration were indignant in early 1981 when I suggested that they were smoking something strange in contending that we could cut taxes, boost defense spending, treat the runaway "entitlement" programs as sacrosanct—and still balance the budget by 1984. We can make progress, but not without making choices.

Interestingly, though, even as Reagan faltered, the old statist steamroller did not instantly reappear. Such wise Democrats as Reubin Askew, former Governor of Florida, quickly noted about their own party: "First of all, we must persuade the people that we can still be practical. We must move beyond all the old nostrums of the New Deal, the Fair Deal, the New Frontier and the Great Society, beyond the rhetoric and the slogans and the nostalgia for other days. Should the American voyage with the Reaganauts end in the shoals of disillusionment, the worst possible response by the Democratic Party would be to veer our own course back sharply to the left." In other words, we're not talking partisanship here; we're talking arithmetic. The American people, while quirky and diverse and always difficult to capture in a facile label, seemed ready to try something else besides ever more Government programs and taxes. The winds of change were blowing away from Washington. This fundamental shift seemed more important than the results of any one election, or the pangs of any one economic cycle. The people, not for the first time, were ahead of their leaders. Now it was time to turn the screws on the budget —and on those who confect it.

IV

Take the Money
and Slow Down

Many an American mother dreams that her child will grow up to become President. Millions of dads fantasize about their sons becoming baseball bonus babies or football heroes. Parents without number can be found thinking hopefully of the day when their offspring might be doctors or lawyers or corporate chiefs—or movie stars, clergymen or master plumbers. But no sensible parent ever looked at a newborn babe gurgling in the maternity ward, and said wistfully: "Perhaps it's too much to hope, but maybe someday my child could be chairman of the Federal Reserve Board."

The reasons for this conspicuous exception are several. Many Americans are not quite sure precisely what a Federal Reserve chairman does. Among the uninitiated, the title can conjure vague thoughts of conservation, or Indian tribes, or perhaps some arcane outpost of the National Guard. Those who are aware that the Fed chairman is, in fact, the nation's chief monetary-policy officer are likely to remain unentranced; the job pays considerably less than a top private banker can command, and it deals with a subject traditionally regarded as so mind-numbing that its intricacies could put all but the hardiest devotees to sleep. But tedium is not the final reason for avoiding a job that, in reality, often produces exciting, if not downright scary, ramifications in every corner of American society. The ultimate drawback is that, no matter how one

103

feels about anyone else in our country, it is always absolutely safe to hate the chairman of the Federal Reserve Board.

Any President will have those who admire him and those who abhor him. A Congressman, no matter how beleaguered, can console himself with the knowledge that many of those people out there actually voted for him. But a Fed chairman cannot win. Those who worry about inflation are almost sure to regard him as the Profligate Son. Those who consider "tight money" synonymous with hard times are likely to deem him the cruelest man in the history of the Western world. Frequently, both charges are leveled at the same time—at the same policy. Chairman Paul Volcker had the distinction of being castigated simultaneously by Milton Friedman and James Tobin, Nobel laureate heroes of the right and left, respectively (who ordinarily had difficulty agreeing even on what day of the week it was); by union leaders and corporate executives; by François Mitterrand, the Socialist President of France; and Howard Baker, the Republican leader of the Senate. Whenever there was no one else to blame, there was always the chairman of the Fed.

The results of this kind of opprobrium are reasonably predictable. Pushed and pummeled first in one direction, then another, Fed chairmen tend to be less evil than generally supposed, but more wishy-washy. Thus the challenge facing those who would improve monetary policy is not to speculate idly on the degree of individual wickedness of any particular incumbent (or on whether the prime rate will get to Jupiter before NASA does) but to get the Federal Reserve Board to stop what it actually has been doing in recent years—which, as it happens, often was quite different from what the headlines suggested it was doing. If we want monetary policy to play its proper role in a true national economic reconstruction, the authentic task is to get the Fed to stop bouncing like a Chinese Ping-Pong ball, switching every few months between the inflationary effect of pumping far too much money into the economy and the cramping, recessionary effect of supplying far too little. What we need, in short, is neither more generosity nor more stinginess, but simply more competence and dependability. The requirement is not for an unattainable degree of genius but for more steadiness, more consistency, more predictability—and certainly not for any more politics.

It might be useful at this point to lower both the heat level and the bewilderment level where monetary policy is concerned. First, what is it? Monetary policy refers to the regulation of money and credit in an economy, as opposed to fiscal policy, which is concerned with the budget and taxes. Fiscal policy gets far more media attention, but lately virtually everybody has an opinion (usually unprintable) about monetary policy, too. There has been a history of disputation in the U.S. about the Government's proper role in this area; the present setup, in which Congress delegated specific powers to a board appointed by the President, traces to the Federal Reserve Act signed into law by Woodrow Wilson at 6 P.M., December 23, 1913. (As with so many latter-day developments affecting monetary policy, he acted when the markets had closed.) The Fed, as it quickly became known to its friends (who are few), has three mighty powers for affecting the course of short-term interest rates: (1) In its "open market" operations, it can choose to buy or sell Government securities. When it sells such securities, it removes money from the private economy, thereby contracting the available supply of credit. When it buys such securities, it writes what for you or me would be a rubber check: it creates the funds out of thin air, thus in effect "printing" money at will. Nice work if you can get it. (2) The Fed can raise or lower the "discount rate" at which it lends to the banks in its system, thus sending a loud and clear signal of its overall policy intentions. (3) It can change the "reserve requirements" governing the amount of money banks must keep in relation to their deposits; higher reserve requirements mean "tighter" money, since the banks then will have less available for loans.

But while the Fed's powers to regulate interest rates are theoretically enormous, a funny thing happened on the way to their actual implementation. The world lately has not worked the way it was supposed to: creating more money did not bring interest rates down, as many believed it would, but in fact sent them higher. In contrast, when the Fed clamped its most severe restraints on the available supply of money, interest rates fell sharply. The glib clichés about "easy" or "tight" money seemed to have been turned on their heads. We must try to figure out why this has happened, what it suggests about proper monetary policy for the future and how the shift to a more effective and productive policy can best be accomplished. (Our discussion will be conducted entirely in the English language, and we will attempt at all costs to avoid the stupefying "MEGO" syndrome—"My Eyes Glaze Over"—that seems to come over so many otherwise intelligent people when discussion of this subject rises to any intellectual level higher than a growl.)

"TOO CLEVER BY HALF"

The British have a marvelous expression that illuminates our recent experience with monetary policy, and suggests how we might improve on it. The expression is "too clever by half," and it refers to someone or some idea that is defeated by its own seeming brilliance. Our monetary policy has been too clever by half. In the belief that the Federal Reserve Board could adroitly fine-tune the behavior of interest rates in a vast modern economy, we have wound up with a historically high level of interest rates and a fitful, hesitant economy. If the Fed wasn't pushing us into inflation, it was squeezing us into recession—or both. (Always, of course, with the very best of intentions, and the most modern econometric tools.) Meanwhile, the markets, which learn faster than the politicians, grew ever more suspicious. In the Nineteen Eighties a higher rate of money growth translated with unprecedented rapidity into higher, not lower, interest rates. The Fed's old tricks had earned the cynicism of the nation's lenders, frightened at the prospect of seeing their savings eroded by a new burst of inflation. What was worse, and notably baffling to traditional economic thinkers, was the record gap between current inflation rates and current interest rates. It was, quite simply, a risk premium on top of the usual inflation premium (long-term lenders historically were thought to want a return about three points higher than the rate of inflation), and it was compounded of elements of fear: fear of continuing volatility in Federal monetary policy, fear of business failures and other economic accidents, fear that brief respites from inflation were illusory and would be followed by new explosions. The way to calm such fears, and lay a more solid economic foundation, is not to be more clever but to be more reliable.

DOES MONEY MAKE THE WORLD GO ROUND?

While economists had in fact been talking about "the quantity theory of money" long before the birth of modern monetarism, its real heyday did not begin until after World War II. Arthur Burns, then director of research at the National Bureau of Economic Research, persuaded a bright young University of Chicago economist, Milton Friedman, to rejoin the bureau's staff and undertake a major project in this area. Burns later had occasion to rue this decision. Friedman began producing, in collaboration with Anna J. Schwartz, a series of seminal works,* the last just published in 1982, whose importance on the modern economic scene is comparable to the impact of Keynes and even of the man whose face Friedman proudly wore on his necktie, Adam Smith. When Burns, two decades later, became chairman of the Federal Reserve Board, his own refusal to follow the tenets of this new monetarism created controversies that linger and bedevil the economy to this day. The teacher, it turned out, was loath to fall in line behind his pupil. The monetarist school, led by Friedman, argued that there was a clear link between the rate at which the Government created money and the subsequent levels of inflation and economic growth. The wisest policy, the monetarists contended, was a steady, moderate, preordained rate of growth in money—avoiding the damaging extremes of expansion and contraction. Burns rejected any such mechanical approach to his job. It was left to a later Fed chairman, Volcker, to give even nominal allegiance to monetarism, by which time it was already having notable influence elsewhere in the world—and particularly in the British Government of Margaret Thatcher, who saw it as an indispensable tool in her eleventh-hour effort to resuscitate a socialized and gasping United Kingdom economy.

A personal story may be illuminating here. On the day President Nixon announced his intention to name Burns as chairman of the Fed, I called Friedman and asked him what he thought of the choice. "Lou," he said, "it's the best single appointment the President could have made"—words that may seem historically ironic in view of the later strains that developed between the two. I told

---

* Notably the 1963 classic *A Monetary History of the United States, 1867–1960*.

108 What's Ahead for the Economy

Friedman that I was surprised at this degree of enthusiasm: that while I was aware of their long-standing personal and professional friendship, Arthur Burns, as I understood it, did not accept Friedman's theory calling for a rigidly controlled rate of growth in the nation's money supply. Friedman paused, giving me the feeling that he had been getting away with the simple ringing endorsement in all his previous telephone calls that day. "Well, no," he confessed, "he doesn't." Pause again. "But he'll probably come closer than any of the other people they were talking about." Longest pause of all. "And you know, Lou, if I were in public office, I might not be so rigid about it myself."

Despite that engaging sally of humor and moderation, however, the monetarists led by Friedman clearly believe in a great deal more rigidity and predictability in this area than the nation has been getting—from Burns or his successors. And since this argument is likely to grow louder rather than softer, it is important for us nontheologians to see what evidence the monetarists have gathered on their side. This evidence is, in many aspects of economics, impressive and revealing. What becomes apparent to anyone who examines even the most rudimentary monetary historical data is the relationship between the amount of money pushed into the economy and the rate of inflation that economy will produce. This link emerges repeatedly in the exhaustive scholarly studies published by the Federal Reserve Bank of St. Louis, for example. In fact, you can check the relationship yourself on any hand-held calculator capable of doing "correlation coefficients"; a friend of *Fortune*'s Daniel Seligman quickly found a near-perfect (0.9) connection between the inflation rate for each year between 1953 and 1977 and the growth rate for the basic money supply during the preceding five years. At some point, then, the evidence begins to move beyond the rival claims of competing economists into the realm of demonstrable fact: stepping on the monetary accelerator produces a higher price level throughout the economy; stepping on the monetary brakes, as we did in the early Nineteen Eighties, can be counted on to slow inflation.

While that still leaves us with two key questions—"With what kind of a lag?" and "At what price in economic damage elsewhere?"—it is a significant new starting point in any discussion of inflation. It means, for example, that geometric increases in the OPEC oil price don't cause inflation, and corporate profits don't cause inflation, and high wages don't cause inflation—unless and until these or other events produce an increase in the nation's money supply exceeding the nation's economic growth. It is normal, in any economy, for some prices to be going up and some to be going down. That's not inflationary, unless the monetary authorities try to hide the consequences by printing more confetti. Despite the intellectual confusion engendered by Washington, OPEC's actions were in truth deflationary: effectively, a tax on Americans paid into foreign treasuries. This reality is not altered by the fact that our own Government then seized on these frustrating events as the excuse for printing even more money—and causing even more inflation. The energy culprits may have been in Riyadh, but the money culprits were in Washington. Those who maintained that we were no longer captains of our monetary fate were merely admitting their own unwillingness to take command. As we saw in the early Nineteen Eighties, there was nothing "inevitable" about endlessly increasing rates of inflation if the Fed was willing to restrain the presses. One can argue about the other costs of this policy, but it should now be evident that inflation is indeed a money disease, impure and unsimple.

Interestingly, this means that the best forecasters around often were those who struck the uninitiated as most "simplistic." For example, in 1979, when U.S. inflation was launched into a horrendous two-year double-digit cycle, I asked Leif H. Olsen, a monetarist and the chief economist for New York's Citibank, whether we could reduce inflation even if we didn't get a tighter budget. Olsen replied that we could, indeed: "I'd like to see tighter expenditure control on Government primarily because I prefer to see a shift from Government resources to the private sector . . . but the way you're really going to correct inflation is through a more restrictive monetary policy." Olsen added presciently: "I know there are many arguments by people who suggest that inflation is a social phenomenon, it's a political phenomenon, and it's not just money. But money is the important necessary ingredient to a continuing ongoing inflation, and the only way we're going to correct it, basically, is through a less expansive monetary policy over time. Now, that's going to require some pain, and it will be a tough adjustment. But increase and growth of money has been associated with inflation for as far back as the Third Century B.C."

Some pain. A tough adjustment. When you hear phrases like

that, you know it's not a politician talking; the classic political error, into which Reagan is just the latest to tumble, is promising a series of economic miracles at no identifiable cost. Restraining the money supply can indeed reduce (even ultimately eliminate) inflation, but if monetary policy is asked to do the nation's economic work all by itself, it seems overwhelmingly probable that the country will not tolerate the discomforts involved in staying the course. A one-armed man is at a disadvantage in a fight to the finish. And, in the real world, the Federal Reserve Board seems incapable of operating in a monetarist vacuum. Consider what Fed governor Henry C. Wallich said to me about inflation back in 1977: "I don't think there is a single cause. Saying that it's the movement of the money supply is a little like saying that when somebody is shot, the cause is the gun. Well, it's in a very approximate sense the cause, [but] there was a reason why the gun was fired. And in that sense the movement of the money supply itself has to be viewed against what forces were driving the economy."

But all that has changed, hasn't it? Since October 1979, we are told, the Federal Reserve Board has been transformed into Milton Friedman's dream. It has become monetarist itself, has it not? Well, yes and—mostly—no. But first, a word on what all the shouting was about. The dominant Keynesian school of economics traditionally did not pay much attention to the money supply. (Indeed, Friedman once suggested that I do a television piece simply showing the ever-increasing space devoted to the subject in succeeding editions of Paul Samuelson's textbook. I declined, on the ground that the seven people who would be interested might not all be watching that night.) Keynesians, in contrast, tend to be preoccupied with interest rates. They argue that changes in the money supply are unpredictable in their effects, depending on such factors as the public's desire at any given time to spend or save. To a good Keynesian, the thing to worry about at all times is interest rates, which (in the typical disciple's analysis) should be kept low to encourage investment. Hence the Fed, which like most of the economics profession has been under Keynesian sway, focused its policy on targeting the "Federal funds" rate, which is the interest rate on overnight borrowings between member banks to obtain required reserves. This was fine in theory, but it became disastrous in practice; by constantly tinkering with interest rates, the Fed wound up accentuating (rather than mollifying) cyclical swings in the economy. And something even stranger was happening: when the Fed decided, as it tended to, that interest rates were too high, it responded by increasing the supply of money—more supply means lower price, right? But, increasingly, it didn't work out that way: investors who had been burned repeatedly by this tactic recognized that more money meant more inflation, so they demanded even higher interest rates than those the Fed had acted to combat.

With disillusionment and cynicism all around, with the soaring price of gold a daily mockery to the U.S. dollar, the Fed thus moved on October 6, 1979, to an at least theoretically monetarist stance—although more in desperation than because of any perceptible profound change of heart. The Fed's traditional goal, expressed by former chairman William McChesney Martin, Jr., as "leaning against the wind," was no longer being implemented; beyond question, the Keynesian policies had been fanning the winds of inflation. And so chairman Paul Volcker announced that the Fed henceforth would concentrate on controlling the money supply rather than controlling interest rates. How well it has done since then is a matter of considerable disputation. There are some leading experts on money who confess, very quietly, that they don't actually know what they're talking about. In this case, as it happens, they mean it literally; they're just not sure what "money" is today, and that makes them dubious about what they regard as overly glib talk about the "money supply." When I chatted with George W. McKinney, Jr., on the eve of his retirement as the Irving Trust Company's highly respected economist, he observed that "it doesn't have to be money that you print . . . there's lots of other things that can be spent besides money, there's savings-account money, there's the new 'sweep' accounts [in which funds above a certain minimum are transferred automatically from bank accounts into money-market funds], all kinds of money." This was beginning to get fascinating, suggesting a whole new world out there to bemuse the professors. "Is it then," I inquired innocently, "that we just don't know what money is these days?" "Never did know," admitted McKinney—and then, while listeners to our conversation chuckled nervously, made clear he wasn't kidding: "A couple of hundred years ago you talked about money and you talked about coins of some kind or other. Then you start adding in currency, then you add in bank deposits, now [there are] a lot of things you never even heard of before. These changes are coming so fast these days that if you talk only in terms of what was money yesterday, the definition's walked out from under you today.''

McKinney's wry perspective seemed plausible to many lay observers in the wake of growing confusion over which of the Federal Reserve Board's several measurements of the nation's money supply was the "real" one to watch. In 1981, for example, M1 (the basic money supply, which includes checking accounts and currency) fell sharply, but M2 (which added the explosively growing money-market funds, plus savings and time deposits) increased above its target range at a frothy 9.5 percent pace. To many, it seemed a dangerous game of mirrors; if the authorities didn't like the results of one "M," they could always point to another. Frightened and befuddled financial markets reacted badly; so did many average citizens. The Fed's "M & M's" seemed like deceptive, and potentially perilous, candy. This suspicion deepened in 1983, when the 1981 performances were reversed; this time, it was M1 that seemed to be running out of control, wildly exceeding its targets, while M2 rose much more moderately. This time, the Fed's apologists naturally told us to focus on the broader measurements, which seemed to be performing satisfactorily, and to ignore M1. To monetarists like Friedman, though, the entire game was an evasion: the problem was not so much selecting the right target as selecting any target and then sticking to it. It was there, they pointed out with considerable force, that the Fed had fallen down; it had changed its rhetoric far more than it had changed its policy.

To a neutral observer, this complaint seems valid. It's true that the Fed occasionally has to redefine its tools to deal with monetary innovations, but this is not an insuperable problem: the relationship between M1 and the nation's nominal gross national product has remained quite consistent. More relevant has been the stop-go nature of monetary policy, even during a period when the public's perception was of a policy of "consistent tight money." The reality has been disturbingly different from this perception. The growth rate of the basic money supply actually has been more erratic since October 6, 1979, than it was in the years before the alleged policy reversal. There were indeed times of overly tight money—when, as Beryl Sprinkel (the Treasury undersecretary who was the Reagan Administration's point man on monetary policy) suggested, the Fed unwisely tried to achieve the anti-inflation goals of four or five years in four or five months. But those squeezes were separated by periods in which the Fed relapsed into excessive money creation. The result was an abatement of inflation, since the average rate of money growth was so much slower, but tremendous—and unnecessary—volatility for the general economy along the way.* Volcker thus gets a mixed report card. His overall effort to moderate the inflationary growth of money worked dramatically (and earned him his reappointment by President Reagan in 1983 to a new four-year term as Fed chairman), but the erratic month-to-month implementation of this policy served both to keep interest rates higher than they should have been and to worsen and prolong the 1981–82 recession. Some decline of economic activity invariably accompanies any effort to check a serious inflation, and those snake-oil salesmen who glibly promise otherwise have read no history. But the ill effects can be mitigated and shortened by clarity of policy and consistency of execution—two areas in which Fed policy recently has continued to falter.

It's not necessary to steep yourself in all the refinements of modern monetary policy, then, to understand that it is far from living up to its boogeyman reputation of being a perennial demand for "tight money and high interest rates." Those are understandably frightening words, and they have been bandied wildly by discontented and distressed Americans, terrified at the specter of heartless, mechanical monetarists precipitating a new American

---

* Friedman codified some of this by noting the annualized rate of M1 growth during each of five distinct periods following October 1979, and then recording in each case the interest rate on ninety-day Treasury bills one month later and the totals for industrial production three months later (which he considered the normal lags in giving monetary policy time to work). Invariably, both interest rates and industrial production went down after each period of slow money growth and up after each period of rapid money growth. So much, incidentally, for the discredited view that "easier" money will bring down interest rates. It won't: it just scares lenders into demanding greater protection against inflation.

Depression. The reality is reassuringly different. Friedman, for example, complained that the 1.3 percent money-growth rate in the first half of 1982 fell well short of the monetarist prescription ("Monetary growth of 1.3 percent per year cannot sustain a recovery in an economy in which the basic rate of inflation is still something like 6 to 9 percent"). In other words, true monetarism in early 1982 would have meant significantly looser money. And here's something even less widely understood: so far from being the precipitating cause of the Nineteen Thirties Depression, a consistent policy of monetary growth might well have averted that earlier economic catastrophe. We now can see the extent to which the economy was devastated by a lack of understanding of the same principles that are imperfectly grasped even today. The more we learn about the horrifying economic events of half a century ago, the more monetary policy emerges as a genuine culprit: the Fed not only failed to keep the nation's money supply growing at a steady, moderate and predictable rate, it actually allowed the money supply to collapse—shrinking by an astounding 35 percent. (We argue now only about how fast the money supply should grow; nobody suggests that it would be a good idea to decapitate it.) In retrospect, we can begin to recognize faulty monetary policy as perhaps the critical factor in producing those Nineteen Thirties traumas: massive layoffs, unemployment running 25 percent of the work force and an unprecedented economic disaster. We didn't know enough about the impact of monetary policy then. But we will have no such excuse if we repeat yesterday's follies tomorrow.

A POLICY, NOT A PANACEA

But if indeed, as the monetarists like to say (in what passes for humor in academe), "money matters," monetary policy is no more a panacea than any of the other recently proposed miracle cures for the economy. Much has been made of the clashes within the Reagan Administration between "monetarists" and "supply siders," but in my view that's like an argument over whether a baseball team needs a pitcher or a shortstop. It needs both. Some of

the more combative "supply-side" theorists, such as Jude Wanniski, can be as venomous toward advocates of steady monetary
growth as toward any of the economic gurus of the Nineteen Sixties. "Milton Friedman is a demand sider," Wanniski told me
scathingly, "and Walter Heller is a demand sider." The words, as
he used them, seemed to imply a particularly virulent form of
leprosy. The monetarists, more sensibly, have concentrated on
trying to find a common ground. Friedman generally has praised
the supply-side philosophy as one that encourages people to move
in the direction of higher rewards and away from activities where
rewards are lower (though he correctly faulted some adherents for
overpromising what they could deliver), while Beryl Sprinkel put
it this way in a speech in Atlanta: "The supply-side promise of real
growth and prosperity is sound. The incentive effects will work in
America in the Nineteen Eighties just as they have worked
hundreds of times before in our own country and in other countries. But they will not work unless there is a fertile, stable monetary environment. You can have the best seeds in the world, but
they won't grow without the proper soil." In any event, neither
the "soil" of a truly steady monetary policy nor the "seeds" of
meaningful supply-side tax incentives were getting anything resembling a consistent test. The economists were arguing about agron-
omy, but the politicians were ripping up the lawn.

Here, though, I think it's worth noting that, just as I believe
President Reagan has been overpraised (and, in turn, overcriticized) for what was, in reality, a tentative and ultimately conventional fiscal policy, so I believe he may have been underpraised in
the monetary area. For, despite some occasional ambiguous blips
and squeaks from both the White House and the Treasury, the
Reagan Administration essentially spent a large part of its early
years in office trying to change fundamentally (and, in my judgment, for the better) the historic relationship between the Oval
Office and the Federal Reserve Board. Sprinkel, the former Harris
Bank economist who took on the thankless task of top Administration monetary officer, commendably concentrated not on winning
easy headlines but on encouraging the Fed to behave itself: to live
up to its own announced policy of gradually, predictably, steadily
slowing the growth rate of the money supply. That this won him
notably few plaudits even within the Administration is scarcely

surprising. It was a 180-degree reversal of the conventional politics in such situations. Traditionally, of course, the White House posture, under Democrats or Republicans, has been to nudge the Fed to ease up on the money supply at all times and under all conditions: to say, in effect, "Come on, now, you guys, what are you, just a bunch of hardhearted bankers? The people are complaining about high interest rates. Aren't you the guys who are supposed to be able to bring them down? Well, will you please get in there and do it—fast?"

What usually happens when the Administration of the day puts that kind of pressure on the Federal Reserve Board of the day? Well, the Fed's governors really are human beings, too—and they want to be liked. So the tendency is to give way at least a notch, to ease up, to pump out a little more money. And, sure enough, that does tend, most of the time (depending on precisely how crowded and how frightened the markets are at the moment the Fed acts), to bring down interest rates a bit in the very short run. When this happens, the nation breathes a great collective sigh of relief, and the conventional view is that we have just been saved from a very close call.

But then what happens? The new money pumped out by the Federal Reserve Board finds its way into the economy as new inflation. This, in turn, creates even higher inflationary expectations. Those who are able to borrow race to do so, while those who are capable of lending, equally understandably, demand greater premiums as protection against the even worse inflation they see ahead. And so, every single time, this wonderfully humanitarian effort to bring down interest rates through easier money winds up by actually producing even higher interest rates than those the Fed started out so humanely to combat. You would think we would learn, after so many trips around the identical merry-go-round. But somehow there always seem to be plenty of people, in Government and out, who appear to believe that all our economic problems would be solved if only we could keep the money-printing presses rolling nonstop, twenty-four hours a day, for the next six months. These folks always have reminded me of the old story of the young woman who wanted to be a little bit pregnant: like her, they just love the initial stimulation, and they don't want to contemplate the consequences nine months down the road.

A GOLDEN RULE?

Before giving my own suggestion for a more modest, and more successful, monetary policy, let us pause for a moment and dream about gold. There is scarcely a word in the English language so evocative of emotion, aspiration and desire. From the inlay that fills a cavity to the finely wrought chain that sparkles enticingly on a lady's throat, gold serves and delights us. On the third finger of the left hand it symbolizes love, while in hot-blooded rhetoric of another kind it symbolizes love's enemy, greed. In recent years, it has been on public view primarily as a medium for investment, yet the overtones were inescapable: to some, its mere purchase was anti-American, to others it was a talisman they believed would assure unending prosperity in an otherwise doomed world. Other investments usually operate at a lower level of hysteria; one is likely to feel less theological about U.S. Steel or a thirty-year municipal bond. I have seen the appeal of gold stir thousands of convinced believers at investment seminars from New Orleans to Honolulu, and I have crawled on my belly in the shallow tunnel of the world's deepest gold mine, in South Africa, in pursuit of the origins of this mystical metal. Now, frustrated and confused by the persistence of America's economic agonies, we are urged to consider gold in a role both new and older than history: as money.

To the true "gold bug," this is simply a matter of recognizing reality: gold is money and always has been; it's this other funny paper stuff that is the impostor. Gold is not just "sound money" but "honest money"; the U.S. will not recover its heritage, these believers insist, until the nation returns to the good old gold standard.

While such moralists formerly seemed a quaint fringe on the edge of serious economics, their influence has gained for two main reasons: (1) Nothing else appeared to be working very well. (2) A number of eminently respectable people, including most conspicuously the President of the United States, seemed to have a soft spot for gold as an immediate or eventual building block of U.S. economic policy. While the Gold Commission appointed by Reagan concluded that there should be "essentially no change in the present role of gold" at this time (though refusing to rule out an enlarged role "at some future date"), Reagan himself appeared to be the Administration's not-so-closeted gold bug. The former economics major at Eureka College occasionally lectured Oval Office visitors on his belief that history showed the need for a link between a nation's currency and gold. Moreover, such key "supply-side" advocates as Jack Kemp, Arthur Laffer, Lewis Lehrman and Jude Wanniski repeatedly beat the drums for a gold standard.

What is a gold standard? There are hundreds of possible variations involving different degrees of linkage of the money we print to the gold we hold, but in its purest form a gold standard would mean that if you didn't want to hold dollars, you could walk up to a teller's window in a bank and exchange your roll of greenbacks for a specified amount of gold at a fixed price. (That option has been unavailable in the U.S. since 1933; for four decades after that, it was illegal for Americans even to own gold bullion or standard gold coins—an unwarranted interference with individual freedom that was patently offensive even to those who had no interest in the monetary question.) Under such a restored standard, the dollar would truly be "as good as gold." We would thus reverse the monetary course of the last half-century, a course on which we accelerated in 1968, when President Johnson weakened the international connection between the dollar and gold, and 1971, when President Nixon abolished the dollar-gold standard. The latter, which had emerged from a 1944 meeting in Bretton Woods, New Hampshire, was an agreement under which all other currencies were tied to the dollar, and the dollar to gold. For decades it was a beautiful agreement, from the American point of view. We could inflate all we wanted, and other countries had to take our dollars at an artificially high exchange rate. When foreigners began catching on and demanding gold, the semi-gilded house of cards collapsed, and the international gold standard went the way of the domestic U.S. gold standard. Since then, as the gold advocates fervently point out, we have been on a dizzy and undisciplined round of inflation.

Okay, so we haven't been doing so terrifically without gold. Why would a gold standard be a cure? Supporters contend that the monetary discipline imposed by a gold standard protects an economy from inflation. Prices would stabilize and interest rates fall, they argue, with a finite resource like gold controlling the money supply. With inflation under control, they continue, public confidence in a gold-backed dollar would grow, and so would savings and investments. People would more willingly tuck their bucks away once the value of money was assured. As gold put faith back in the dollar, supporters maintain, gold also would take politics out of the economy: with gold governing the governors, the power of the politicians would be diminished; no longer could capricious mortals crank the printing press at will. And finally, the gold advocates say, gold would ensure a stronger currency: once it was backed by gold, the dollar abroad would jump 20 to 30 percent in value in foreign-exchange markets, and U.S. international policies also would be strengthened. A golden future indeed, and what are we waiting for?

Closer inspection reveals a potentially less glittering scenario. Critics say a return to a gold-backed dollar would squeeze the money supply so tightly that a deep worldwide recession would result. (Under a gold standard, all Federal credit operations would have to be financed out of the nation's net savings. In other words, the ability to "monetize" the Government's debt—a fancy word for printing inflationary dollars—would disappear.) With a new, golden lock on the money supply, says credit analyst David M. Jones of Aubrey G. Lanston & Co., "the gold standard would lead us straight to a depression." Some argue, too, that a gold standard works only in a stable economic environment, which we plainly don't have now. ("The notion of combating inflation by a return to gold is like putting the cart before the horse," Rainer Gut of Credit Suisse told the National Press Club. Though a certified "gnome of Zurich," Gut also declared unambiguously: "From the Swiss banks' point of view, the debate over a return to the gold standard seems like something of a red herring. It cannot render a major contribution to effecting an improvement in the international price and exchange rate climate. It is even of less use as a means of lowering interest rates or restoring confidence in money. All these goals can only be achieved if governments, backed by a broad public consensus, are willing to work for them in an energetic and constant manner.") In addition to creating domestic turmoil, opponents say, a return to gold would wreak havoc overseas and endanger trade. They conjure visions of a return to the dog-eat-dog days of protectionism, of modern-day versions of the Smoot-

Hawley Tariff Act, a sweeping measure of the Nineteen Thirties that set record tariffs, disrupting trade and contributing to the Great Depression. They warn that a U.S. shift to such "hard" money would bring perilous deflation to many of the European countries battling high unemployment and would devastate less developed countries, which would have diminishing trade, higher oil bills—and little gold. Indeed, oil bills for practically everyone else would soar, it is assumed, because OPEC would continue to price its product in (comparatively more expensive) dollars. Far from being a golden stabilizer, the metal's critics contend, the change would produce a gilded vise, compressing the planet's economies into catastrophe.

One need not be so apocalyptic to have serious reservations about the gold standard as an economic panacea. To begin with, the historical record is by no means as reassuring as is often implied. Tying a nation's money supply not to its economic output but to its supply of a finite metal turned out to be a dangerous straitjacket; between 1815 and 1914, the U.S. underwent fully a dozen "panics" in which the growing legitimate demand for currency and credit could not be met. (Ironically, in discussing hard economic times, we now deal with a euphemism for a euphemism. Franklin D. Roosevelt sought to soften "panic" with the coinage "depression." That, in turn, developed such terrifying emotive power that we now call periods of industrial slowdown and high unemployment "recessions.")

Even gold's anti-inflation role is not nearly so persuasive as rhetoric suggests. The basic pro-gold argument is that, unlike paper, the metal cannot be produced at will by feckless politicians and bureaucrats. Gold output over the centuries has risen by about 1.5 to 2 percent a year, which by happy coincidence matches what many experts, of all schools, believe to be a healthy, noninflationary long-term growth rate for money. It sounds great—until you remember Lord Keynes's cynical reminder that in the long run we're all dead. In the short run, as it happens, new gold discoveries have been highly inflationary over the centuries. The last hundred years have been typically erratic: output soared between 1890 and 1910, fell for the next decade, rocketed until the start of World War II, tumbled again, etc. Rising production depended not only on gold-field discoveries but on such other unpredictable developments as new recovery techniques. As Alfred L. Malabre, Jr., of the *Wall Street Journal* observed, "It's no surprise that inflation in the U.S. began to worsen severely around the turn of the century, even though the dollar was on a gold standard at the time; this was precisely when vast new fields in South Africa were emerging and the gold rush was underway in Alaska."

Moreover, the impression that the gold standard kept prices stable during the Nineteenth Century depends on taking a century-long average, a method reminiscent of the old line about statistical wordplay in Washington: "Seasonally adjusted, the Great Lakes would never freeze over." Along the way, we had quite a few heat waves and deep chills. Economist Edward Bernstein calculated that wholesale prices in the U.S. fell 60 percent from 1815 to 1843, rose 15 percent from 1843 to 1864, fell 49 percent from 1873 to 1896, rose 50 percent from 1896 to 1913 and fell 33 percent from 1922 to 1932; he concluded understandably that "the view that the gold standard provided the discipline necessary for monetary stability is an illusion." (Interestingly, in the immediate post–Civil War period, one of the few times in the century before 1933 that the U.S. was not on a gold standard, prices declined sharply.) In a similar study, Rudiger Dornbusch and Jacob Frenkil reported that the gold-standard period in the U.S. in fact evidenced "short-term price variability substantially in excess of the post–World War II experience." As if that were not sufficient condemnation by itself, they cautioned that any longer-term appearance of price stability in those bygone days was "to a large extent accidental," the result of "fortuitous gold discoveries rather than the systematic operation of the system."

There are two final objections, as far as I'm concerned. The first is that the world's largest producers of gold happen to be two foreign nations whose future, from an American viewpoint, is considerably less than reassuringly guaranteed: South Africa and the Soviet Union. This could work either to reduce or expand supplies in a way unhelpful to U.S. economic stability. In South Africa, for example, racial tensions could lead to untimely production stoppages, or a future government could force heavy new supplies on the U.S. at an artificially fixed gold-standard price. Once gold's price was set well above gold's production costs, these major suppliers could force inflation on the U.S. by compelling us to come up with piles of new dollars. "The Soviet Union would buy us out," said Charles Stahl of *Green's Commodity Market Comments*. Even well short of that, an array of mischief-making possibilities arise, leading to the conclusion that strong U.S. reliance on gold could be unwise on strategic grounds.

The most important objection of all is merely a reminder that, even if we did turn to the alleged magic of gold, we would still be dealing with politicians. They have never shown much fidelity to principle, or to putatively "automatic" disciplines. The history of expedient tinkering goes back to Solon the Athenian, who in 594 B.C. countered a run on government coffers by reducing the amount of gold and other metals the Greeks could buy with drachmas. Solon has had many imitators in the intervening generations. It does not require a high degree of skepticism to conclude that any gold standard adopted by politicians would again be susceptible to political alteration whenever it became inconvenient, as has been done throughout the centuries and most recently by Franklin Roosevelt and Lyndon Johnson and Richard Nixon. As far as jettisoning a gold standard completely when it made us chafe is concerned, we did it before and we can do it again.

One is left with the impression that we are dealing with what is an outright diversion for some and a futile golden straw for others. But the argument will not subside unless and until we show greater success in achieving monetary stability. Professor Amitai Etzioni of George Washington University put it heatedly in a 1982 article for *Business Week*: "The best response to the gold nuts is to evolve an economic policy that makes sense and that works. Until that is done, the door will be open to all kinds of snake oil." More temperately, the Fed's Henry Wallich, though equally suspicious of gold as a panacea, said in a Paris speech: "The simple arrogance of saying that the gold standard is ridiculous and not worth talking about is not supported by any superior performance of alternative methods of regulating our monetary affairs. A negative view of the gold standard, which I believe to be justified, must be based on the assumption that in the future we can handle our affairs better than we have in the past."

And that, I think, is the ungilded nub of it: if gold is not the answer, something else will have to be—something giving reasonable people a basis for assuming "that in the future we can handle our affairs better than we have in the past." Those who are convinced that gold must be the solution have despaired of such a change within the present machinery. I think such pessimism is premature, though it is certainly understandable. I don't believe we need a closer connection of our currency to gold, or that such a link would necessarily be an improvement. But I have no doubt that demands for such a policy will increase if we continue to create the kind of monetary mess that has been the American specialty for the last generation. Sneering at gold bugs does not cleanse the sorry record on which they have fed. Ideological diehards and ordinary Americans alike are rightfully distressed by our failure to have done better. If we do not improve our present economic tools and our future performance, calls for a return to a misremembered and outdated monetary standard may be the least of the extremist demands on American society.

A MODEST PROPOSAL

Well, then, what should we do? The yearning for an immediate, enchanted remedy through returning to a metallic standard looks, on closer examination, suspiciously like a search for fool's gold. On the other side, the recent siege of brutally high interest rates produced demands that the Fed cease its new monetarist experiment and resume its former targeting not of the money supply but of interest rates. This desire has obvious popular appeal: knowledge of the subtleties of the monetary aggregates is limited, and controversial even among the initiated, whereas we all encounter (and occasionally are penalized by) interest rates. As we have seen, though, the Fed turned to monetarism not because it no longer wanted lower interest rates but because it found its conventional techniques no longer able to produce them. With growing understanding that loose money equals higher inflation equals higher interest rates, the marketplace had rejected the old ways of conducting monetary policy long before the Fed was forced to throw in the towel.

The answer would appear to lie in recognizing what monetary policy can and cannot do, and then finding a rather modest and passive way of achieving that limited result. Monetary policy alone cannot perform economic miracles: it cannot eliminate all fluctuations of the business cycle (though it can diminish them); it cannot revitalize an outdated industrial machine; it cannot reform and reduce an overblown, arrogant bureaucracy; it cannot substitute for the freedom-generating effects of lower Government spending and meaningfully reduced taxes. But it can perform a crucial stabilizing function—first and most obviously on prices, but also in providing a degree of assurance and predictability about the future whose absence fostered the historic investment timidity of the Nineteen Seventies. By being less ambitious itself, the Fed can nurture job-creating boldness in the private sector.

This requires a change not just of methods but of overall posture. On methods, it seems time for the Fed to stop confusing the public, and itself, with endless redefinitions of the money supply —and instead to make clear its intention of concentrating on a single narrow measurement that does not change and that it truly can control. The most logical such measurement is the so-called monetary base, which consists of currency in circulation plus bank reserves.* This fundamental gauge, sometimes referred to as "high-powered money," has two compelling advantages: the Fed's power over bank reserves makes this the one measurement it can easily and accurately control, yet it is also a reliable proxy for what is happening in the broader and more familiar standards (its growth rate rarely varying more than a percentage point from that of M1). Switching attention to the monetary base would mean outside guessers would no longer have to wonder which of the other measurements was the one we really should be watching this week, or this month, or this year. Unlike the various well-publicized "M & M's" of money-supply measurement, which can be distorted hopelessly by such new developments as money-market mutual funds, the monetary base can be controlled steadily and

* The monetary base should not be confused with the more widely known M1, which is often called the nation's "basic money supply." M1 is a broader measurement that is intended to represent funds readily available for spending, including cash in circulation, deposits in checking-type accounts at banking institutions and nonbank traveler's checks. In an era of rapidly changing banking rules, and an unprecedented variety of new kinds of accounts, money can shift misleadingly between M1 and M2. The monetary base, on the other hand, is not subject to constant redefinition.

precisely by the Federal Reserve Board. The monetary base thus fills two other valuable functions for anyone willing to bypass the prevailing rhetoric and actually look at the numbers: it tells you what the Fed truly is up to, and it provides the best available hint of what future interest rates will be. (As Joel M. Stern, then president of the Chase Manhattan Bank's Chase Financial Policy division, put it to me, "The monetary base is the one thing the central bank controls. Stepping on the monetary-base accelerator results in a highly predictable underlying money-supply figure.") In recent years, the monetary base has been an impressively efficient prognosticator for short-term market watchers, but this was because of a characteristic, and ultimately perilous, volatility that over the longer run made it difficult for even the most trusting outsider to know for sure what the Fed was planning. If the Fed cut out the roller-coaster fun and games, and instead worked on slowly, predictably bringing the monetary base to a steady annual growth rate of about 1.5 percent, this would provide an environment for stable prices and an atmosphere in which savers and investors could breathe with confidence. Announcing such an intention and visibly, systematically pursuing it would end the violent shifts that have immobilized progress even when the Fed was trying to do the right thing. The costs of the present uncertainty were suggested when Karl Brunner of the University of Rochester said in mid-1982: "We now know that the Fed has pursued an anti-inflation policy for the last two and a half years. But no one could have known it during the period, and no one can say with any confidence that the policy will continue." Focusing on a single, narrow and eminently controllable benchmark measurement like the monetary base would make Fed policy considerably less exciting but considerably more useful.

It doesn't take an advanced degree from the University of Chicago to recognize why there has been so much resistance over the years to what seems such a simple solution to monetary instability. To the Fed's august governors, the proposal that their intuitive genius should be replaced by a mechanical standard is understandably troublesome. To politicians who have made a career of demanding ever looser money, the prospect of being denied such a surefire target borders on sedition. That is why, once the necessary array of technical changes were implemented, it would be essential

to alter the overall position of monetary policy in the economic
mix. At the moment, monetary policy is almost an afterthought:
budget and tax programs come first, and the results get dumped on
the Fed, with the expectation that it will do its best to be accom-
modating. Despite the Fed's proud claims to independence, a
study by Robert Weintraub of the Joint Economic Committee indicated that Presidents since World War II have gotten the monetary policy they wanted. What is needed is a monetary policy that
is independent in more than name of the big spenders and endless
deficit creators. Ironically, some think this would have to come
from Congress itself—in the form of a "monetary rule" ordering
the Fed to proceed much as I have suggested it might. One would
hope that the Fed would not have to wait for such legislative authorization to resolve to stick to a more responsible course. The
alternative has created record prolonged inflation and, as part of
the periodic effort to contain its excesses, pain for American industries and American workers on a scale not seen since that earlier monetary catastrophe of the Nineteen Thirties. To falter now
would guarantee an even higher price the next time we struggled
to conquer the inflationary demon.

Lest anyone conclude that we are merely speculating with weird
and untried theories here, it should be noted that we have a positive model abroad of such an altered role for monetary policy. In
West Germany, which over the years has done a markedly better
job of controlling inflation, the central bank establishes and announces monetary policy with power, believability and success.
The Bundesbank tells the rest of the government how much it will
allow the money supply to expand, and fiscal policy has to fit with
monetary policy—or take the consequences. Credibility is the key.
The contrast with the U.S., where fiscal policy traditionally has
been dominant (and where the Fed's announced monetary targets
are seldom taken seriously by anyone—sometimes, it appears,
even by the Fed), is embarrassingly evident. I discussed this
superior West German performance with the man who ran it,
Bundesbank chairman Karl Otto Poehl, and he was quick to
acknowledge that such sturdiness of purpose came easier in Germany, which has suffered two searing postwar inflations in this
century, than in the U.S., whose overriding economic concern
since the Nineteen Thirties has tended to be unemployment. As he

diplomatically put it, "I think that the people in Germany are extremely sensitive as far as inflation is concerned due to the historical experience of my country, and therefore maybe they are more ready than other people to accept anti-inflationary policies and all the repercussions of an anti-inflationary policy." Poehl also told me firmly, and significantly: "I can assure you that the Bundesbank is absolutely independent from the government, and from political parties, and that we will pursue our policy of maintaining price stability." Ponder for a moment the extent to which a similar, credible stance in the U.S. would galvanize investors and spur the kind of long-term job-creating undertakings that seem so questionable in times of recurrent inflation. Suddenly the issue of monetary policy becomes neither boring nor irrelevant; by entering a sort of public prison itself, monetary policy could liberate and expand the lives of private citizens. We would hear less about it, but we could rely on what we heard. Instead of the well-intentioned volatility that breeds insecurity and fear, augmented by the atmosphere of self-conscious secrecy in which the operations are conducted, a monetary policy announced in advance and delivered on schedule would enable Americans to plan their lives with greater confidence, boldness and prosperity. All that would have to come down would be prices, interest rates, unemployment and governmental hubris. I can take it if you can.

GET A HORSE?

Finally, a story: Over the years, for those discouraged by our seeming inability to get even the purely technical details of economic policy right, I have presented my own version of the view expressed by Milton Friedman. Milton, I would say, has his own unique solution to the problems of monetary policy: Milton would abolish it. Friedman would like to replace all those bureaucrats in that great Grecian temple in Washington, the Federal Reserve Board, with one highly trained quarter horse. On the first day of each year, the horse would be brought out on the steps of the Federal Reserve Board building, and a junior bureaucrat would be assigned to approach the horse and say to him: "Trigger"—or maybe that should be "Professor Trigger"—"what should the growth rate of the money supply be this year?'' Trigger, who would have been highly trained, but only to do one trick, would then lift his right front hoof and bang it on the pavement precisely four times. (Only one and a half times, presumably, if Trigger were familiar with the monetary base.) And the junior bureaucrat would say, "Oh, I get it—four percent growth in money supply again this year. Well, thank you, Trigger." Everyone would go home, and that would be monetary policy for that year.

Well, I have to confess that I had always thought that might be just a hair simplistic—that it might not work quite as easily as Milton had always assured us that it would. But on the other hand, I have to confess that I am no longer convinced that it would work notably worse than the system we have tried in recent years. And that system involves only half the horse.

V

You Can Bank On It

Not long ago, the typical American picked his bank more or less the same way he picked his mailbox. If it was nearby and federally endorsed, that was about the most he could ask. The price and the rules were the same everywhere in town. Now changes are coming so swiftly that what seems sensible in January may appear foolish by July; the customer has an ever-growing variety of choices from an ever-growing variety of competitors for his funds. None of these competitors is entirely delighted with this radically altered U.S. financial situation. The rivalry has become bitter and most unbankerly: the name-calling in newspaper ads, of bankers by brokers and brokers by bankers, is startlingly remote from the traditional image of good gray financiers in three-piece suits. Happily, the one clear winner in this battle of the big-money men is the customer. The only thing keeping him or her from a total knockout is the continuance of an outmoded regulatory system, which pretends to serve the ordinary citizen but in fact conducts a series of rearguard efforts on behalf of assorted and conflicting vested interests. It's time to make the consumer's victory complete.

The financial area remains today the single most overregulated sector of the U.S. economy, and plainly not to or for the consumer's benefit. Major improvements, such as the money-market funds, came as the result of innovative end runs around the creaky regulatory apparatus. Not only do Federal agencies compete, often at cross-purposes, in this outmoded arena, but each of the states has its own additional setup—which in practice usually performs no function loftier than continued protection of the interests of entrenched local institutions. Part of the rationale for this labyrinth is the myth that banks, savings and loans, insurance companies and securities firms are all vastly different entities, defined by their historical industry classifications. In reality, both new financial products and outright interindustry mergers have obliterated many of the traditional distinctions. It's hardly surprising, then, that regulatory conflicts and overlaps abound. We must streamline this maze before we can exit from it.

As just one example of the endless proliferation of would-be overseers, the securities markets alone are now subject to the jurisdiction of at least ten Federal and more than a hundred state agencies. While talk of regulatory reform is one of the politicians' hardiest perennials, it tends to proceed on a conventionally parochial footing. Chairman John Shad of the Securities and Exchange Commission has wisely suggested that one solution might lie in the establishment of a task force to recommend consolidation and simplification of existing rules and—perhaps most important—"regulation by functional activities rather than by outmoded industry classifications." But since each industry tends to feel most cozy with the overseers it knows, there has been no discernible rush to join Shad's bandwagon. It's far easier to gripe through lobbyists about allegedly unconscionable invasions of one's turf than to plan intelligently for the U.S. financial system of the Twenty-first Century.

A more productive policy on banking and credit would begin by recognizing that competition is what everybody wants—for the other guy. The bankers who now demand a "level playing field" would initially have preferred the total banning of money-market funds. The newcomers who advertise their "one-stop financial supermarkets" would be delighted if the banks they seek to replace were forever uniquely restricted with such things as reserve requirements. The large California S&Ls joyfully cut through archaic banking limitations by buying troubled thrift institutions in New York, Florida and elsewhere—but grew indignant when New York's Citicorp took over ailing Fidelity Savings of San Francisco. (What? A commercial bank allowed to buy an out-of-state S&L? Next thing you know, they'll be smoking.) And even those daring money-market mutual funds, the saver's best friend since the piggy bank, became irritable when the banks and S&Ls got approval to invade their turf with money-market accounts of their own.

The funds feared—correctly—that their monopoly would prove no more enduring than the banks' had turned out to be. The jolt was even harsher than most fund managers had expected. On December 14, 1982, U.S. banks and thrift institutions were freed to create money-market deposit accounts, with whatever interest rate the institutions chose to pay; on January 5, 1983, they got the same right for checking accounts. The banks and S&Ls moved in aggressively, offering premium initial rates and emphasizing the convenience of branches and the security of federally insured deposits. Success was instantaneous: the money-market deposit account grew more rapidly than any other consumer-deposit account ever authorized. By May 1983 banks had attracted more than $350 billion with the account, and savings and loan associations $100 billion more. Meanwhile, the older money-market funds run by brokers and other nonbank financial institutions saw their assets fall from more than $230 billion to less than $170 billion in the first six months of competition from the banks. The decline had begun to slow by midyear, as the initial premiums the banks offered disappeared, bringing the bank account rates more in line with money-market rates. The money-market funds took advertisements hammering home some of their own convenience features and emphasizing a fundamental difference: while the funds' rates always directly reflect their investments in the short-term money market (Government securities, top-rate commercial paper —corporate IOUs—and large certificates of deposit), banks can use the customer's money any way they choose and arbitrarily decide the rate to be paid. Customers, attuned by the money-market mutual funds themselves to the attractions of an extra inch or two of interest, did not seem panicked by this. The likely outcome was a niche for both kinds of funds, depending on the needs of the particular customer for the particular funds being deposited. In other words: that almost unheard-of condition for individual savers known as free choice. Both bankers and brokers were grumbling, though, that there ought to be some new restrictions on the other side.

No wonder it has been so difficult to concoct financial legislation that takes a broader view than a constituency-by-constituency count of local votes and dollars. But the financial shape of the future is becoming clearer, nonetheless. Like it or not—and the consumer generally should, even if some established institutions do not—the lines traditionally separating different kinds of financial institutions in America will surely continue to blur. The state lines, too: when New York tried to maintain an unrealistic 12 percent "usury" ceiling on credit-card loans, Citicorp stunned the doctrinaire locals by moving its credit-card operations to Sioux Falls, South Dakota. Other governors, such as Delaware's astute Pierre S. du Pont, quickly took the point and began luring significant chunks of business from less alert states. Those who refused to move with this tide of greater financial freedom were destined to be swamped by it.

A SAVING GRACE

It's worth noting, as we chart a future course for banking and credit, that the array of new opportunities for savers that has appeared in the last decade was not a bounty bestowed by Washington. On the contrary, both legislators and regulators played catch-up after innovative private firms had found ways around the old rules—and then quickly won such wide customer support that the rulemakers were loath to exercise a veto. A similar situation occurred in the spring of 1983, when Congress bowed to a popular groundswell and moved to repeal the 1982 provision calling for withholding taxes on dividends and interest starting July 1, 1983. Superficial media coverage termed this a victory for the "bankers' lobby," but this was a misreading for two reasons: many of the larger banks assiduously avoided the crusade (preferring to save their legislative firepower for more parochial concerns, such as a bailout on bad foreign loans), and masses of individual Americans were genuinely angry, correctly seeing that the provision would create a nuisance, an administrative cost and a net reduction of returns to savers and investors.* The actual impact would have

* The claim that the real purpose of this revenue measure was to catch cheaters is low-grade political baloney: the voluntary compliance rate on reporting interest and dividend income is already 97 percent—on payments that are reported to the

been to encourage present and prospective savers and stock-market participants to seek tax-free investments instead. It was a misguided idea that had been rejected by Congress six times between 1942 and 1980—when Jimmy Carter proposed it, the House turned it down by 401 to 4 and no fewer than sixty Senators spoke out against it. Among those who saw things more clearly then was Kansas Republican Robert Dole, who was the measure's chief advocate in 1982 and 1983 in his new role as a tax increaser, but who had written a constituent on June 4, 1980, asserting—with greater wisdom—"I oppose such withholding because it is a disincentive to savings and capital formation at a time when we need to encourage both." Dole would doubtless disagree with the acerbic Kansan, a former supporter, who maintained to me that the shift was entirely political: "The *New York Times* and the *Washington Post* raised him from a hatchet man to a statesman when he raised the taxes." But the Senator might well have listened to his own earlier counsel on the economic need for savings.

There is nothing new about leading legislators pushing prospective savers in the wrong direction, by encouraging debt and penalizing thrift. Indeed, the unmistakable message from the capital for more than a generation has been that Polonius was only half right; when the Shakespearean character advised, "Neither a borrower, nor a lender be," he obviously hadn't consulted a good tax lawyer. Being a borrower in an inflationary economy proved an excellent strategy. Not only could one count on being able to repay the loan with significantly cheaper dollars than those originally borrowed, but the interest on the loan would be tax-deductible all along the way. In contrast, those foolish enough to practice the ancient virtue of thrift found that their overlords in Washington (a) ordered financial institutions to pay less than the market interest rate to small savers, and (b) then had the temerity to tax away a sizable portion of this below-market return. You could get a better deal than that from Torquemada.

Grudgingly, and in excruciatingly limited stages, the Government has been allowing that indefensible anti-savings policy to

---

Treasury by paying institutions on Form 1099. The only substantial compliance problem is on interest paid by Federal agencies. Solution: make the Government file the same forms as everybody else.

erode. Yet even within the last couple of years, in the unending debates as to precisely how much justice it might be reasonable to allow to the thrifty, the idea has been presented to Congress with awesome heat that the entire direction of this effort is misguided: that the most dreadful threat to the U.S. economic system today stems from that dastardly moment when our masters first unwisely consented to give the small American saver something resembling an even break. This view was presented both by S&L executives, seeking to recapture a lost paradise of fixed interest ceilings, and by bankers, who until they were permitted their own money-market accounts spoke darkly of the perils of bypassing the established system of institutions and accounts. Significantly, neither Congress nor the multipronged banking-regulatory apparatus had much to do with the changes that have most helped small savers. Left to their own devices, legislators, regulators and industry lobbies would presumably have been content to see consumers getting no more than a taxable 5.5 percent on passbook savings, and never mind that fat cats with $100,000 or more to invest could be raking in a double-digit return.

The traditional financial community and its Washington allies were—not for the first time—staring in the wrong direction. Even today, the country banks spend much of their time looking over their shoulders in nervous, preoccupied glances at the big-city banks; what energy is left is often dissipated in largely outmoded antagonism between the bankers in general and the savings and loans. Meanwhile, more venturesome financiers such as Walter Wriston of Citibank and (before he became Secretary of the Treasury) Donald Regan of Merrill Lynch have been effectively dynamiting many of the geographical and regulatory Maginot Lines of finance. The single most significant financial development of the last decade, the money-market mutual funds, mushroomed entirely outside the rivalries that traditionally preoccupied industry lobbyists. When these nonbanking bank accounts—for they are, in truth, nothing less—captured more than $200 billion of the nation's savings, many old-style financiers denounced this as unfair competition, involving as it did the payment of market interest rates to the former suckers. What a horrible and un-American act! Later, of course, these same financiers rushed eagerly to offer their own money-market accounts. But to hear some of my friends in the more traditional financial bastions discuss these matters, you might conclude that all the much-ballyhooed problems of the U.S. banking system would disappear if only they could revert to what has been called the 5-9-2 system: pay 5 percent for your deposits, charge 9 percent on your mortgages and be on the golf course by 2.

Well, sorry, gang, but you're not going to keep them down on the farm after they've seen the Paree of market interest rates. A sounder basis for progress in this area of banking and credit would begin with demands not for more Government interference but for considerably less than already exists. Both the interests of potential savers and the national interest in their encouragement would be served by moving more rapidly and purposefully toward elimination of the remaining unrealistic ceilings and restrictions—on both sides of the financial equation. (For savers, for example, this might entail elimination of requirements of stiff penalties for early withdrawals; for banks and S&Ls, it would involve greater freedom to offer other financial services.) And you have to do it on both sides to make it work economically; it's merely demagoguery to urge deregulation of what the institutions pay out while advocating continued outmoded restraints on their profit-making activities. You can't practice single-entry bookkeeping—unless, of course, you're in Washington.

This route toward greater freedom and competition could lead to a number of important public advantages. It would, for example, entirely stop penalizing ordinary Americans—middle-class depositors—as opposed to their wealthier or more sophisticated neighbors who have had the sense, in times like these, to move in and out of the open money market. And the more equitable competition for funds, long opposed by regulation advocates as a threat to the nation's housing industry, could actually have the opposite effect: making vastly more money available for mortgages at times like those that have recently been upon us, when interest rates have climbed agonizingly and money has left the banks and thrift institutions—thereby creating hardships for would-be home-buyers all over America. The real threat to the nation's financial structure, despite the alarms of frightened traditional financiers, does not come from Merrill Lynch or Sears Roebuck, and it certainly doesn't come from giving a long-overdue break to the average

American saver. It comes from an inflationary and irresponsible Government.

BUT WILL MY MONEY BE SAFE?

The idea of less regulation for the nation's banks is frightening to many Americans. At home, the 1981–82 recession brought well-publicized bank failures—stirring fears of old-style panics and desperate runs on the bank, of the loss of a family's lifetime savings. Abroad, we heard of big U.S. banks in trouble because they forgot the golden rule of banking: it's good to make loans, but it's better when the borrowers actually pay the money back. (Looking at the roster of bad foreign and domestic loans amassed by some of our more eminent big-city banks in recent years, cynics have wondered whether these institutions ever managed to make any good loans.) Some of our more apocalyptic prophets foresaw imminent collapse of the world banking system, and a downward spiral into bottomless Depression. No wonder many depositors grew uneasy.

The task here is to reassure the understandably jittery without creating new travails through further gratuitous interference with the marketplace. There are indeed troubling problems within the U.S. (and international) financial system, but the notion that they will be solved by still more piecemeal legislation or ham-handed regulation should by now be terminally unconvincing. To begin with, the effectiveness of present regulatory practices in safeguarding the consumer tends to be badly overrated. The Federal Deposit Insurance Corporation's list of "problem banks" mounted from 217 in 1980 to 277 in the summer of 1982, for example, but somehow managed not to include the Penn Square Bank—which did collapse.

On the other hand, the private marketplace already has punished some banks, here and abroad, that operated on the apparent theory that all loans to foreign countries were equally riskless in this best of all possible worlds—and then suddenly found, to their horrified surprise, that such major borrowers as Mexico, Brazil and Argentina kept needing new loans just to pay old interest. Part of the answer, as Treasury Undersecretary Beryl Sprinkel suggested on "Wall $treet Week," lay in beefing up the emergency-aid capacity of the International Monetary Fund, but part lay simply in some old-fashioned research, judgment and discipline. In the short run, too, it might help to recognize that, as the *Financial Times* of London put it, "lending with no illusions" will now sometimes be needed "to support earlier loans that had been full of them." However, we should be vigilant against the suggestion that the full brunt of such bad loans should fall on the U.S. taxpayer; such costs belong properly to the shareholders of the erring banks.

Suggesting that we move to a less regulated atmosphere does not mean eliminating such widely trusted provisions as the insurance of bank deposits. But we can find a better way to carry out that reassuring process. At present, there is considerable confusion between insurance of bank deposits and insurance of banks. The former has worked pretty well at steadying the customers' nerves over the last half-century, during which time there have been banking failures without banking panics.* But the latter, as exemplified by some spectacular multimillion-dollar bailouts of spectacularly mismanaged banks, has been neither necessary nor advisable. One effect has been the widespread (though, as the 1983 resolution of the Penn Square case demonstrated, unjustified) assumption that the $100,000 statutory limit on insured deposits is merely theoretical, and that the Government will in fact rescue everybody down to the last penny. This leads as well to the corollary conclusion that careful bankers are simply suckers; since everybody will be protected in the end, according to this dangerous line of reasoning, you might as well be a little bit reckless in going for the extra inch of profit. One possible solution was suggested by the *Wall Street Journal:* make banks, and perhaps those that act like banks by offering things like interest-bearing checking accounts, buy their insurance from the Government or the private sector on a variable-rate basis, one that would openly penalize an institution with what the newspaper called "a weird portfolio and

---

* Despite the dark prophecies of professional fear merchants, I'm convinced that small savers can sleep soundly at night, in the justified faith that their federally insured deposits are safe.

skimpy capital." In other words, bigger credit risks would pay bigger insurance premiums, just as with individuals. By translating the understandable desire to protect small depositors into near-total insulation of the financiers from the realities of a competitive marketplace, officials typically have lost sight of the original sup-posed motivation for all this proliferation of regulation and coun-terregulation. A move back to Square One, and a rethinking of the purposes of such financial legislation, would seem a useful place to start.

WAS IT SMART TO BE THRIFT-Y?

A classic illustration of Congress's bent for substituting narrow-based bailouts for broad-gauge economic thinking has come in the ongoing saga of U.S. savings and loans, next to which the Perils of Pauline seem downright placid. The "thrifts," as they like to be called, are creatures of regulation that recently threatened to be destroyed by it. (William Shakespeare, where are you when we need you?) For years, they survived nicely in the hothouse of a comfortable environment where they took in short-term savings, at federally mandated below-market levels, and then loaned the money out on higher-rated long-term mortages. Favored over the commercial banks by being allowed to pay a then-whopping extra one-quarter point on savings accounts, the thrifts flourished. In 1966, passbook savings made up 91 percent of their deposits, and it scarcely required the financial acumen of a Bernard Baruch to run a prosperous S&L. Then came a period of rapidly increasing interest rates and—most disastrously for those who had reveled in the old order—rapidly increasing alternatives available to the for-merly docile passbook saver. To keep these savers in the fold, the S&Ls had to offer higher-yielding certificates; by 1980, only 21 percent of S&L deposits were still in low-paying passbook savings —and thrift executives complained that they were cannibalizing their own assets. The nervousness of this industry, with its formi-dable political clout, led to some historically foolish legislation. In 1981, one result was legislative restrictions on competing invest-ments: as if it were the Government's job (or area of competence) to tell you whether you should be allowed to put gold bullion or Chinese ceramics in your retirement account. As for the money-market funds, they were described by some skittish S&L executives as the biggest threat to the American home since the demise of the Big Bad Wolf. It soon became apparent, however, that what would rescue the thrifts was not an assault on "collectibles" or money-market funds—or even such passing ploys as the tax-favored "All Savers" certificates—but a less inflationary environment, accompanied by lower interest rates.

The plight of the S&Ls was undoubtedly real (the net worth of federally insured associations fell by more than 20 percent between mid-1981 and mid-1982), but the reasons for it could be grasped by a bright second-grader with a rudimentary knowledge of simple arithmetic. In early 1982, the typical U.S. savings and loan was paying 11.31 percent on its deposits and earning 9.79 percent on its loans. Now, you can't make that up on volume. Clearly, lower interest rates would help both halves of this equation: most obviously, by reducing the cost of deposits, but also by encouraging a better return on loans (while new mortgages would be made at rates below the stratospheric—and prohibitive—levels then being demanded, they would for quite some time likely be made at rates higher than 9.79 percent). What emerged from Congress, however, was precisely what was not needed; instead of grasping the opportunity for sensible and far-sighted deregulation, our noble legislators passed one more narrow-based bailout bill. The so-called Depository Institutions Act of 1982—oh, gosh, if Congress were only as good at making sense as it is at confecting imposing titles —authorized Government-backed pieces of paper to shore up the S&Ls' balance sheets, allowed the thrifts to put 10 percent of their assets in commercial loans (in contrast to their traditional emphasis on housing) and let S&Ls as well as banks offer money-market accounts. A study by *Fortune* magazine a mere month after the bill's October 1982 passage concluded that it was already "a bailout the S&Ls no longer need." The much-ballyhooed capital assistance program had become "largely irrelevant"—some 100 of the nation's 4,100 S&Ls were too sick to qualify; of the rest, only an estimated 282 would be eligible, and as interest rates dropped, most of them would be returning to profitability anyway. Even one of the bailout's leading advocates, chairman Richard Pratt of the Federal Home Loan Bank Board, admitted: "With interest rates where they are today, we could have managed without the capital assistance program." On such long-range statesmanship do our leaders plot the rules that guide our financial futures.

ARE WE BORROWING TROUBLE?

One of the best-kept secrets in the world of credit is the extent to which the American people have been rationally self-policing. They had better be. Even throughout a period in which we were told continually how "tight" money was supposed to be, the pressures on the innocent to go further into debt have been all about us. I have before me as I write two recent examples from my own unsolicited mail:

(1) A major New York City bank has sent me what looks like (but is not) a check for $15,000; this sum can truly be mine, the bank's computer informs me, if I will merely complete a short form and return it in a postage-paid envelope. These swell guys want to give me this money, it seems (no mention of anything so vulgar as interest rates appearing anywhere in the friendly letter—though the figure, it transpires, would be 19.75 percent), simply because I'm exactly their sort of fellow. "We believe," the word-processed billet-doux continues, "an appropriate 'get acquainted' step is to provide you with an opportunity to borrow funds you may need right now." Can you imagine anything so thoughtful? Why, my newfound pals even suggest a number of ways I might think of spending this windfall, not even neglecting our mutual friend Uncle Sam. "Many professionals tell us they experience a temporary cash flow difficulty for months after income tax time," they advise me reassuringly. (The letter has arrived in September.) Golly, Mom, we've got nothing to be ashamed of, wanting to go to Cannes for Thanksgiving: even the professionals get caught short now and then. And, as a final fillip, these generous-hearted computer punchers are gracious enough to tell me that I can be their buddy even if I don't take everything they're offering: "Should you require less money, simply cross out the $15,000 and write in the amount you wish—minimum $3,500." (Anything less, I presume, is regarded as such petty cash as to be unworthy of us both.)

(2) Two more unsolicited checks arrive almost simultaneously,

this time from some pals I didn't know I had at a big bank in Chicago. One of these checks has already been filled out for $500, and requires only my greedy signature to be negotiable; the other is for me to write myself, for what could be a much greater amount. And why am I so fortunate, so beloved by the financiers along the shores of Lake Michigan? Why, because my First Card credit line is being raised substantially, in tribute to the bank's "determination," after a "careful review" of my credit history, that I have managed my account "in a superior manner." Gosh, isn't that terrific? And these fellows don't mention interest rates even in the finest of print—though, to be sure, there is something cryptically informing me that "the checks are for use in obtaining credit under the terms previously disclosed." But who could cavil at that, when dealing with such obvious philanthropists? Only someone who (a) wondered what all that talk about "tight money" was about (money apparently being loose enough, for anyone able and willing to pay 19.75 percent for it), or (b) was aware that the credit trade's new secret internal definition of a "deadbeat" is a customer who pays off each month's bill in full, thereby avoiding any juicy interest charge. Could it be that these grand new friends were simply trying to get me in over my head—so that I would have to stop being such a deadbeat and start foundering in debt like I was supposed to be? Perish the ungenerous thought.

But if the stern and prudent banker of archetypal lore has in fact been replaced by a new breed feverishly peddling bill-consolidation and home-equity loans, kitchen-appliance and Easter-vacation loans, plastic-card and over-the-telephone loans—not to mention enough toasters to provide breakfast for all the armies in NATO— the remarkable thing is not that so many Americans have gotten in over their heads, but that so few have. Implored regularly by bankers, credit companies, auto dealers and retailers of all descriptions to achieve instant gratification on what the British shrewdly call the "never-never" payoff plan, American consumers on balance have shown a degree of responsibility that contrasts vividly with the devil-may-care approach the politicians have taken toward the debt they themselves were amassing in Washington. While the dollar value of individuals' debt rose dramatically over the last decade, these IOUs actually shrank as a percentage of net worth. The average person is far from the dummy his would-be guardians are forever trying to make him out to be. When rapidly escalating home prices in the Nineteen Seventies necessitated the allocation of a higher portion of the family budget to mortgage payments, households simply—wisely—cut back elsewhere: consumer credit as a portion of all U.S. debt fell from 24 percent to 21 percent between 1971 and 1981, keeping the overall individual share steady. Moreover, far from tumbling deeper into debt when conditions worsen, the typical family tends sensibly to cut back on borrowing as the headlines grow gloomier. This has been the predictable pattern throughout recent economic cycles; when the country entered recession in late 1981, individuals again quickly began paying off bills at a record clip. Even in the hardest of times, when rising bankruptcies capture the headlines, the people display consistently better character than their Government: the National Commission on Consumer Finance found unemployment, illness and overextension the three top reasons for loan defaults—while simple wrongful refusal to repay ranked last. The unheralded fact is that the overwhelming majority of individuals do not require a watchdog, public or private, to get them to behave more dependably than perennially palms-up foreign governments, subsidy-hungry corporations or spend-happy Congressmen. With the U.S. recession at its worst in 1982, Leonard Druger, vice president of credit policy for the New York banking division of Citibank, noted with appropriate respect the resurfacing of this traditional phenomenon: "People are tougher on themselves than we are. They'll just not buy. They'll defer purchases. They won't borrow. They're afraid of rejection. The irony is people are self-qualifying much more stringently than the bank." (Characteristically, Government efforts to protect borrowers from themselves often wind up being counterproductive. An example is the 1980 change in the Consumer Bankruptcy Act: hailed by consumer groups as a victory for the little guy, for whom it made it easier to claim bankruptcy, it actually served to limit loans to deserving little guys. Since courts were forbidden to consider a would-be bankrupt's future earning power—only his existing assets—finance companies naturally began to restrict their loans to people with assets. All of which meant that lower-income groups, because of this wonderful new effort to "protect" them, were deprived of loans they previously could have obtained. As Finn Caspersen, chairman of the Beneficial Corporation, put it to me: "Consumer credit by its very nature is credit that's made available to an individual based on his ability to pay it back. [But] the existing law says consumer credit can only go to those people who have assets, i.e., the wealthy. . . . The creditor doesn't want to attach assets, [but] right now, we will not lend to people who don't have assets.")

It is, of course, always easier to tut-tut about the awful ease with which our fellow citizens allegedly take on debt than to deal with two more valid problems: the truly damaging way in which the Government accumulates IOUs it has absolutely no intention of ever repaying, and the practices by which that same Government encourages individual borrowing while simultaneously discouraging individual saving. For, as we have seen, consumers did not take on their current pile of debt unabetted by Washington. But this never inhibited any politician from trying to make us feel guilty about it.

AN OSCAR FOR MR. CARTER

One reason we are forever seeking makeshift solutions to more fundamental problems is that our governmental apostles have such an unparalleled talent for shifting the blame. I have to confess, though, that even I had underestimated that capacity until the start of this decade. I had thought that successive Administrations in Washington had found every possible scapegoat on this planet for their own continuing failure to get our long-range inflation problem under control—from the anchovies off Peru to the sheiks of Araby. But I had to admit that they were even more creative than I had assumed when in March of 1980 the Carter Administration announced that it had discovered that Public Enemy Number One was actually the Visa card. This, surely, was the Academy Award winner in the category of Inventive Scapegoating. Never mind that, even before May was over, the perpetrators had to say, in effect: "Whoops, sorry, guess it wasn't that, either"—and change that policy, too. The experience was more instructive than intended. First, there was the spectacle of a Government that was unwilling to consider more than purely cosmetic cuts in its own burgeoning budgets for 1980 and 1981 now suddenly discovering that the real cause of inflation was credit-card purchases and bank-overdraft loans. An entity whose own unpaid bills were edging merrily toward a trillion dollars turned with righteous indignation on the American housewife. Second, the Government acted against the background already detailed here: that the private use of credit had been considerably—and consistently—more rational than the Government's own borrowing excesses. Not only had this been routinely true in the past (the average U.S. family reduced its debt dramatically as we moved into the deep mid-Seventies recession), but it was identifiably true at the very moment of the Government's grandstand play: the latest monthly figures had indicated that the growth of consumer credit already was slowing in anticipation of another economic downturn. Third, the incident demonstrated that the beleaguered average citizen was still notably more patriotic than those who would chastise him. For all the talk about the alleged new cynicism of the populace in the wake of Watergate, double-digit inflation and assorted other governmental disasters of the previous decade, the typical American clearly still listened respectfully when his President offered counsel—no matter how spurious. When Jimmy Carter blamed an important share of our inflation woes on irresponsibly high consumer debt and spending, millions of Americans took his (highly inaccurate) words to heart—and did more in fifteen days than Congress had done in fifteen years. So devastating was the impact of this radical consumer-spending cutback that Treasury Secretary G. William Miller was sent racing to the barricades to announce grandly that consumers had "done their job" and could now—please!—"go back to more normal spending." Thus ended, in a few shameless weeks, the third-fastest economic battle of the decade, surpassed in brevity only by Gerald Ford's button-happy campaign to "whip inflation now" ("WIN") and Carter's own ephemeral "moral equivalent of war" on energy ("MEOW"). Fourth and finally, it rapidly became evident to anyone not hopelessly adrift in an ideological fog that inflation was no more caused by overuse of credit cards than it was caused by workers trying to get a raise or businessmen trying to boost their profits; the authentic villains were the guys in Government, the ones doing all the finger-pointing. For, sure enough, at the very time the misguided consumer cutback was slicing into retail sales and sharply worsening the recession, the Federal Reserve Board was reopening the floodgates in panic: a massive easing of the money supply that led to a quick recovery and, equally predictably, a devastating resurgence of inflation and record interest rates. The correct slogan for our economic policymakers should have been: "Common sense—don't leave home without it." For what they genuinely should have been preaching would have involved a discomforting look in the mirror, and the revelation of a well-kept secret: If the Government of this country had conducted its debt one tenth as responsibly as the private citizens of this country have conducted theirs, we wouldn't have this inflation problem to be talking about in the first place.

ADJUST SOCIETY

To say that individual consumer behavior is by no means a root cause of the country's economic problems (despite periodic political efforts to pretend that it is) is not of course to say that personal prudence is not still advisable in taking on debt. Some of the old rules, which became unfashionable in an era when rising inflation could be depended on to salvage even the most foolish of excesses, again become persuasive as the inflation rate subsides. It seems sensible, for example, to recall the useful dictum that no loan ought ever to last longer than the object purchased: a guideline that may approve a home or auto purchase, for example, while leading us to forgo the temptation to "fly now, pay later." Individual and family responsibility remains a better guarantee of financial security than any governmental intervention or hortatory zeal, no matter how high-minded. It is interesting to note, moreover, that while such emphasis on the necessity for private judgment may seem unstylish in a period when we have been conditioned to rely on bureaucrats and "consumer advocates," it actually corresponds more closely to the way our economy really works. When the economy favored debtors, that's what it produced; when economic conditions (and the tax bills of 1978 and 1981) slightly shifted the odds, people's habits became more thrifty. As economic consultant Raymond T. Dalio observed, "In late 1979 the transition was from a decade of inflationary expansion (in which being in debt and owning hard assets paid) to three years of liquidity crisis (in which having liq-

uidity and investing it in short-term debt instruments was best)."
The point is that it didn't take legislation or new regulations to
induce Americans to change their habits. An increase in the savings rate didn't make everybody happy, to be sure: it was accompanied, for example, by severe troubles for the U.S. automobile
industry and by the first decline in the rate of U.S. home ownership
since the Census Bureau began keeping track. There was an inevitable period of shock treatment for those sectors of the economy
that had been geared to the comfortable assumption that tomorrow
would always be the same as yesterday. But people, as individuals,
were more flexible; on balance they tended to respond sensibly to
changes produced by erratic governmental policies. While the conventional wisdom was that "everybody" was devastated by high
interest rates, I regularly received many letters from retired people
and other savers who thought high double-digit returns were the
most pleasing music since Lawrence Welk. Headline writers like
to deal in bold generalities, but the truth is that an economic situation is never either all good or all bad; and prudent individuals
adjust their behavior to the new realities. It's the Government's
job to create the conditions that will inspire private individuals to
deploy their money in the public interest—not to hector those
individuals for showing a higher financial IQ than their elected
masters.

For institutions as well as individuals, the challenge in this period of rapid change in banking and credit will be to sift intelligently
through previously unavailable alternatives without grabbing every
piece of candy on the counter. As the adaptability of such old-line
institutions as Citicorp has demonstrated, the fading away of old
territorial rights—geographical and financial—does not necessarily mean that the winners will be exclusively the new arrivals.
More venerable institutions, if they prove flexible, creative and
wise, can flourish in this more open environment. Those that know
and take care of their customers need not automatically fear the
spread of plastic and other interlopers. Some years back, before
giving a speech for one of the largest S&Ls in America, I chatted
with its chairman and reminded him of my view that more freedom, not more gimmicks, should be the golden rule for financial
policymakers in the decades ahead. I was surprised to find that he
not only agreed but eschewed all the conventional industry rheto-

ric about the need to preserve such previous crutches as the quarter-point differential so beloved by the S&Ls. (They traditionally were allowed to pay a fraction more in interest than the commercial banks, an advantage that became meaningless when money-market mutual funds arrived.) Here was one S&L executive who already had begun to think of himself not as the hero of an old Jimmy Stewart movie but as a modern marketer of financial services to a sophisticated public. Asserting that his institution heartily welcomed the chance to compete aggressively in a less confined arena, he declared—accurately, as it turned out: "When the time comes, we're going to be ready." It seems even more obvious today that the financial future will belong to those, regardless of the nominal niches formerly occupied by their institutions, who can adjust to competition and think in terms of wooing the customers and not just the Congressmen. You can bank on it.

VI

Laboring Under Some Delusions

Having been a sacred cow for the last half-century of U.S. economic life, the American union movement now threatens to become a sacred dinosaur. The real news is that traditional unionism is becoming extinct at a rate that would have made the brontosaur seem like a slowpoke. Numerically and economically, the movement declines—doomed by its own inherent flaws, not by such storied foes as harsh employers, repressive police or hostile Government (all of which were in fact often among its coziest partners). If it is to survive at all in the economic world of the Twenty-first Century, U.S. unionism must now adapt with uncharacteristic rapidity to a radically changing environment; otherwise, it will expire on the battle lines of conventional confrontation, as surely as those misfit giant reptiles of yore. Understandably, neither prospect enthralls the conventional titans of U.S. unionism, whose receptivity to new ideas, at the best of times, frequently resembles that of the pterodactyl. Less understandably, the rest of us have been slow to recognize and adjust to the dramatically altered essence of modern American labor. Yet though the facts, as we shall see, lead ineluctably to this still-unfashionable conclusion, it is one of the great untold stories of the popular press—and the prevailing bipartisan politics. Politically, unions retain a legislative clout that, while diminishing, remains ludicrously excessive in terms of their actual modern role in the economy; "labor reform," at best an occasional item on the pre-election rhetorical menu, invariably turns out in practice to be a potato too sizzling to be served. Far safer to hail organizational hacks as "labor statesmen," and to make whatever ad hoc accommodations may from time to time become possible: the public, after all, might not be prepared for outright candor on this subject. And why should it be? Though workers increasingly avoid (and even shed) unionism, as yesterday's answer to tomorrow's problems, too many journalists tend even now to act as if the words "labor" and "union" were identical. This basic intellectual confusion then frequently leads them to the dangerous assumption that "anti-labor" and "pro-labor" are useful and objective terms, which can be defined authoritatively as being against or for whatever happens to be on the mind of some individual AFL-CIO leader on some particular day.

Long before the statistics had reached their present inescapable message of union discredit, I marveled at how positions that ultimately damaged the interests of the average American worker could be routinely (and unquestioningly) presented as "pro-labor," while proposals that could build the prosperity of that same worker, if not necessarily of his union bosses, were consigned unthinkingly to the "anti-labor" junkheap. When I first began publicly criticizing what I regarded as specific anti-worker ideas of specific union leaders, I was surprised to be told that I was a courageous fellow: didn't I know that the word would quickly be put out that "Rukeyser is anti-labor"? At first I was amused by the notion: I had, after all, always worked pretty hard—including, for extended periods, as a member of two AFL-CIO unions. And I liked to think that the First Amendment should be operative in this country even for somebody who had the temerity to criticize George Meany or Lane Kirkland. I still do, but a personal experience of mine in early 1981 may be cautionary for anyone tempted to follow in my tracks. More important, it illustrates why I am convinced that many of today's most influential union leaders fall short of informed and responsible statesmanship.

The incident began with a newspaper column in which I twitted Douglas A. Fraser, president of the United Auto Workers, whose stature in trendy circles unaccountably seemed to rise in inverse proportion to the economic health of the workers he led. Pity poor

Douglas Fraser, I opined. Every time he tried to branch out into high finance, he seemed to come up with a clinker. First, I cited his massively ill-timed effort to get himself put on the Chrysler Corporation board of directors—a breakdown of the traditional U.S. labor-management separation that he nonetheless regarded as a tremendous historical precedent. (Two years later, Fraser finally resigned from the Chrysler board for the duration of contract negotiations, in belated recognition that he could not, in fact, simultaneously serve two antagonists.) I went on to observe that Fraser also had shown little sense of history in proposing, during the latest negotiations, an economic package that would offset wage concessions with a profit-sharing plan involving Chrysler preferred stock. What made this particular Fraser venture so outlandish, I suggested, was its classic bad timing, coming at a time when Chrysler was on its financial knees. A generation earlier, in contrast, the UAW had coldly snubbed an automaker offer of genuine profit-sharing—at a time when there were profits aplenty to be shared. The U.S. car industry dominated the world, and was in the middle of one of its most glorious periods of expansion in productivity and earnings. But the late union president, Walter Reuther, showed no interest in deviating from standard contract demands, and thus turned down what would have been a dramatically good deal for his workers.

Nor did the issue stop there, for one of the key things that had gone wrong with the U.S. auto industry was the UAW itself. By raising costs unduly and failing to alert its members to their own roles in assuring their financial futures, the union had contributed significantly to the deterioration of Detroit's competitive position, both worldwide and within the U.S. itself. Japan, which had not learned the hip lesson that hard, careful work was out of style, had reaped the benefits of this shortsighted UAW approach. I was at pains to point out, for several paragraphs, that "no fair-minded person would place all the blame for Detroit's woes on the union," and I detailed a number of the culpable actions of management and Government. On this, there was no kickback: business and bureaucrats apparently are fair targets—or at least thicker-skinned.

Fraser not only heatedly denied all my allegations concerning the UAW but reacted so vehemently that he managed to bulldoze a number of people into accepting his version of the story without checking. Accusing me of "editorial malpractice," he wrote in letters to editors all over the country: "Rukeyser's basic argument was that it was 'outlandish' that the UAW rejected auto company offers of profit-sharing decades ago, yet bargained profit-sharing with Chrysler when the company is not earning profits. The only thing 'outlandish' about such a proposition is Rukeyser's gross inaccuracy. Time after time, the UAW went to the bargaining tables at the Big 3 seeking a genuine profit-sharing program. GM, Ford and Chrysler not only did not offer profit-sharing, they consistently rebuffed the concept. . . . The only exception to this was in 1961, when the union negotiated profit-sharing at American Motors."

Remarkably, though, Fraser apparently was patently misinformed about the negotiating history of his own union. The facts, as I subsequently recalled them in a second column, are these: In 1955, General Motors offered the UAW an extremely attractive profit-sharing proposal. It was the very first point in the ten-point offer made by GM on May 17, 1955. The GM economic package included a savings plan, a loan plan and a severance-pay plan. The Stock Purchase Plan was to be patterned after the old Savings and Investment Plan that had been in effect for GM's hourly and salaried employees from 1919 to 1936. The plan would have permitted employees with at least one year's seniority to contribute up to 10 percent of their gross pay into a "Savings Fund" from which the money would then be invested equally in U.S. Government bonds and GM common stock. In addition, for every two dollars contributed by an employee into the Savings Fund, the corporation would pay one dollar on the employee's behalf into an "Investment Fund," which money would be invested entirely in GM common stock. There were a number of other sweeteners, including a guarantee that employees couldn't lose money—that they would receive at least what they had put in, plus interest figured at the Government-bond rate. It was, in short, not just a profit-sharing plan but an extraordinarily generous one.

Anyone with even a vague notion of how magnificently GM stock performed in the decade or so following 1955, in addition to paying dividends all along the way, knows how excitingly those UAW workers would have shared in their company's profits. A mere two days later, however, Walter Reuther summarily rejected the plan. Such a capitalistic profit-sharing proposal simply did not fit into his then-current demand for a "guaranteed annual wage," on which the UAW had been working for nearly five years.

Now the point of all this is not merely that hell hath no fury like a union leader tweaked, or that anyone with the audacity to point out the human fallibility of an individual union leader runs the risk of being denounced as an enemy of the working people of America. That sort of personal vendetta would be of no general interest were it not symptomatic of a lack of intellectual preparation on the part of too many union leaders. Fraser even in 1981 did not seem to understand the extent to which his union had contributed to its own economic problems, led by outmoded combativeness into policies that, over the years, had damaged both the industry and the well-being of his own workers. We cannot grasp a happier labor-management future if we refuse to acknowledge the self-defeating errors of the past.

WHO LEADS AMERICAN LABOR?

The routine intimidation practiced by U.S. "labor" leaders, and their embarrassing tendency to stub their toes on economic reality, is significant both because these leaders seem perennially at odds with the arithmetic of the marketplace—and because the real labor marketplace increasingly is rejecting them. In this connection, the death of George Meany on January 10, 1980, marked a historic turning point, signaling that the new decade would be a time for new thinking about the role and prospects of American labor. In Meany's lifetime, that role had changed dramatically, even though you might not have guessed it from much of the reporting of his passing. The obituaries all referred to him as "the leader of American labor"—yet that, despite his many other achievements, was the one thing he never got to be. Indeed, when you filtered the facts through the sentiment and propaganda, you found unmistakably that his claim on even a share of that title had dwindled throughout his twenty-four years as president of the AFL-CIO.

I know, from my own meetings with this colorful and assertive character, that he did not hesitate to present himself as the voice of every worker in America. But to have accepted him as that was something else. It required two critical suspensions of belief: first,

in assuming that the words "labor" and "unions" were synonymous, which they clearly and increasingly were not, and second,
in ignoring the numbers that told a story of American labor quite
different from the one Meany presented. The truth is that Meany's
power base was eroding almost from the moment he led the craft-
oriented AFL and the industry-organizing CIO into their merger in
1955. Even then, only 16.8 million of the 68 million work force—
one in four—were union members. But, given their discipline and
political clout, their economic influence was at a peak. By 1979,
though the work force had grown to 104 million, union membership
had inched up only to 20 million—or fewer than one in five workers. Even more strikingly, there were fewer in the AFL-CIO than
on the day it was founded. When George Meany retired three
months before his death, only 14 million U.S. workers called him,
even nominally, their leader, which means, however disconcertingly, that the other 90 million in "American labor" did not.

Part of the problem for Meany, and his successors, was the
changing nature of the U.S. economy, with more workers entering
the harder-to-organize "service" industries. Part lay in squabbling
within the union colossus itself. But an important part arose because the U.S worker was changing in more fundamental ways,
and men like George Meany did not always keep up. In the diction-
ary sense, Meany may have been the most conservative man in
American public life—he was rarely disturbed by the prospect of
a new idea. Much was made of his social conservatism (his support
of the Vietnam war, his antagonism toward dissenters, his slow-
ness to push civil rights objectives, his brusque anti-communism),
but it was in that most basic of union concerns, economics, that he
fell farthest from his claim to represent all U.S. labor—and thus
pushed the creaky AFL-CIO machinery along its present faltering
course.

I remember once interviewing him on national television, on one
of his regular Labor Day appearances, and listening to a conventional Meany denunciation of the rapacious high profits of U.S.
business—the kind of raw meat that feeds the old-time religion of
unionism. I asked Meany whether it was in fact true that business
profits were currently all that high, given the relevant statistics on
return on investment and other traditional measurements. Taken
off his familiar oratorical footpath, Meany was uncharacteristically

at a loss for words, finally allowing somewhat lamely that he had never said the boss shouldn't be permitted to make a decent profit. Plainly, he had been unbriefed on such technicalities. After an uncomfortable pause, we went on to other areas.

The point is surely not that Meany was an evil man: he most certainly was not. Incorruptible, patriotic, frequently warmly human and appealing (despite his carefully cultivated image of "crustiness"), George Meany brought verve to a Washington that, in his final years, had been marked depressingly by personal bland-ness. But he was not the voice of all American labor in periodically advocating still another round of wage and price controls, which would have further limited profits, investment and job creation. He was not the voice of all American labor in insisting on an unrealistically high minimum-wage rate, which protected the com-fortably unionized by barring disadvantaged workers from holding entry-level jobs. And, as the numbers showed, most American workers knew he was not their leader, even if the press did not. He was a mighty force in a dwindling force—American unionism —and it honors neither him nor his authentic achievements to pretend he led us all.

LABOR'S FUTURE: DILEMMAS AND POSSIBILITIES

Today's union leader could play a significant role in working through the economic difficulties we face, but he must show a depth and breadth of understanding we have not customarily seen in such leaders in order to face the authentic dilemmas and possi-bilities of modern American labor. Labor, the workingman or -woman, as any fair-minded student of the U.S. economy must conclude, is both a victim of every problem discussed so far in this book and, in addition, one of the causes of our American economic malaise. But what, if anything, are we going to be able to do about it (especially given the reluctance of our politicians to consider anything so perilous as a new idea in this connection)? I suggest that we may, however improbably, actually be able to make some progress on this one. I submit that it is evident to a growing num-ber of Americans that the time unmistakably has come to think again on both sides of that harmed/harming equation. We must think, for a change, as a nation united in search of a common prosperity, and not out of some ideologically rigged, but economically senseless and obsolete, feeling of class war, management against labor. Ironically, adversity may have made possible what prosperity could not produce.

The labor-management news of the latest U.S. recession centered around unprecedented union "givebacks" in industries as varied as steel, autos, rubber, farm equipment, construction, trucking, newspaper publishing, railroads and airlines. It was not clear how much of this change of heart represented short-term contract concessions under the imminent threat of plant closings and job cancellations, and how much represented a more thoughtful shift in traditional attitudes; in some industries, such as autos, militantly indoctrinated workers were notably balky in accepting even the limited sense belatedly suggested by their union leaders. The point is certainly not that the U.S. should now embark permanently on a low-wage, low-reward economy: what is at stake is more fundamental, and at the same time more promising. The genuine message is that our country can no longer afford the luxury of endless, mindless labor-management confrontation—of a pervasive "hate the boss" or "hate the worker" psychology—if we are ever going to manage to stay ahead of some of our international competitors. I suggest that it is now imperative and in the interests of all of us that we approach this sensitive, emotion-stirring issue of labor-management relations in a new spirit of "one nation," and not with the traditional and destructive antagonism of "us against them." This requires leadership on both sides of the labor-management table, and it requires politicians who will drop easy sloganeering when looking for votes.

This approach will not delight hidebound thinkers, conditioned by an earlier era in which corporate executives and union chieftains could engage in mutual denunciations, eventually agree to outlandishly overstuffed contracts and then repair to their respective headquarters muttering invective but confident that the marketplace would accept the higher prices required to cover these uneconomic costs. Them days, as even the most myopic should have discovered by now, are gone forever. But while a shift away from traditionally hostile confrontation, toward a deeper and more open recognition of common economic interests, is not a happy prospect for the more indelibly old-fashioned labor-union bosses of America—who thrive on the endless repetition of ancient demagoguery—it would clearly improve the lot of millions of ordinary workers, whose dues now frequently support the ideological blowhards.

Lest you conclude dourly that this kind of fresh approach to the labor-management negotiations of this country (and, indeed, to the obsolescent labor-management legislation of this country) is wholly impossible, let me point out a fact that the Lane Kirklands and Douglas Frasers of this world understandably do not parade: increasingly, their influence dwindles even among their own membership. As one striking example, fully 44 percent of the card-carrying rank-and-file labor-union members in America rejected the conventional advice they received from their union leaders in 1980 and went out and voted for Ronald Reagan to be President of the United States. This was only one of many recent demonstrations that the union bosses, despite the continual media inflation of their roles, cannot in fact deliver the numbers for whom they profess to speak. Just as the working people of America are not as politically monolithic as they often are depicted, so they are not stupid. In significant numbers, they know that they, too, are the victims of a historic inflation caused by runaway Government; that they, too, suffer from lagging American productivity and failing American competitiveness; that, indeed, as the succession of recent recessions has demonstrated, they are often among the first to be hurt by words said and deeds done ostensibly in their name.

It is not just economic theoreticians who have begun to find the old union ways ultimately unworkable: both workers and the general public have caught on. A 1981 review of a broad range of survey data, reported by Seymour Martin Lipset and William Schneider in *Public Opinion,* found that unions had become "one of the least trusted institutions in American life," adding: "There is considerable evidence that labor stands lower in public regard than business, and in some cases it is held in even lower esteem than government or politics." (How low can you get?) Even more uncomfortably, unions have been losing steadily in the representation elections for which they historically fought: not only has the union share of the work force been declining since World War II, but unions now win fewer than half the elections held under the supervision of the National Labor Relations Board to determine whether workers want to be organized. (In 1937, they won 94 percent.) Unions also must contend with a tenfold increase since the late Forties in so-called decertification elections, in which workers can vote out a union. Workers have, in fact, decided to do so in three quarters of such elections.

The sentimental rationale for the decline in union power and prestige is that the unions' efforts have brought the workers up to such an economic level that the ungrateful wretches turn their backs on their benefactors. This is engaging bravado, appealing at least superficially to anyone who ever sat around drinking beer and singing such stirring anthems as "There Once Was a Union Maid" and "Joe Hill," but it also happens to be nonsense. While most economists agree that unions do take advantage of their legally authorized monopoly power to force up wages in organized industries, the evidence is overwhelming that they do so at the expense of the non-union sectors, the overall efficiency of the economy and the ability of new entrants (notably including those from minority groups) to find jobs. Moreover, even the apparent successes in heavily organized industries are illusory when economic conditions change: it is scarcely coincidental that the latest U.S. recession hit worst in those areas where unionism was strongest. Professor Yale Brozen of the University of Chicago reported that steel and auto wages over the last three decades moved from about 15 percent above the manufacturing average, which roughly reflected the higher skills required, to 86 percent above. At that time, to the unions' surprise and indignation, unemployment in those industries mounted disastrously and they were unable to compete with "unfair" foreign competitors. The unions routinely deny any responsibility for the bad times they have helped produce. The incumbent AFL-CIO president, Lane Kirkland, who was frequently described as a professorial labor statesman, declared in 1982: "I don't think wage increases are in any way responsible for past recessions nor for the difficulties we are in now." Similarly obtuse is the frequent argument that all improvements in worker benefits can be traced to union militancy; this contention is akin to the belief of Chanticleer, the fictional rooster, that it was his crowing that brought on the dawn. As Milton Friedman wryly observed in 1962 in his book *Capitalism and Freedom,* "The wages of domestic servants have risen very greatly in recent years. Had there been a union of domestic servants, the increase would have come through the union and would have been attributed to it.''

In sum, a balanced look at the pluses and minuses of union influence in modern American life at least raises questions as to whether we have not let sentimentality replace sense in retaining outmoded laws that give unique, and potentially destructive, power to one anti-competitive section of the labor force. As *Fortune*'s perceptive Daniel Seligman wrote, in reviewing the rash of recent union ''givebacks'' of previously won gains, ''If we tell ourselves that this extraordinary display of collective-bargaining-in-reverse is preserving output and jobs, then shouldn't we also tell ourselves that *ordinary* union behavior destroys them? . . . [And] if unionism does have perverse effects, shouldn't we be re-examining a variety of public policies whose stated purpose is to bolster collective bargaining?'' Even those who do not accept that conclusion must come to recognize that America's unions will either fundamentally change over the next century or vanish, and that this disappearing act may be hastened by changes in legislation that now continues to treat an ever-shrinking fraction of the American work force as an unduly privileged class. To say this, as we have seen, is to risk the opprobrium of the wreckers of Youngstown and Detroit. Not to say it, though, may ultimately be more perilous to every American. I submit that we have just two basic choices in this area. We can fall to the ground as a nation, continuing to fight an old-fashioned class war. Or, by reorienting traditional prejudices and offering enlightenment instead of die-hard union-management confrontation, we can begin to rise together to something resembling the economic stars. But if we are going to make it, or even come close, we have to stop letting the professional architects of envy and hate set all the terms of all this nation's economic debates. That First Amendment is indeed a good one, even if someone dares to talk less than reverently about the unions.

"UNEMPLOYMENT, UNEMPLOYMENT, UNEMPLOYMENT"

One reason it is so difficult to galvanize the nation into meaningful economic progress is the tendency for those who shape our view of the news to concentrate exclusively on one issue at a time. Most recently, the issue receiving that kind of this-is-it, forget-every-thing-else attention was unemployment—the economic subject that is traditionally, if not correctly, considered easiest to report. If the unemployment rate sets a new post-Depression high, it's very simple to send the cameras out and get some moving, human shots of the unemployed and their families, kids and all—and ask 'em what they think of "Reaganomics" now. Who says they can't do in-depth coverage on television? One of our most senior network commentators, David Brinkley, contemplating an economy in which the most devastatingly prolonged inflation in our nation's history might be coming under some control at last, announced that the only valid economic question in America today was "unemployment, unemployment and unemployment." Even though the declining inflation had delivered significant, measurable benefits to millions of the nation's poorest citizens, all his colleagues nodded gravely, and no one even ventured to enter the mildest of dissents.

The single-minded approach ignores cause and effect, failing for example to relate the undeniable problem of unemployment to such underlying sources as the nation's pernicious inflation. This media omission can encourage counterproductive legislative efforts to "cure" unemployment with more of the poison of unchecked Government spending and excessively loose monetary policy, thus guaranteeing the future arrival of even worse unemployment. By such a simplistic, incomplete approach to a complicated economy, news coverage can feed faulty public policy.

Similarly dangerous is the temptation, among newsmen seeking a good story or opposition politicians seeking a good issue, to exaggerate the unquestionable severity of today's unemployment. Bad and in need of attention, it certainly is. But to compare our present job problems with those of the Nineteen Thirties is, quite simply, to engage in ideological fantasy. When unemployment peaked at 24.9 percent in 1933, we had a much more narrowly measured work force. Those figures overwhelmingly represented true nationwide tragedy—families without a breadwinner or visible means of support, would-be workers who couldn't find any kind of a job. What we have now is often quite different: people who cannot find a job they consider appropriate at a wage they consider fair, and who frequently are seduced into indolence by a benefit system that discourages the acceptance of lower-echelon jobs. The merits of this change may be endlessly arguable; the impact in artificially swelling unemployment statistics is patently less so. As Vermont Royster, the sagacious former editor of the *Wall Street Journal,* has observed, "An ill-remembered past unconsciously affects our view of current economic statistics. . . . The number of working-age people employed today is greater than when the unemployment rate was 3 percent. The unemployed today do not suffer the same destitution. There are 36 million on Social Security, 23 million receiving food stamps, 11 million getting special aid for families with dependent children. Nearly 4 million get housing assistance and 22 million are on Medicare. Millions more still draw unemployment compensation. Some people get more than one of these benefits, none of which existed when the Great Depression hit."

The growth of two-income families, whether through social change or economic necessity, also has a significant bearing on today's unemployment figures—both in increasing the numbers and in sometimes making the apparent pain deceptive. Even at the end of the Depression, barely more than one in four American women were counted in the work force; since 1978, the participation rate has been more than one in two. And while pessimism is quite obviously the trendy order of the day, reality may be more encouraging: the worst impact of the economy's adjustment to profound demographic changes may already be behind us. Year by year, America's work force is becoming notably older and more seasoned. The U.S. in the Nineteen Seventies took the brunt of the postwar baby boom; workers in the 16–24 age group, peaking at the end of the decade at 17 percent of the total population, were at their highest proportionate level in half a century. That share will dwindle over the next decade. Those who came to maturity in recent years will have more age, stability and experience—encouraging both for their own job prospects and for the country's economic performance. Similarly, the impact of female workers on the economy should be increasingly favorable, both for them and for the economy generally. Productivity growth was unquestionably slowed over the Nineteen Seventies by the entrance into the work force of 11 million women (an annual increase more than two and a half times that for men), not because they were female workers but because they were new workers. Experience will surely enhance their job skills, and the nation's badly lagging productivity, too. So while change in the nature of the country's employment mix is inevitable, and healthy in an expanding economy, some fundamental population factors will be working in our favor for a change. Not every young worker is inefficient, of course, nor every middle-aged male a dynamo, but the employment and productivity trends are unmistakable; in the next decade, as new equipment comes on stream following the nation's shift to a more pro-capitalist orientation in tax and other policies, this equipment will be used by a more mature and therefore more stable and skilled work force. In short, darling, we are growing older (don't weep; the alternative is worse), and that's excellent news for jobs and productivity.

The untold story, moveover, is the growth not of unemployment but of jobs: as record numbers of young people, women and other new entrants sought employment in recent years, the U.S. private economy demonstrated an amazing capacity to take them on. Fully 20 million workers were absorbed into the labor force between 1970 and 1980—a 25 percent increase. And even at the depths of the latest recession, the percentage of working-age Americans actually holding jobs remained near all-time record levels. What is remarkable is not that unemployment has been running high in such declining sectors as manufacturing (which now employs barely a fifth of all workers) but that, despite the worst anti-job excesses of misguided Government policies, the overall American economy has in fact remained what economist William C. Freund aptly called "an unsung miracle . . . a job-creating machine." We must do even better in the years ahead—a challenge that requires the sort of dynamic economic growth that can be produced only by greater savings and investment—but we will be deluding ourselves, and courting future failure, if we fail accurately to assess our strengths.

Meanwhile, as we grope for solutions that will provide a job for every American who really wants to go to work, it is essential to remove the taboos against asking the truly important questions. For example: there is perhaps no more sensitive issue in America than the question of whether all the unemployed are genuinely unable to find work. Yet it is an issue we had better have the courage to confront if we are ever going to lick the problem of chronic high U.S. unemployment—and growing dependence of succeeding generations of our fellow citizens on Government handouts.

There are two main reasons why the subject has not received a more honest airing. First, it is considered a political untouchable. Employment is not a qualification for voting; nor is diligence in seeking work. Second, such discussion as there has been has tended to degenerate into an emotional slanging match between "compassionate" liberals and "tough-minded" conservatives, more useful for venting self-satisfying anger than for dealing with (and improving) reality. Hence President Reagan, when he answered questions about rising unemployment in 1982 by citing pages of newspaper want ads, was denounced as the reincarnation of Marie Antoinette, callously suggesting that the starving, untrained suffering masses ought to race to fill openings for advanced computer technicians. But was it quite as simple as that? Not long after the President was generally vilified for this seeming indifference to the anguish of recession, the anti-Reagan *New York Times* (scarcely a bastion of U.S. conservatism in any Administration) printed its own account of a raid by immigration authorities on several companies in the New York metropolitan area. Many illegal aliens rounded up the previous week had been released from custody and were back at their old jobs, the paper reported. And while the Government had acted on the conviction that it was freeing jobs that rightfully belonged to unemployed American citizens, it appeared that few, if any, unemployed Americans had actually bothered to apply for these newly opened jobs. "American citizens don't want to work for the minimum wage," said one company official. A spokesman for the New York State Department of Labor, while pointing out that some unemployed people might not have known of these openings, readily conceded that "it also may be true what the employers are saying, that these are marginal jobs that most people are not interested in."

"Marginal" jobs? Unattractive because, although paying the statutory minimum wage, they are not more remunerative? It would appear that we have moved beyond a simple media melodrama about an allegedly desperate unemployed population. Seven months later, the *Wall Street Journal* front-paged the news that "the aura of success" had "faded" nationwide from the U.S. Immigration and Naturalization Service's well-publicized "Project Jobs," in which foreigners thought to have sneaked into this country were to be ousted from "better"jobs to make room for out-of-work U.S. citizens. The Service, which itself had assumed that unemployed Americans wouldn't take jobs at the lowest level, consequently had largely ignored aliens working as busboys and field hands; those undocumented workers it did seize had been earning an average of $4.81 an hour. However, not only were these openings soon being filled once again by "illegal aliens," but nearly all the U.S. workers who had taken the temporarily vacated jobs had left within days—apparently because they viewed such tasks as beneath them. "We simply don't bring up our children to be manual-service workers," said Wayne Cornelius, head of the center for U.S.-Mexican studies at the University of California at San Diego, and the kinds of positions opened up by "Project Jobs" were looked on as "Mexican jobs or Haitian jobs." It would be nice, of course, if everybody could be an executive vice president; but we serve neither the truth nor ourselves by ignoring the continuing erosion of the old American work ethic.

Such erosion is particularly troubling when it comes under governmental auspices. In Chapter III, I discussed some of the research of Professor Arthur B. Laffer of the University of Southern California concerning what he calls "the inner-city trap"—studies that may ultimately prove more profound than his lavishly publicized "Laffer curve," which provided the philosophical underpinnings for the original Reagan tax program. According to Laffer's findings (which challenge conventional thinking on both sides of the ideological spectrum), we are sending precisely the wrong message to the working—or potentially working—poor. "Legislative changes in various entitlement programs for the poor and disadvantaged," he concluded, "have increased the disincentives facing the working poor." Laffer found that when a previously unemployed person took a job, the combination of taxes on wages and the loss of old means-tested benefits often left the person less well off than before. It was Laffer's persuasive conclusion that "as a result, for an inner-city resident, it has never been truer than today that it pays to be poor." The real question, given the continuing counterpressures on those contemplating relatively low-level entry into the work force, is not why so many Americans stay home and take Government benefits but why so many, nevertheless, gallantly and with pride try to contribute.

Government disincentives to those who might otherwise go to work? A feeling that some legal jobs are simply "beneath" U.S. citizens today? It begins to get a little more complicated than just the saga of an understandably puzzled auto worker, or Hollywood-style emotional oversimplification. This problem will not vanish with economic recovery, and it deserves, finally, to employ both our hearts and our brains.

HOW TO DO THE JOB

Much has been made of the distressing and seemingly inexorable climb of the unemployment rate, over recent economic cycles, to ever higher plateaus. Less widely understood are the Government's own inadvertent contributions to this continuing unemployment: a list of contributions that is frighteningly long. It includes a perennial tendency to punish business profits through the tax system, profits that to a revenue-hungry politician can often be interpreted as "excess" or "windfall" or worse. Hardly ever can it be even hinted that profits are essential to a business, the true key to more jobs and rising living standards. Is there a problem with financing Social Security? Why, just solve it by greatly increasing the cost of employing new workers; figure that most people will be too dumb or too distracted to recognize that you are really putting still another surtax on labor. (The higher the payroll cost, the greater the incentive to replace people with machines.) Is there an energy problem? Emphasize conservation rather than production; who among the unemployed will realize that you're victimizing them—by limiting the creation of new jobs? Is safety a popular issue? Then carry it to ridiculous extremes, and let self-important Government regulators go into small and large businesses all over the country with extravagant power and unending fine print; if this so escalates business costs that new hiring is diminished, count on the fact that few Americans will make the connection. And be sure to behave the same way about the environment: nobody is cheering for pollution, are they? Be a good conventional politician and demand that we create a test-tube-pure ecology, banishing the last 1 percent of filth; if production and employment remain sluggish because of overambitious environmental timetables, that's a mighty small sacrifice—for the employed. And so on into the gloomy but marvelously well-intentioned night.

Most of all, if you want to be truly, identifiably "humane," be sure to defend at any cost the single most anti-youth, anti-black, anti-job law on the books of the United States of America: the minimum-wage rate.

Now I've really done it, haven't I? It was bad enough to speak critically of the effect on workers' ultimate interests of those legal cartels known as labor unions; it bordered on the intolerable to suggest that, in the name of such glorious ideals as welfare or safety or the environment, we have frequently wound up discouraging work and diminishing the number of workers; but how could anyone but the most elephant-skinned reactionary employer say anything unfavorable about that wonderful minimum-wage law, which as we all know assures a decent wage to every working person? Right?

Wrong. Consider, for starters, some differences between the historical situation of American workers and the situation we find today. We have grown so used to hearing devastating figures about black unemployment, particularly black teenaged unemployment (which climbed over 40 percent when the overall national rate was still below 9 percent), that we may have come to think of these tragic statistics as a continuing remnant of our racist past. In fact, it is nothing of the kind: it is a phenomenon produced over the last three decades by repeated increases in the minimum-wage rate. Not only is the gap between adult and youth unemployment historically high, but the present highly publicized and deeply ominous spread between the unemployment rates of white and black teenagers is unprecedented. Back in 1948, the unemployment rate for blacks sixteen to seventeen years old was actually less than that for whites (9.4 vs. 10.2 percent). And until 1954, black teenagers (indeed, blacks in every age group) were more active in the labor market than their white counterparts—the reverse of today's situation.

As one outraged black, Professor Walter E. Williams of Temple University, incisively saw it, the change since then was no coinci-

dence: "In addition to discriminating against unskilled labor, minimum-wage laws foster racial discrimination as well. That is, if an
employer is faced with a white and black employee of equal productivity and he prefers white to black, then if he must pay the
same wage no matter which is hired, he can entertain his bias at
zero cost." In a 1979 article for *Lincoln Review,* Williams observed
that with each increase in the level and extent of coverage of the
minimum-wage law, black youth unemployment had risen relative
to white. He commented tellingly: "We cannot account for this
dramatic reversal by saying that employers are *now* more racist
than they were in the past. No, Federal or state minimum-wage
laws make it uneconomical to hire highly disadvantaged young-
sters." Williams also was scathing about the notion that labor
unions are blacks' loving allies, noting that the union movement
historically "sought, with but few exceptions, to exclude Negroes
and other minorities from many job markets," even now imposes
seniority rules that "tend to make permanent the disadvantages of
past discrimination," and lobbies for a lofty minimum wage not to
protect its own members, who earn much more, but to discourage
employers from replacing one skilled union worker with two less-
skilled beginners.

This is not the stuff we are used to hearing from those generally
referred to as "black leaders" (whom Williams derides as "the
inept black leadership"); Williams is part of a small but intellectually significant coterie of free-enterprise blacks who have come
to recognize that an apparently benign series of Government-inter-
ventionist policies in practice has served to widen the gap between
whites and blacks. His concern in fact extends to all poor Americans, a group in which blacks are disproportionately represented:
"Jobs for the lowest-skilled persons have all but been destroyed,"
Williams observed in a 1980 speech at Michigan's Hillsdale College. "In this sense we have cut off the bottom rungs to the economic ladder. . . . Poor people today need just what the poor of
yesterday had: a life with Government off their backs." Before
you reject such unconventional thinking as interesting but bizarre,
keep in mind the deeply racist character of the idea we have been
sold for a generation: that the groups trying to struggle out of
poverty today, unlike all their predecessors in American history,
are so uniquely feeble that they need Government to help them at

every step along the way. Keep in mind how disastrously this idea has failed in terms of actually helping human beings into the economic mainstream. Then you may well reach the conclusion, as wise men like Walter Williams and Thomas Sowell have, that the laws of economics—like the laws of arithmetic—do not vary according to one's pigmentation. The insulting contrary theory—that we need a special, benign economics just for those poor blacks—may be one of the most degrading and debilitating contributions, however unconscious, of Twentieth Century "liberalism."

Why are blacks—and youths of all hues—special victims of a law like the minimum wage? Because the law makes it impossible for an employer profitably to hire an unskilled worker whose output will not match the minimum. The unskilled worker is thus effectively shut out of the opportunity for learning skills on the job; he or she is denied the chance of gainful employment of any sort. Teenagers generally are the lowest-skilled group of workers, so more of them get pushed aside each time the rate goes up. Black teenagers are doubly handicapped, as Williams puts it, "because of poorer family backgrounds and past and present discrimination." The authentic question is not, as the demagogues have stated it, "Isn't it fair to pay every American worker at least the minimum wage?" In the real world, employers must calculate their costs, and if the benefit of hiring a particular worker is less than the price, that worker will not be hired. So the true question is "Is it better to have masses of workers unemployed at $3.35 an hour —or working for (say) $3.00?" The so-called minimum-wage law in fact too often becomes a minimum-work law, assuring only that a grotesquely large number of Americans will in fact be paid $0.00 an hour, will not get vitally needed initial work experience and will be excluded from entry to the ladder of economic success. If that's "humane," make mine pistachio.

It is fashionable to make fun of economists, and to pretend that they can never get together on anything; I confess that I have contributed something to this derision myself on occasion, tempted irresistibly by the profession's tendency toward faulty, and conflicting, conclusions. But, in truth, this is one issue on which virtually every serious independent economist in America —"liberal" or "conservative," black or white—has concluded that an apparently compassionate law is having an identifiably harmful effect. For example, Andrew F. Brimmer, former member of the Federal Reserve Board, a certified "liberal" and undeniably black, declares unambiguously: "A growing body of statistical and other evidence accumulated by economists (particularly those outside the Government and not connected with the trade-union movement) shows that increases in the statutory minimum wage dampen the expansion of employment and lengthen the lineup of those seeking jobs. Advances in the minimum wage have a noticeably adverse impact on young people—with the effects on black teenagers being considerably more severe." So the economists, the facts and common sense are now speaking unmistakably on this one. It should not now be too much to expect of our politicians that, if they have one tenth the concern they routinely profess for those without jobs in our society, they move swiftly to remove this unarguable barrier to full employment—at a minimum.

One final thought, which applies to the minimum wage, to welfare, to habitual seasonal applicants for unemployment insurance, to intransigent negotiators, to excessive taxation—and to a vast range of other issues that perennially confront the modern American economy: it seems time to make one basic rule, already suggested in Chapter III, that might aid us in devising proper and productive policy in all these areas. That rule would be, quite simply, that we will never again have a law in this country that makes it more desirable for any American not to go to work. It's a revolutionary thought, to be sure, but who knows? It just might help do the job.

VII

Giving Us the Business

We turn now from labor to business, but the turn is not nearly so abrupt as our politics suggests. Far from being antagonists between whom the Government must mediate, labor and business tend to be siblings in the same economic family—and not always squabbling siblings, at that. When a common interest is perceived, such as protection against overseas competition or the continuance of friendly anti-competitive domestic regulation, apparently warring managements and unions routinely unite to exert identical pressures on Congress. The popular image of die-hard opponents, wrestling endlessly for bigger shares of the same pie, can be perilously misleading. Executives and assembly-line workers in, say, the widget game frequently are defined more by their firm's product than by their role in its production. Contrary to the impassioned oratory of "redistribution" and "social justice," in the real world their fates tend to be inextricably entwined. It is scarcely coincidental that those aging industries with perennial labor problems, such as steel, happen also to be the businesses perennially regarded most warily by investors; a sick industry spreads its maladies generously from boardroom to union hall. Conversely, when a glorious new boom began in the high-technology frontierlands of California's Silicon Valley and Massachusetts' Route 128, it wasn't necessary for any bureaucrat or "militant" union czar to demand that high salaries be paid to those whom these growing industries wanted to attract.

Just as the role of industrial confrontation is exaggerated as a force for economic progress, so are the benefits of special-interest business lobbying. And so I want to come at business exactly the same way I just came at labor, not in terms of its current—and often conflicting—demands on Congress but in terms of where the authentic long-term national interest in the area actually resides. (We thus avoid the conventionally empty political approach: "A lollipop for you on the left, a lollipop for you on the right, and a lollipop for you over there in the corner. Now, don't you all love me?" Serial handouts are a poor substitute for serious analysis.) Where business is concerned, that national interest centers on the necessity greatly to improve U.S. productivity over the next decade by greatly encouraging U.S. investment over the next decade.

We have made a faltering, and highly belated, start in this direction at last, but there is plenty more we can and should be doing if our nation is to go forward and justify the fundamental optimism that underlies this book. Let me be specific on that, because I know every reader has been exposed to an inordinate amount of gloom and doom over the last few years—and it's fairly obvious, too, that even amid economic recovery many important statistics have fallen well short of becoming extravagantly cheerful. Let me, then, state unreservedly what I see as our economic potential, not in some remote and theoretical future, but right now in the Nineteen Eighties: I believe we have the capacity to transform this into a golden decade for the American economy.

If we keep our heads we can finally rein in the horrible inflation that has trampled our economy for a generation: we can capitalize on the slowdown in inflation that accompanied and followed our last recession as the opportunity to enforce a permanent halt. Similarly, we can seize the opportunity provided by the temporary world oil glut as the chance to move decisively toward a long-range solution of our country's massive energy problems for the next century. I believe, too, that we can take advantage of the recession-induced intermission in reflexive labor-management hostility to build a better national relationship in that area, and one more suited to the authentic requirements of the Twenty-first Century. And I devoutly believe that we can provide a job—a genuine productive job in the private economy—for every American who truly wants to go to work in the next decade.

If any of that is going to be more than just wishful thinking, however, then I think we're going to have to make much more significant changes in the way Government and business interact over the next ten years. That means we must continue to revamp our tax code to reflect economic realities and not social spite. It is dazzlingly foolish to move backward with additional debilitating tax increases, and this applies whether we are candid enough to call them "tax increases" or whether we try to disguise them with euphemisms such as "loophole closing" or "revenue enhancement." When the Government ups its already-exorbitant take from the private economy, that's a tax increase. Vindictiveness, moreover, makes notably bad grounds for tax policy. Consider that example previously cited from the 1982 tax bill: a provision cutting back on maximum contributions to corporate pension plans. The motive was to stop letting all those rich dentists and pediatricians have an advantage that the rest of the folks don't have. Certain actual result: money that formerly went, via pension plans, into the socially useful stock and bond markets will now be going into whatever tax shelters can be found. Scarcely a major economic advantage for the nation at large—or for that wondrous cause of "equity."

We can preoccupy ourselves with "fairly" distributing unending economic misery, a task for which the Government appears supremely well suited, or we can re-evaluate what truly breeds prosperity—and how a more modest role by our bureaucratic saviors might genuinely encourage its reappearance. For starters, for example, we might proceed forthwith and without any further political pussyfooting to remove from the tax code such foolishly anti-investment provisions as the ongoing double taxation of corporate dividends. (Company profits are taxed once at the source, a second time at the stockholder level after they are distributed as dividends.) There could scarcely be a worse signal to those with investable funds in this country than to continue a tax system that handsomely rewards various forms of rampant speculation (and encourages the growth of Government by making the interest on state and municipal bonds tax free), while doubly punishing investment in dividend-paying, job-creating American corporations. Any self-respecting politician should be at work to get that one off the books by sunrise.

We ought, moreover, to be open about our new intention as a nation not to go on penalizing savings and investment (as we did in 1969, as we did in 1976, as Jimmy Carter wanted us to do again in 1978, and as the Dole-led Congress did do in 1982) but instead to move in precisely the opposite direction: directing far more of this country's savings, current and potential, into productive investment—the investment that is, in the end, when all the politicians' larynxes have been exhausted, still going to be the only authentic route to more jobs for American workers. Every major econometric study of the last decade reached exactly the same conclusion: the best way to promote jobs in America is to promote investment in America. Those who loudly complain about unemployment, but turn around the next day and seek to erect even more roadblocks in the way of investors and employers, have to be either total dumbbells or total hypocrites. Where in the world do they expect all these badly needed new jobs to come from? The Social Security Administration? Delivered by the Post Office? (No, don't knock the Post Office: they do a terrific job for 22 cents. That's 5 cents for postage, and 17 cents for storage.)

CAPITAL FORMATION: THE ONE THAT PRODUCES ECONOMIC TOUCHDOWNS

The problem of capital formation is immediate and vital in the U.S. today; it has nothing to do with quarterbacking, penmanship or geography, but everything to do with how well we and our children will live in this country a generation from now. In language that even a politician should be able to understand: we simply are not taking enough of what we earn as a nation each year and putting it back into America's future, either by our own historical standards or by the standards of the more successful nations with which we must compete in the modern world. We are not only failing consistently to confront and conquer this massive threat to economic progress; at critical junctures, we are substantially ignoring it— preferring to make tax legislation the old-fashioned way: swapping and swindling and avoiding at any cost a coherent economic philosophy.

If the average American is perceived by his elected representatives as essentially indifferent on this subject, that is hardly astounding. As Charles D. Kuehner observed in his book *Capital and Job Formation: Our Nation's Third Century Challenge,* neglect of the subject by the nation's news media is "almost total," union leaders have never focused much attention on it, Congressmen put it low on their priority list, regulatory agencies have "largely neglected" it and even the nation's graduate schools of business "virtually ignore" it in their course offerings. Kuehner likened awareness of the problem to awareness of high blood pressure ("Both involve millions of people who don't know they have it"), and warned that such symptoms as unemployment and inflation would continue as long as we languished in "American provincialism" and refused to learn from the experiences of others. Pointing out that West Germany and Japan, which "have given capital formation highest national priority for over a quarter century"—taxing dividends far below the U.S. rate and capital gains virtually not at all—had "miraculously" produced up-to-date plant and equipment, high productivity, strong currencies and low unemployment. Kuehner also noted, in contrast, that Britain, which went the other way for so long, wound up with an antiquated industrial plant, low productivity, chronic currency weakness, endless labor strife and relative economic slippage.

Those who would write off this problem as the parochial concern of financiers and investors should ponder two relevant facts: (1) since 1969 the U.S. has been failing notably to maintain private capital investment at what had been normal postwar levels; (2) starting precisely the same year, the U.S. ceased making progress in reducing the number of its citizens in the lowest income bracket. In other words, capital formation is, among other things, a remarkably effective anti-poverty program. In earlier years, when business was booming and profits were healthy, the private economy took millions of Americans out of poverty (and sent millions more into affluence). Then the Government moved twice, in 1969 and 1976, to make tax changes that strongly favored immediate consumption over job-building investment. Such steps did indeed disappoint and discourage investors and business people; what they didn't do was help the poor. On the contrary, as business economist Norma Pace, of the American Paper Institute, observed, it was "not coincidental that the failure to reduce the number in the lowest income brackets coincides with the period when the stock of capital itself failed to grow in line with the man-hours available." That's an important point: in terms of real buying power, discounting the effects of inflation, the amount of capital stock in place for each manufacturing man-hour worked advanced steeply between 1947 and 1969. This aggressive investment created better tools and more jobs. It increased the size of the economic pie and therefore the size of the slice that each worker could obtain. Though there were bumps along the way, few would have doubted that the course of the American economy was essentially upward. Then, in 1969, just as we needed more jobs than ever to accommodate the postwar baby boom, the trendline of capital stock began to dip sharply. There were several reasons: Government-induced inflation squeezed business profits and reduced the real return on equity investments. The stock market reacted in terror, further discouraging potential investment. And the Government botched things completely by making tax changes that, under the banner of equity, actually served to retard the expansion of the national economic feast.* The worst victims, as usual, were those in whose names the anti-business legislation was enacted—for the resulting economic conditions made things immeasurably tougher for those poorer Americans struggling to get a larger share of that fabled pie for themselves. No wonder Mrs. Pace concluded that "ironically, the failure of the U.S. economy to continue to make progress in the distribution of income is a direct result of Government policies aimed at improving it in the United States. These policies not only failed to accomplish that purpose but left a trail of heavy inflation which continues to work counter to the goal." More telling still, doing the right thing in this area doesn't even involve the customarily advertised trade-offs. When Congress eased capital-gains taxes in 1978, in defiance of President Carter's desire to do precisely the opposite, the result once again surprised the big-government theorists: capital-gains revenues went up, not

---

* The so-called Tax Reform Act of 1969, together with its subsequent revisions, raised the maximum tax on capital gains from 25 percent to 49 percent, reduced the write-off of capital losses by 50 percent and sharply curtailed the deduction of interest expense on borrowed funds used to make an investment. As the *Wall Street Journal* commented, "All in all, the rewards for success were cut in half, and the penalties for failure were doubled."

down. Lowering the tax increased the attractiveness of taking long-term profits, thus freeing funds for new investment. Similarly, ending the double taxation of corporate dividends would surely result, before long, in more corporate profits to tax. Measures that encourage business investment thus eventually have a double payoff: the tax collectors win, and so does the country.

In the end, it becomes a sort of economic Rubik's Cube. A number of seemingly diverse elements—a frustratingly slow and inflation-prone economy, a tax system that rewards debt and penalizes thrift, a disappointing performance on productivity, the failure to produce anything like the investment capital needed for solid national growth—fall neatly into a pattern. Perhaps the most obviously necessary twist right now would be a major U.S. effort to bolster productivity. The problem can scarcely be evaded: we have been on a sort of three-two-one-zero countdown to catastrophe. Annual increases in productivity, as measured by output per worker per hour, averaged 3.2 percent from 1948 to 1966, 2.1 percent from 1966 to 1973, 1.0 percent from 1973 to 1978—and then actually slipped below zero in 1979 and 1980. These are not just statistics to beguile the academics in our midst: they are a message that we have been kidding ourselves with wage increases we did not earn. When productivity rises smartly, so can wages, not just in theory but in true buying power. Those who worry endlessly about "redistribution" ought instead to be worrying about productivity: get it moving, and we can live better—as we did in the first two decades after World War II. With rising productivity, it's possible to raise wages without raising prices. But unless workers actually are producing more each year, wage increases just add more pressure to the inflation machine. Only rapidly improving productivity, an achievement in which the U.S. once proudly led the world, can make it possible once more for all of us to elevate our standards of living, and not just our prices.

How do we get U.S. productivity rising vigorously again? We can ignore short-term trends: it's quite normal, for example, for productivity performance to deteriorate in the early stages of a recession and improve later on. When the economy first slows, factory orders decline, plants have more "downtime" and industries tend to work well below capacity. Typically, though, employers don't lay off workers as fast as business worsens. Bosses as a group may be more softhearted than legend holds, or they may just assume that conditions will be improving soon and they don't want to go through the agonies of rehiring. Whatever their motivations, with a still-large work force producing less during the slowdown, productivity per worker naturally declines, which means more bad news on inflation. (The rate at which prices rise tends to parallel with frightening exactness the extent to which wage increases exceed productivity increases.) On the other hand, when the economy begins to pull out of a slump, the productivity rate usually climbs rapidly—because the work force, trimmed down during the bad times (and, of course, painfully aware of the possibility of unemployment), is producing at top efficiency as demand for its products accelerates.

Clearly, though, we can't depend only on routine cyclical improvements to bail us out of our long-term U.S. productivity problem. As we've already seen, there are many explanations for our lagging performance, and some of them are even valid. We are told, for example, that it is impossible to maintain speedy productivity growth as the economy moves toward an ever more pronounced "service" orientation: give a farmer or factory worker better tools and he can produce more each day, but how are you going to achieve a significant boost in the output of your neighborhood barber? That explanation is a bit too glib, though: some of our most conspicuous "service" industries, such as financial institutions, have made historically dramatic productivity improvements in the last decade, thanks in large part to the computer.

Other old-line institutions have made striking gains simply by smarter management. Philip L. Smith, the able and independent-minded president of General Foods Corporation, told me in mid-1983 that he was convinced the next big advance in U.S. industrial productivity would come not from fancy new technology but from plain old people. While corporations obviously need modern facilities and up-to-date technology, Smith said, there is a limit to how much automation can be brought to a given plant. That's the point at which emphasis must turn to "better utilization of people," both in blue-collar jobs and in management itself. Smith contended that most individuals at any corporate level "really don't work anywhere near their potential as human beings—not because they don't want to but because we give them a working environment that denies them satisfaction. Finding a working environment that gives them that satisfaction will produce real productivity benefits for us.''

As one example of what General Foods has accomplished in this area, Smith cited a new approach to quality control, putting responsibility directly on the production line rather than depending on checks after the fact by special quality-control departments, which have been a significant (if not always brilliantly effective) part of most U.S. plants since the Nineteen Fifties. What General Foods calls ''TQS,'' for Total Quality System, replaces most of the previous off-line checks, except in such highly specialized areas as toxology. Smith pointed to the company's dog-food plant in Topeka, Kansas, where microprocessors allow line workers to read the moisture and weight of the products being prepared, whereas previously samples would have been pulled at the end of the line. General Foods has found that such workers on automated production lines are better motivated when ''given accountability as responsible people.''

Another method the giant multinational corporation is using to increase worker output rejects the conventional view of blue-collar employees ''in neat boxes''—that is, in their traditional craft-union designations as, say, plumbers or electricians or mechanics. Under the old system, such workers would wait around in the maintenance area for their respective turns at a particular job. Now, at plants like that in Topeka, workers are encouraged to learn more than one skill—and get a raise for each new ability acquired. (Usually, it also means that one—or no—union wins out where several competing unions existed before.)

While it remains easier to make work-rule changes in plants that are not unionized, Smith reported ''increasing cooperation'' from some union leaders in readjusting to the needs of today's economy. At the company's Hoboken, New Jersey, coffee plant, for example, General Foods was able to negotiate a contract in which workers gave up any wage increase for two years (in return for a one-time bonus) and agreed to significant work-rule streamlining, after management pointed out that, without such changes, it could produce coffee at its Houston plant and deliver it to New York City more cheaply than the coffee turned out across the river in Hoboken. The central task for wise corporate managers is to be sensitive simultaneously to possible uses of new investment dollars and to the human task of motivating workers to perform better with existing tools. As Smith put it to me, "This time is a golden opportunity to produce a climate of greater cooperation between labor and management."

Most businesses, then, will find that they can bolster their individual productivity performances when they creatively put their minds to it. Both management and labor plainly have key functions here, and it is one more area where traditional unions, and traditional corporations, must either adapt or perish. It is scarcely unnoticed by other businesses that some of the most successful companies in modern America—including such titans as IBM, Eastman Kodak and Delta Airlines—have combined outstanding corporate performance with excellent labor-management relations while operating largely outside the normal trade-union structure. (Delta, traditionally the "blue chip" of the troubled airline industry, stirred such remarkable loyalty among its employees that 65 percent of them signed voluntary pledge cards and bought their employer a brand-new $30 million Boeing 767 in December 1982. The plane was dubbed the *Spirit of Delta,* and you can be sure its maiden flight was watched with interest in places like Japan, which cynics keep telling us are the only countries that know how to keep their employees happy anymore.) The productivity challenge is big enough to employ us all.

Those gloomsters who insist that our country is on an inexorable downhill slide maintain that our disappointing productivity record in recent years is just one more sign of the decline of the American spirit. This position is not wholly lacking in evidence (the tax system, as we have seen, frequently provides a disincentive to extra effort; and we have not yet fully expunged the "anti-materialist" excesses of the Nineteen Sixties, when many young people apparently were taught that prosperity was achieved not by labor but by demonstrating against the rotten system), but the malady should not be exaggerated. I recall talking in 1980 with Karl Otto Poehl, chairman of West Germany's central bank, and telling him that there was "an occasional suspicion in this country that one reason that West German productivity improves so much faster than ours does is that your population hasn't learned the lesson that work has gone out of style." Poehl, interestingly, immediately rejected the idea that West Germans work harder than Americans. Calling this "an image" and "a prejudice," the Bundesbank chief noted that the West Germans were losing as many working days because of "our many religious holidays" as the British were losing because of strikes. "I don't think this is the real difference," he said. "The main reason [for the more rapid rise of productivity in West Germany than in the United States] is the fact that we have a much higher savings rate in Germany. We have a savings rate of 16 percent of national income, compared with about 4 percent in the United States, and this high savings rate is partly, at least, the result of a very tough [monetary] stability policy. People have the confidence that we do everything we can to maintain the value of the currency. And therefore the saving is high, and that means that private and public investment can be high and can be financed without creating inflationary pressures."

Savings as the key. That does take us a step beyond dolorous moralizing. And, significantly, Poehl's perspective on the American economy is widely shared beyond our shores. Describing "America's panoply of tax breaks given for borrowing," *The Economist* wrote in 1982: "A nation raised on the folklore of thrift unaccountably forgot to enshrine that virtue in its tax laws. The United States is unique in this—and therefore has a uniquely low savings ratio. Last year America's personal savings amounted to 4 percent of its gross national product, compared with Japan's 13 percent. . . . This is why Japan can run a budget deficit up at 4 percent of its GNP, and have commercial bank prime lending rates down to 6 percent; while an American budget deficit of 3 percent drains away so much of the few available net savings that commercial prime rates go to 15¾ percent."

The idea that savings are important seems self-evident, but is at odds with the populist notion that the borrower should invariably be king, and that low tax-deductible interest is the key to all good things. As long ago as 1954, Professor Seymour Harris of Harvard University commented that the then-revered English economist John Maynard Keynes "won a signal victory because he attacked the last unassailed fortress of capital—saving." The trend so disturbed Ludwig von Mises that he took pains to point out in 1956 that "every step forward on the way toward prosperity is the effect of saving." In other words, the saver is ultimately the worker's best friend; and, as Kurt Richebaecher, executive manager of the Dresdner Bank, put it, "Inflation is the feedback of using capital for consumption rather than production." By now, American economists of many ideological persuasions have come to recognize the damage we have done to our productivity and eventual living standards by failing to place adequate emphasis on savings and investment.

PRODUCTIVITY GROWTH IS EVERYBODY'S BUSINESS

The effort to make American industry more competitive becomes a job that begins in Washington (with better control of inflation and more intelligent tax legislation to encourage savings and investment), but ends, inevitably, on the factory floor. It is too late in the game for unperceptive union leaders to ignore their own roles in this effort and to resist modernization with an antagonistic mind-set shaped by Charlie Chaplin's *Modern Times* or the officious and ridiculous "time-study man" in *The Pajama Game*. Failure to keep productivity growing has led not to more employment but to less, not to higher living standards but to lower. As Egils Milbergs, director of the Commerce Department's Office of Productivity, Technology and Innovation, noted in a 1982 article for *Enterprise* magazine, "When productivity growth decelerates, many problems become more difficult. Some people argue that productivity improvement will lead to unemployment. I submit that our problems in steel and autos, for example, are caused by a lack of productivity improvement, not because of it. So productivity is not just a statistical abstraction. It is a reflection of the capacity and will of a people to sustain a certain way of life."

But the broader national realization of our joint stake in sustained productivity growth comes slowly. The problems of the beleaguered steel industry, for example, illustrate the dilemma vividly. Not long ago, that industry's position in American and international economic life seemed unassailable. Blazing furnaces, modern factories, enormous commitments of capital and labor—the epitome of U.S. big business, the titan of the world. So mighty was steel, it seemed, that it was an ineffectual politician indeed who didn't occasionally take a "populist" poke at it. A succession of postwar Presidents, starting with Harry Truman, found occasion to make the American steel industry a favorite whipping boy. Meanwhile, strange things were going on: we helped West Germany and Japan rise from the rubble of World War II with factories more up-to-date than our own; we gloried in Presidents like John F. Kennedy who claimed great patriotic successes in compelling lower prices—and profit margins—for steel; we passed laws that discouraged capital investment, and apparently were astonished to discover that this had a particularly bad effect on capital-intensive industries like steel; we were so outraged by any taint of pollution that we passed legislation whose costs soared zanily beyond its benefits; we applauded "labor statesmen" who kited steel-union earnings beyond any reasonable correlation with the output of their workers. And then—wonder of wonders—suddenly the American steel industry wasn't so almighty anymore. Suddenly it dawned on people that you didn't have to buy steel from U.S. Steel or Bethlehem, and that there were other places elsewhere in the world where you could get the same product at a lower price. Sentiment in the world of international business lasts about as long as campaign pledges in the world of politics. Yet the sense of misdirected outrage at the employers, and of worker "entitlement" to unrealistic settlements, dies hard: in the winter of 1982–83, major steelmakers, disappointed by their failure to get wage concessions from the steelworkers' union, faced the prospect that they might be deserted by some of their biggest customers. It seemed that many of those traditional buyers of American steel—including, ironically, the import-battered U.S. automakers—had been warning industry officials that simple economics might soon force them to switch orders to foreign suppliers. How the alleged "robber barons" had been humbled! And how much poorer all Americans were as a result.

With wage costs out of line in our basic industries, with the nation's savings rate still disconcertingly low, with the promotion of investment still honored more in rhetoric than in legislation, the challenge of revivifying U.S. productivity growth is unlikely to be susceptible to overnight solution. But one area where every individual can contribute is in matters of the spirit: of caring just a little bit more about the quality of the final product. This isn't the whole story, to be sure, and it cannot realistically be viewed in isolation—but it surely is time we stopped deriding as "company men (or women)" or "nitpickers" or "workaholics" any Americans who take the trouble to make their work better than it absolutely needs to be. A national attitude of "it's not *my* job" is a national prescription for disaster. Excellence, not adequacy, is what powers a country's prosperity. Yet pride in America's workmanship fades unmistakably and, with it, confidence in America's future.

I am reminded of a conversation with former Secretary of State Henry A. Kissinger in which Kissinger unhappily contrasted today's attitudes with those that had impressed him as an immigrant GI four decades ago. "During World War II," he told me, "the German tanks were clearly superior to our American tanks, but none of my fellow soldiers would admit this. The general attitude was 'If better tanks could be built, we Americans would build them.' " What, Kissinger wondered, had happened to that confident American attitude? What had happened to our seemingly boundless pride in U.S. workmanship? Why had standards slipped so unarguably that the Japanese—once known for shoddy imitations of fine American products—were now widely acknowledged, by Americans themselves, to produce better products ranging from cars to television sets? At least part of the answer, I would contend, can be found in our following false leaders, who were so busy arguing about what was "fair" that they forgot to emphasize what was fine. Every country in the world has philosophers of redistribution; what makes some countries unusual is that they manage to produce more good products to distribute. And the production of quality products is a task that, historically and completely, baffles every government on earth—for it is something that only motivated people can accomplish. A sense of "that's good enough—now pay us our share" is a sense of imminent decline.

While business executives are quick to applaud the suggestion that more should be done by educators, politicians and union leaders to encourage quality workmanship and productivity growth, they are often dilatory in recognizing their own responsibilities for modern American problems. (Recognizing the other guy's faults is a breeze.) Yet no account of the dwindling American position in, say, the international automobile business would be complete without a few more critical words concerning the role of U.S.

management. At least part of the lack of good workmanship in this and in other industries proceeded from management's failure to emphasize it. Some shortsighted automotive executives concluded years ago that genuine quality control was too expensive; instead, in a "disposable" society oriented to packaging and "planned obsolescence," it was simpler to change the tail fins than to perfect the transmission. A business built on serving the consumer began to develop a suicidal arrogance toward the people buying the product. Indeed, I have long felt that the nation's struggling automobile companies would be entitled to more of our sympathy if their executives had not committed what should qualify as an unforgivable economic sin: they appeared to take John Kenneth Galbraith seriously. Revering Professor Galbraith is a pardonable offense for sophomores engaged in learning, as H. L. Mencken once put it, how to hate their fathers. That, after all, is a time-tested academic function. I have enjoyed Galbraith's engaging company myself, in India during his ambassadorship more than twenty years ago and on other continents since, and I certainly have no quarrel with anyone captivated by his diverting prose. But I wouldn't buy a used theory from him. And when the nation's most highly paid group of business executives, the lofty auto chieftains, operate their concerns on the apparent thesis that Galbraith must know what he is talking about, it really does become time to blow the whistle—and honk the horn.

I am not suggesting that these managers sat down, read Galbraith and then applied his analysis. That surely would be to over-intellectualize the commercial process. But the disastrous way they did proceed, with predictably terrible results in a market economy, would have made sense only if the world had truly been the way Galbraith described it in his treatises on our industrial society. Consider what the Harvard economist told them (and the rest of us). He told them, first, that their market power was so immense that they could devise any product they chose and, through the wiles of Madison Avenue, induce us to buy it. And he told them, second, that this uncontrolled power enabled them to price this product wherever they chose—and still shove it down our throats. It was an appealing analysis for business's critics, and won Galbraith quite some celebrity in their ranks, but what in the world made businessmen themselves believe such nonsense?

Yet that is exactly what seems to have happened in the boardrooms of Detroit. First, the auto executives, despite their strato-spheric six-figure salaries, stupidly ignored the perennial message of the Volkswagen: that millions of Americans really did want smaller, more economical cars. As late as 1969, when the Ford Motor Company was getting ready to introduce the subcompact Maverick, Henry Ford II confessed to a reporter for *Fortune* mag-azine: "I keep thinking that the Volkswagen will turn out to be another Model T—that one of these days, it will go down the drain. I keep saying that, but it doesn't seem to happen." Meanwhile, while most American auto executives continued to view small for-eign cars in a manner that one wag compared to Thomas Hobbes's view of life ("poor, nasty, brutish and short"), the imports grabbed a hitherto-unimaginable share of the key American car market.

The battering Detroit took from the imports when it tried to elevate itself to a position above supply and demand might have been enough for most people. But the auto executives then went right ahead and acted as if they believed the second part of Gal-braith's thesis: that they were above the normal market restraints on price. In the fall of 1974, with the nation slipping into a deeper recession, the automakers blithely raised their prices. Unsurpris-ing result: the cars didn't sell. So the executives came up with a daring and brilliant solution: they lowered their prices. (They called these price cuts "rebates," partly because they were scared that if they openly lowered their official level of prices the Govern-ment would institute a new controls program and freeze them there.) Wonder of wonders, they began to move a few cars.

More recently, the automakers found it necessary to learn both halves of the lesson over and over again. The "rebates" became more frequent and more sizable. And, belatedly, the manufactur-ers were trying desperately this time around to figure out what the public really wanted—and were discouraged to find that some of the enchantment appeared permanently to have vanished from the traditional American love affair with the car. A public scorned had become, in significant measure, a public scorning.

Three decades ago, ex-GM boss Charles E. Wilson was mocked by the Washington wise guys for suggesting that what was good for General Motors was good for America, and vice versa; but it turns out that he was right. And, conversely, what was bad for

General Motors has been bad for America: in rising joblessness, lagging productivity and an enlarging trade gap. We do indeed have a national stake in a healthy, internationally competitive U.S. auto industry (though, as we shall see in the next chapter, it does not follow that it is incumbent upon us, or desirable for us, to provide taxpayer bailouts for those who can't hack it in the marketplace). But it would be useful for all of us—and possibly instructive for any business executive tempted in the future to imitate the auto-makers' old self-defeating arrogance—to note the moral: just as it would be naive to assume that large corporations possess no power in our economy, so it is equally naive to accept the stylish view that they have total power. Supply and demand, however impeded, have a way of resisting extinction; they represent one law that no government has been able to repeal. And Detroit's painful readjustment to this fact would have been easier if we had not all been dazzled by economic theories whose lavish coatings of intellectual chrome did not prevent them from being exposed, in the end, as lemons.

"NEO" NONSENSE

If such once-dominant American industries as autos and steel sometimes seem like elephants lumbering toward the graveyard, the fault is not entirely their own. An eagerness to write them off has spread from Wall Street to academe, where it has begun to be noticed that other newer and smaller sectors of the U.S. economy have been doing notably better: that we are creating new businesses six times faster than we did in 1950; that the amount of venture capital available for nurturing them has doubled since 1974; that high-tech entrepreneurs are giving us a window on the future; that during one recent seven-year period, when U.S. big businesses didn't add a single net new job, U.S. small businesses added fully 6 million. And so, since the market asserted itself when the "planners" failed, the natural, and apparently supremely logical, academic solution is: more planning. Only this time, instead of telling the big guys exactly what to do at all times, we're going to tell them to get lost. (This sort of thing is considered highly intellectual in some circles. Honest.) There's nothing like giving a tired idea a shiny new label, and it's a heck of a lot easier than actually thinking. And so we suddenly have been seeing a bunch of the failed nostrums of our recent economic past resuscitated and repackaged under such glittering titles as "neo-liberalism," "national industrial policy" and "new *[sic]* economic ideas." Feeding on the widespread perception that "Reaganomics" has so far been stronger on promise than performance, ill-wishing critics now propose to remedy the lingering maladies of our economy by giving us further doses of the original diseases: even higher Government social spending, even more massive Government intervention in the economy, and (with U.S. business as their special target) even more arrogant Government "planning" of our future. These folks seem to have walked right past the essential lesson that the greatest job-creating business success in recent years has come in precisely those areas where the least official "planning" and control had occurred.

These fashionable nostrums take a variety of forms. Timothy E. Wirth, a Democratic Representative from Colorado, advocated the establishment of an "Economic Cooperation Council" to map long-term economic strategy. Robert B. Reich, a Harvard professor and author, frankly urged that the Government coordinate all its policies affecting business so as to support high-valued high-technology industries at the expense of mass-production industries. Similarly, Lester Thurow, economics professor at the Massachusetts Institute of Technology and a frequent adviser to Democratic politicians, favored a greatly enhanced Government role favoring industries that, in his view, have the best chances of competing worldwide. Felix Rohatyn, an investment banker at Lazard Freres, scorned "a mere belief in the virtue of the free marketplace" and called for a modern-day Reconstruction Finance Corporation, like the one Herbert Hoover set up in 1932.

Euphemisms abound in this discussion, for two obvious reasons: (1) called by their right names, such interventionist policies look uncomfortably like the failed panaceas of earlier big-government apologists; (2) kept vague, talk about "coordination" of assorted, presumably messy existing endeavors can seem attractive even to many who would despise the probable result. (One strong advocate of "industrial policy" is Owen Bieber, new president of the United Auto Workers, but he sees it as a means to safeguard and rehabilitate waning industries—rather than as a way to hustle the newcomers to the front of the line.) Frank A. Weil, who served as an Assistant Secretary of Commerce in the Carter Administration, when talk about such a "national industrial policy" began, candidly acknowledged the attention given to the choice of words. "We were faced with the question of how to deal with inflation and lagging productivity," he told the *New York Times* in 1983. "Incomes policy—which is another form of microeconomic policy where the Government intervenes in setting wages and prices through various methods—was one answer, but that was a no-no. Industrial policy became another way to talk about the same subject."

Indeed, the concern with altering the labels, if not the content, often seems obsessive. Since the word "liberal" appeared to be at least temporarily in voter disfavor, some of these economists and legislators started to call themselves "neo-liberals," presumably to dissociate themselves from those who were content simply to continue funding the existing social programs. "I will confess to being a liberal," Lester Thurow told me in 1982, "but I think liberals need to do some rethinking about what their objectives are." Thurow, whose recommendations include a radically expanded role for Government in investment banking, is also wary of the term "planning"—possibly because of its demonstrably disappointing worldwide track record—and instead favors the word "strategy," a distinction that in practice might require a microscope of wondrous intensity. Here's how he himself drew the line to me: "I think by planning, people traditionally mean you're going to have some Government authority that sets the price of everything and gives production orders for everything. By strategy, I mean that you have a strategic vision of the direction in which the economy ought to go, and you help push it in that direction. You say, 'Well, hey, we ought to move toward semiconductors,' and then the question is, what if anything can the Government do to help you move in that direction." Now, who in the world could be unkind enough to confuse that with "planning"?

The problem with such "neo" thinking is that, despite its ambitious goals, its practical effect might be to reduce what remains of the healthy private economy to its knees. It is hardly insignificant that the areas of impressive U.S. growth lately tend to be precisely those where the Government has had least involvement. Why should we allow armchair "planners"—or "strategists"—to muck things up in those sectors, too? In reality, there is nothing new about the idea that the state should play a role in guiding industry. It was fundamental to the thinking of the mercantile protectionists in Europe during the Sixteenth and Seventeenth centuries. It is flopping conspicuously today in the sputtering economy of François Mitterrand's France. Those who advocate such policies in the United States would of course reject such comparisons. They really want the private economy to flourish, they contend; it's just that it doesn't know how to do it on its own. What's needed, we're told, is brilliant new Government "strategists" to decide which businesses are getting too much money and attention, and which should now be favored and supplied with special coddling and priority handling from Washington. (Never mind that Washington's ability to think sensibly about our productive economic future would have to quadruple to become infinitesimal. Never mind that turning such critical decisions over to the United States Congress would be akin to turning brain surgery over to a herd of rhinoceroses. We're not talking reality here; we're talking "new ideas.")

The purveyors of this much-vaunted "neo-liberalism" are just the latest in a stale and discredited intellectual tradition whose advocates are most easily distinguished by one indelible characteristic: they absolutely adore "the people," but they appear to have absolute contempt for "people." "People," you see, always make the wrong decisions: the cars they want are not the cars Ralph Nader wants, they insist on spending their money on all the "wrong" things. And so the "neo-liberal" Lester Thurows of today, precisely like the John Kenneth Galbraiths of yesterday, are readily distinguishable by their eagerness, on all occasions, to substitute their own elite judgment for that of the vulgar marketplace. (That such governmental substitutions have, in fact, repeatedly led to a less productive, less competitive, less prosperous America is a minor irritant to be ignored. Let's prime the pump once again, and authoritatively direct its spray.)

A related folly that surfaced during the tax debates of 1982 and 1983, and one directly relevant to the long-range future of aging but still-critical industries, was the notion that it made no sense for Congress to encourage further private investment just now, since

—as any academic could plainly see—we weren't using the factory capacity we already had. (Factory use, as measured by the Federal Reserve Board, dipped to the lowest percentage in the thirty-four years those records had been kept.) Here was a classic case of intellectuals who understand everything but reality. They assume, time and again, that the U.S. economy is static: that people's behavior will not change significantly just because we alter their incentives. In truth, that factory-use statistic is virtually meaningless (though it is always good for a headline), because it doesn't answer the authentically vital question: Capacity for what? Capacity to produce for the economy of 1960 or the economy of 1990?

A sense of history again is instructive. For these self-assured would-be governmental "planners" (or "strategists"), so anxious to let their own choices supersede those of the unpredictable marketplace, never learned the simple and apropos lesson so brilliantly taught by steel magnate Andrew Carnegie at the turn of the century. Carnegie astounded competitors—and built enduring success —by scrapping existing plants and constructing more efficient new ones. He wasn't buffaloed by theoretical figures about available current capacity; he seized the future. And he didn't get, didn't need, and surely would have scorned, a governmental nudge—just as no Washington "planner" would have been able to come up with the original Henry Ford's decision to pay a then-lavish wage of five dollars a day (and thereby significantly boost his own firm's productivity). The entrepreneurial instinct is alien to academe, yet essential to genuine economic progress. And Carnegie's boldness has an important message for anyone who takes the current plant-capacity figures too seriously: theoretical capacity is utterly meaningless if the plants are outmoded and uncompetitive. The way to boost production, and provide permanent job expansion, is once again to encourage savings and investment in America—and then allow the marketplace, not the bureaucrats, to allocate resources for a more succesful tomorrow. What the discouraged U.S. worker really needs is conditions that will hearten not "neo-liberals" but "neo-Carnegies."

We will not cure the ills of our uncompetitive industries either by special Government aid or by a unique Government cold shoulder. Government's job is to create conditions that will help make long-term investment something more than a fool's game in America. Then it will be industry's job to focus on the longer term, too. A common criticism of American managers (some insist it's a specific disease of MBAs) is that they cannot think beyond the next quarter's profits. This is said to limit U.S. executives' effectiveness in comparison, say, with the Japanese, who are always thought to be casting their corporate eyes a minimum of three generations hence. This sweeping complaint is not without some justice, but (a) a good many brighter American managers actually always have been able to take a bifocal look at their company's short- and long-range futures (doing what could be called planning, as opposed to "planning"—which is what bureaucrats do with somebody else's company); and (b) the best way to get the majority of U.S. managers to adopt a more farsighted orientation is to provide a less volatile economy, with more stable prices and interest rates. Given the recent wild fluctuations, a businessman doesn't have to be a hysteric of Wall Street proportions to develop the idea that long term is anything beyond next Tuesday.

WHY BUSINESSMEN DON'T SELL THE SYSTEM

Having said so much about what U.S. business should be doing to meet the challenges of the Twenty-first Century, let me say one thing that I think it ought not be doing—and that is trying to mollify its most mindless critics by posing as Mother Bountiful: a sort of grand and generous charitable institution, only incidentally concerned with making a profit. You would think American business had enough to worry about in recent years, what with recession, brutally high interest rates and the hangover of two decades of inflation. But the guilt instilled by all that jolly anti-corporate rhetoric of the Sixties and Seventies dies hard, and we see firms struggling even now to please their foes by refurbishing the business "image." How else can I explain, for example, the arrival on my desk not long ago of a questionnaire from one of the nation's biggest oil companies, Phillips Petroleum, soliciting my views on the issue of "corporate social responsibility"?

Lest I chuck the questionnaire in the appropriate circular file, an accompanying letter from a company vice president assured me that the questionnaire was going only to a "highly selective" group of leaders of thought, "domestically and internationally," and that the world would benefit immensely from hearing from this "spectrum of informed opinion." (Golly.) But this flattering impression of a disinterested search for truth was promptly dashed by other portions of the letter suggesting that Phillips' own mind was very much made up on this question, and that what it was truly seeking was not so much elucidation as applause. Not only did the firm piously place itself on what it clearly regarded as the side of the angels—"Phillips Petroleum Company has long recognized the need for business to acknowledge the social responsibility a corporation incurs as part of the privilege of conducting free enterprise in an open democracy"—but it made no secret of its real hope that the questionnaire would confirm its own foregone conclusions and persuade other business leaders "to place a higher priority on the role of corporate social responsibility in their own policies and plans." If Phillips was seeking media hosannas for its recitation of these trendy platitudes, it called at the wrong precinct. My own feeling is that more nonsense has been talked lately on the subject of "corporate social responsibility" than on virtually any other subject in the economy—an awesome distinction—and that the primary result has been to contribute to public confusion about what a corporation actually is and what its role in our society can and should be. A corporation is, in reality, just an association of people for the purpose of doing business. Period. Emotional rhetoric to the contrary, it is neither inherently good nor inherently evil. Which leads us to the earnest, high-minded and well-meaning Phillips questionnaire—and my answers thereto.

Having assumed at the top that there was already a "fair consensus" on such "motherhood issues" as equal opportunity and employee health and safety (violations of most of which are, in any event, flatly against the law), the questionnaire said it wanted to focus instead on "community involvement" and "corporate philanthropy." First question: Do you agree that private corporations should engage in community involvement? My answer: Yes, certainly—primarily by producing goods that customers want to buy, making a profit and creating jobs. Question: Do you agree that private corporations should engage in philanthropy? Answer: Only when it advances the interests of their stockholders. It is in the corporate interest of General Motors, for example, to improve the climate of life in Detroit, and Citibank has a legitimate interest in improving education in New York City. When there is no direct connection between the owners' interest, as a group, and the charity soliciting, the corporation should say no—however worthy it may be for individual officers and stockholders to contribute their own money. The basic point is simple: a corporation is not some mean old rich man hiding in a cave; it is an entity formed for the purpose of doing a particular kind of business, within the law, for the benefit of those whose savings financed it. We shouldn't seek to appease those who despise our private-enterprise system by accepting their mistaken metaphors. Running a successful and productive business—and making a profit—can be the most socially responsible act of all.

In the end, then, business people ought to get off the defensive against senseless accusations of "corporate greed," stop apologizing for being successful enough to hire people and make products customers want to buy, and start actively and aggressively selling the best economic system that ever came down the pike. Phillips doesn't merit any special opprobrium for trying to play Mr. Nice Guy instead of getting on with business; possibly it just wanted to distinguish itself from, say, Mobil (whose outspoken "issue" advertising is plainly more to this writer's taste). Indeed, I long ago reached the conclusion that the typical, publicly timid American businessman is mad at the wrong people: he's furious at just about everybody else (politicians, journalists, professors) for failing to defend the U.S. economic system. But he forgets that he does a startlingly rotten job of this himself. The average businessman is so poor a salesman for the economic system—which has been such a key factor in America's unique achievements—that he has contributed significantly toward leaving the field to his professional critics, however misguided or malignant.

What has produced this apparent suicide complex among so many U.S. business people? I've pondered it for years, and reached four main conclusions: (1) The average businessman is afraid he might offend people by speaking out. He sells, he reasons, to Republicans and Democrats, liberals and conservatives, sensible people (those who think as he does) and idiots (those who think otherwise). The less he intrudes on their beliefs and prejudices, he believes, the less likely he is to lose a sale for reasons unrelated to the quality of his widgets. His job, he concludes, is to sell widgets—not save the world. (2) The average businessman does not really understand the system, or his role in it. In this he is scarcely unusual: he is the product of the same inadequate educational system as everybody else. It was nearly eighty years ago that the United States first was described as a nation of economic illiterates by Frank A. Vanderlip, president of New York's National City Bank, and there has been scant reason in the intervening eight decades to alter that appraisal. Lecturing, as I do, at scores of American colleges and universities, I repeatedly encounter audiences who apparently have never before heard a rational defense of a market economy: not in elementary school, not in high school, not in college. Then they grow up and watch TV dramas and multimillion-dollar movies about what stinkers businessmen are. So why be surprised that the American businessman, like the American anything else, typically is ill-educated in economics, ill-served on the subject by most of the media and ill-equipped to do ideological battle with those who sneer at the system and at him? (3) The average businessman thinks he—and possibly, just possibly, his partner—are the only honest ones around. He shrugs at occasional evidences of corporate bribery and malfeasance, reasoning cynically that everybody knows financial reports are not to be trusted. He is insufficiently stirred to anger when he discovers shoddy quality and misleading labeling, arguing to himself that those are the ways of the modern world. And before long, he himself is half ready to believe the propaganda that typecasts business in the role of impure greed, and Government—of all people—in the role of purifier and improver. (4) The average businessman believes that free enterprise is a marvelous system—in every field but his, which of course has special conditions.

What such businessmen (and -women) do not recognize is the ultimate indivisibility of economic liberty. Just as they should be honest in their own dealings, and openly indignant with those who are not, so they should devote more time to preserving the national framework in which all legitimate private endeavors can flourish. Yet the typical American businessman is neither a spokesmah nor an activist for the system that has brought him—and the country —such unparalleled results. With some conspicuous and praiseworthy exceptions (but still far too few), he lets the debate go by default to demagogues who substitute "compassionate" rhetoric for economic sense, and picture the typical private businessman as a villain he never was. The injustice is unlikely to be corrected as long as the average businessman fails to sell the system, as well as his product. For without the former, the latter ultimately doesn't have a chance.

Businessmen forget this at their peril. They tend to fall into helpless obsequiousness in the presence of hostile politicians; the then chairman of General Motors, Thomas A. Murphy, once bizarrely and ludicrously announced to the world that—I kid you not—Jimmy Carter had come up with a wonderfully effective program for conquering inflation and putting the economy on the right track. It's all very well to seek to preserve one's tax breaks, but sometimes it's necessary to speak bluntly and publicly about how wealth really gets created in this country—and by whom. Some years ago, New York's Senator Daniel P. (Pat) Moynihan did for businessmen what more of them should be actively and feistily doing for themselves. Speaking at Yale University, Moynihan asked for a show of hands from anyone in the audience who planned a career in business. Only a very few hands went up. Most of the other New Haven undergraduates apparently viewed a life of vulgar commerce with elitist disdain. As he recalled it in my presence later, Moynihan looked around the auditorium and smiled faintly. "Oh?" he said. "Then all the rest of you just plan to be leeches?" Attaboy, Pat: it's time somebody gave this country the business.

VIII

See You Later, Regulator

Well, okay, I admit it: I'm a very unfashionable fellow. I kind of like business. And that's not a bit trendy. It's not that I adore every person who ever called himself a businessman. Heaven forfend. The business community over the centuries has had no discernible shortage of scoundrels, liars and fakes. It's the system I like. Indeed, those of us who favor a freely competitive system ought to be the most vigilant in exposing any who abuse its opportunities. But my affection has a simple rationale: when business comes up with a clinker, I don't have to buy; but when Government misfires, I have to pay anyhow—just as if it had had a brilliant success. In fact, the price tends to rise in inverse proportion to a governmental program's success. When Ford came up with the Edsel, the customers were free to hold their noses and walk away. But when Washington creates a product with an outlandish price tag and no visible use, my choice has evaporated: the item is on my tax bill, even if I didn't order it.

So, after a generation or so in which the bulk of our media intake has been devoted to savaging business and extolling all those "humane" programs of Government, mine may seem an anomalous perspective. I suggest not only that business has a legitimate role to play in our society, but that that role should expand—in all our interests. Furthermore, and contrary to what we hear regularly from legions of politicians and journalists, I am convinced that business profits not only have not been too high, but that they ought to be a heck of a lot higher if we are ever truly going to get U.S. living standards charging forward again. Most basically, I think we should face a highly unstylish fact: business is the economy. Period. When you ask, "How's business?" that's how the economy is. The notion that you can somehow build a more prosperous America while simultaneously indulging in a nonstop ideological attack on the profits of American business is a form of intellectual lunacy that could only have been devised in Cambridge, Massachusetts, or Washington, D.C.

But having said so many favorable things about American business, let me now step back a pace or two and give American business a well-deserved boot in the behind. I think it's way past time for too many business people in too many businesses all over the country to stop paying lip service to free competitive enterprise —in every business but the one in which they happen personally to be engaged—and start learning how to practice free competitive enterprise a little more, without flying off to Government every time things go awry. (Or driving to Government, in a Chrysler car.) Virtually every business executive in America today will expound, with minimal prompting, on the extent to which excessive Government regulation is holding his company back, ultimately reducing productivity and hampering national economic growth. What is far less widely confronted is the extent to which business itself is responsible for these governmental intrusions.

Every economist, whatever his or her views on other subjects, can cheerfully give you a list as long as Kareem Abdul-Jabbar's arm of restrictions we already have built into this economy at the behest of some special interest—business or labor. These are luxuries we can no longer afford in today's intensely competitive world economy. It is ludicrous for self-seeking business executives to cite these past mistakes as the precedent for present folly. (As far as he was concerned, Chrysler's Lee Iacocca let us know, free enterprise vanished a long time ago. About the same time, it was suggested by Detroit flacks that Iacocca would himself make a marvelous candidate for President of the U.S. It was not immediately apparent whether his chief qualification was that he clearly already knew the way to the public till.) Instead of letting an endless number of subsidy seekers have their corporations' failures rewarded by preferential treatment, it is time now to start systematically rooting out these anti-competitive interventions where they do exist, and where they do hold us back, and certainly not to allow anyone else to use them as the excuse for ever more exceptions every time one more business executive thinks he has the right to go into your pocket to bail out his balance sheet. Business executives are, in the end, the system's worst enemies when they seek special privilege at the expense of the healthy disciplines of a competitive society.

ON THE CARE AND FEEDING OF DINOSAURS

Those who are forever standing by ready to extend the Government's regulations, restrictions and other interventions into the private economy at the drop of a rationale invariably inform us that they are doing so not to destroy the system but to save it. They resemble, in this respect, a character most of them would affect to despise: that legendary U.S. officer in Vietnam who announced that the village had to be destroyed in order to save it. These advocates contend that in the economic context, one cannot be a purist; there are sometimes pressing human reasons for acting contrary to competitive theory in a specific situation. Take Chrysler: when the Government intervened to save that company from almost certain bankruptcy in 1979, it did so, we are told, because (a) it was necessary to preserve jobs, and (b) be sensible—you just couldn't let a company as big as Chrysler, the tenth-largest industrial corporation in America, simply disappear from the scene. Neither argument, as we shall see, had enough intellectual content to fuel a ride from your home to the supermarket.

By Iacocca's own admission, Chrysler in 1979 was "too top-heavy," with three dozen vice presidents "tripping over each other" and 40,000 white-collar workers "who were just pushing paper around": a company whose bloated management had stuck too long with big cars and failed conspicuously—even by Detroit's slovenly standards—to adapt to a changing marketplace. Can you imagine what would happen to any ordinary business person, or to you and me in our personal affairs, if we behaved with anything resembling such financial ineptitude? Chrysler, in contrast, was able to ask for $1.5 billion in Government-guaranteed loans. The suggestion that this was not a taxpayer subsidy is wholly ludicrous: such guarantees enable the borrower to get money cheaper than he otherwise could. Perhaps even more important for a country struggling to improve productivity and competitiveness, the bailout meant that a portion of the nation's severely limited lendable funds was artificially directed to inefficient Chrysler and thus did not go to the businesses the marketplace, left alone, would have chosen as better bets.

Ironically, Iacocca has become something of a business hero for his apparently successful maneuvers in keeping his company afloat and even successful. In a more profound sense, however, this incident has been bad both for the country in general and for business in particular. If Chrysler, thanks to Federal largesse, succeeds in recovering from a situation that otherwise would have been terminal, that will be lovely for Chrysler stockholders, their strange bedfellows in the United Auto Workers, and (should he care, which he says he doesn't) Iacocca's personal effort to get revenge on Henry Ford II, who peevishly fired him as president of Ford Motor in 1978. For the rest of us, though, the benefits are more dubious. Senator William Proxmire, who has made a career of brilliantly vindicating Alf Landon's 1936 contention that a man could be a liberal without being a spendthrift, continues to regard the Federal assistance to Chrysler as a grievous error. "I disagree that any jobs were saved," the Wisconsin Democrat said in 1982. "Any jobs lost at Chrysler would have gone to Ford and General Motors, which have colossal unused capacity."

Even more questionable is the easy assumption that Chrysler, because of its size, simply demanded special attention. Indeed, one of the presumed arguments for having the taxpayer do for Chrysler what the market would not was the notion that, in the normal order of things, industrial giants ought to last forever. But where is it written that they should? As a fascinating study made available to me underlines, the rise and fall of titans is a normal expectancy in a prospering and growing economy. The logical conclusion is that the system functions best when the market is allowed to provide its own rewards and penalties.

Consider: of the hundred biggest U.S. corporations in 1917, only thirty-four remained in that elite grouping in 1977. Meanwhile, such 1917 top-dozen colossi as Midvale Steel and International

Mercantile Marine had gone off the board entirely. Even as recently as 1945, the hundred biggies of the day were a chancy bunch on which to bet: forty of them were out of the first hundred by 1977, and several had vanished forever. Such current giants as Monsanto, Xerox, Caterpillar and Sperry were nowhere to be found in 1945. (IBM just squeaked aboard—in ninety-fourth place.) As the author of the study, Steven C. Leuthold, of Funds, Inc., put it to me, "Current corporate size, wealth and prosperity are no guarantees of continued future prosperity or even survival. Looking at the corporate elite of the past clearly demonstrates this. This rather simple observation is very often overlooked by investors, pension planners, politicians and economists. Diamonds may be forever, but a giant corporation (and its pension fund) may not be. Chrysler's current crisis is hardly unprecedented in American economic history."

So Chrysler-type dilemmas, far from being a unique feature of a troubled modern economy, are in fact a natural by-product of any competitive society. Indeed, Leuthold, who is a highly respected adviser to institutional investors, found it puzzling that the automaker's potential failure should have come as such a shock to so many in Washington—"unless, of course, the experts did not do their homework on the mortality rate of major corporations. . . . Continued corporate success cannot be taken for granted, no matter how healthy a corporation appears at a particular time in history." But it's not just that Chrysler, left to its own devices, might well indeed have gone the way of the buggy-whip manufacturers—joining such long-forgotten, once-wealthy corporations as Central Leather and American Locomotive. Entire industries ebb and flow in a normal, healthy, expanding economy, and we forget this at our peril. In 1917, for example, fifteen of the fifty largest industrial corporations were metal and mining companies; in 1977, only three. Does this mean that the Government should have rushed to the barricades in 1917 to preserve the corporate status quo of that day? Of course not—any more than the Government should have tripped over any semblance of a free-enterprise philosophy in its haste to rescue Chrysler in 1979. As Leuthold wryly noted, "Natural selection, survival of the fittest, has in the past culled a great many then-weak but once-mighty inhabitants out of the U.S. corporate world, just as takes place in the jungle. The U.S. Government now seems at least partially dedicated to subsidizing and keeping these once-powerful creatures at almost any cost. . . . Dinosaurs can be very expensive pets.'' Future corporate welfare clients, please note.

THE BIGGER THEY ARE, THE SOFTER THEY FALL?

My own perspective on the Chrysler affair, and its potential successors, offers two additional thoughts. The first is the silliness of any policy based on the notion that the bigger they are, the softer they should fall. By that reasoning, which seems particularly hollow amid all the unceasing talk about ''fairness,'' the secret of going broke is going broke big. If you're heading for bankruptcy, it would seem, your wisest course is to increase your debts hugely. If your threatened collapse is sufficiently titanic, there will always be a sizable bloc in Washington amenable to the suggestion that the rest of us ought to bail you out. If, on the other hand, you're a poor individual sucker, or some small-business person struggling desperately to get established, forget it, that's the way it goes. (Interestingly, the public is awakening to the lunacy of all this: a Harris poll in 1982 reported that 56 percent of Americans now thought the Government's proper role toward ''companies in important industries that are in severe financial trouble'' should be to ''let them sink or swim.'' What's more, an even larger number—60 percent—specifically opposed bailouts of automobile companies.)

Finally, my thinking is shaped by the experience of having lived almost six years in Britain, the country that preceded us in trying to run an economy on institutional ''compassion'' rather than economic sense, and thereby contributed mightily toward transforming one of Western Europe's highest living standards into one of its lowest. It often seemed to me during my time in England that we were carrying on an unfortunate and unannounced lend-lease program in which the U.S. sent Britain the worst of its culture, and Britain responded by sending back the worst of its economics. The British, characteristically, were way ahead of us in trying to bail out major industries that got in trouble—and thus misallocating national resources and crippling national growth. Ultimately,

the British came up with an apt word for such Chrysler-type foolishness: they called it "lemon socialism." You take from the profitable, the marketable and the successful, and you give to the
"lemons": the unprofitable, the unmarketable and the unsuccessful. Quite predictably, as the British ruefully discovered, what this
means is that each year you increase that portion of your economy
that is unprofitable, unmarketable and unsuccessful. That way,
clearly, lies not the compassionate full-employment economy of
political rhetoric, but the reverse of the more prosperous America
that lies within our grasp: a backward-looking, buggy-whip economy, in which every American suffers and every American's living
standards deteriorate. I don't want that kind of America, you don't
want that kind of America—and, when you get right down to it,
Lee Iacocca and Frank Sinatra shouldn't want that kind of America, either.

SUCCESS AND FAILURE:
THE TWIN ENGINES OF GENUINE PROSPERITY

There is deep irony in the sight of many vote-attuned Congressmen
eager to rush taxpayer assistance to any faltering industry with
sufficient political clout to get a hearing. For those most disposed
to do so are, more often that not, the same folks who have been
trying their darnedest for decades to eliminate success in American
life: a condition they appear to regard as inherently unfair. Now,
with equally nonsensical enthusiasm, they are seeking desperately
to eliminate failure as well. The simple truth that continues to elude
them is that a healthy, competitive, thriving and expanding economy requires both success and failure. Success and failure are the
twin engines of genuine prosperity. The rewards of success are the
incentives that in the real world lure entrepreneurs, investors and
smarter, more productive work. The penalty of business failure is
an equally important part of this equation. Indeed, one of the significant long-term contributions of any recession is cleansing the
economy of inefficient enterprises whose survival has depended on
inflation and the anything-goes mentality of a boom. While such
failures are normally treated by the media as national tragedies,
history suggests that they are often national benefits: clearing the

way for newer, more efficient activities keyed to the future and not to the past. No nation ever raised its living standards by cementing the status quo.

What goes for corporations goes for individuals as well. I have spoken several times over the years in Youngstown, Ohio, an old steel town that has suffered one of the highest unemployment rates in the country. A little-discussed part of the problem is that many multigeneration steelworkers have been reluctant to relocate, industrially or geographically. The fellow who says, "My grandfather was a Youngstown steelworker, my father is a Youngstown steelworker and I'm entitled to be a Youngstown steelworker, too," is voicing an attitude that is alien to the best American tradition. He is, rather, mirroring attitudes long found in parts of the north of England, where a refusal to alter roles or location has depressed living standards and inhibited national progress. The American heritage is one of mobility, and to abandon that heritage and resist further change is to erect needless barricades against a potentially better future. I have often been asked whether I saw any decent future for Youngstown—or for a number of other tired industrial-belt cities in which I have made repeat lecture appearances in recent years. My reply consistently has been that such communities still have much going for them, including a relatively well-educated and skilled population and continuing transportation advantages, and that I can see a very happy future for them indeed —if they will seek that future in the future and not in the past. Those who are waiting for some magical politician to resurrect 1960 are doomed to bitterness and discontent. But those who will prepare for 1990 may yet surprise us all.

THE PROPER ROLE FOR GOVERNMENT

Government's proper role in all this may be less than generally assumed. Its guiding industrial policy should be a simple one: Butt out. Without the unambiguous prospect of economic failure as a key discipline on corporations large and small, we coddle the inefficient and outmoded, discourage breakthroughs in productivity and labor-management relations, and freeze the allocation of resources that might otherwise go to the younger, more daring and more inventive in our midst. The politicians ought to get over their feverish obsession with penalizing success and prohibiting failure. Both these possibilities are essential if we are to go forward vigorously as a nation. I fervently believe that America's economic future can be brighter than anything previously known in this or any other country, but I submit that we cannot find that future by attempting to subsidize and enshrine America's economic past.

And for all those who have agreed with me in principle but perhaps have been privately thinking to themselves, "Yeah, he's right in general—and maybe about Chrysler—but my business is a little bit different; we've got special conditions that require a special relationship with Washington," let me remind you that it has been well said that the Government never did anything *for* you that it didn't do *to* you first. Indeed, they tell me that, according to the latest update of the old joke, the three biggest lies in the United States of America are now these: Number One—"Your check is in the mail." Number Two—"Of course, I'll respect you in the morning." And Number Three—"I'm from the Federal Government—and I'm here to help you."

WHO REALLY WINS FROM REGULATION?

One of the customary rationales for governmental restrictions on the free market is the notion that our public servants are "protecting" us from the savagery of an untamed marketplace. Actually, as even the most cursory examination will reveal, most regulation works ultimately against the interests of the individual consumer. This continues to surprise most people, who then engage in witch hunts aimed at particular regulators, or else whoop on "consumer advocates" who promise that, with them in the van, the nasty corporations will be tamed and the interests of you and me predominate at last—with, of course, an intervening stop in Washington. In reality, while the interests of consumers are inevitably diffuse, the interests of producers are splendidly concentrated, and those who would substitute governmental directives for the free choice of the marketplace should not be astounded when those directives tilt toward the producers. There is no contradiction here with the conclusion that less regulation would be better for the nation's business, for what these interventions tend to promote is not business in general but the interests of entrenched, existing corporations. The least efficient have the most to gain when Government steps in.

There is nothing new about this. Observing that "most regulatory policies have been sought by producer groups," University of Chicago professor George J. Stigler, who won the 1982 Nobel Prize for economics, said consumers generally "are, and in their own interests should be, the supporters of a highly efficient economy, which I will identify with an unregulated private economy." Not quite what we usually hear on this subject, is it? In his pamphlet *American Capitalism at High Noon,* reprinted in *Competition* magazine, Stigler—an outspoken advocate of the view that Government regulation hurts rather than helps consumers—recalled the start of regulatory movements in the closing decades of the Nineteenth Century: "It is quite impossible to believe that large political interferences in the economic system could have taken place without the permission of the industries that were regulated. Imagine the railroad industry under the unwilling control of the Interstate Commerce Commission in 1890. The industry had 700,000 employees, and $10 billion of capital and dozens upon dozens of powerful, able entrepreneurs. The ICC had five commissioners, a staff of 61, a budget of $150,000, and infinite respect for the members of Congress, who in turn were not lacking in respect for the great industry of railroading. If told that the ICC controlled the railroads, the Duke of Wellington would have repeated himself: anyone who believed that would believe anything. . . . What the American business community lacks is the will to eliminate most business regulation."

Today's events suggest that Stigler's barb at the aggrieved business community was on target. The ICC, having presided grandly over the decay of America's railroads, now—for no logical reason whatsoever—extends similar beneficence to the trucking industry. (Entry into the railroad industry was theoretically limited because of the immense capital investment required, but anybody with ambition and the credit to buy a used truck can take to the roads.) As Milton Friedman commented in *Newsweek,* "An ICC permit to operate is a valuable piece of property—to the person who has it. It is valuable because it restricts entry and thereby enables truckers to charge higher prices than they otherwise could. Private wealth, public nuisance." No wonder, then, that established truckers (and the Teamsters Union) relish limited entry and rate protection; and it is noteworthy that the Reagan Administration, despite all its fine initial talk about deregulation, responded to such powerful anti-competitive pressures and actually moved backward in areas like the ICC. No wonder, too, that a host of other industries have been crying loudly about the apparently terrifying prospect of "freedom now": from television to liquor. Michael deCourcy Hinds reported in the *New York Times* that "the nation's distillers, brewers and vintners . . . learned long ago to live with the entangling vines of Federal regulation and do not wish to be freed." Those who might wish to enter the industry, and are currently being discouraged by those "entangling vines," were, of course, not consulted.

Less obvious, perhaps, to those who distinguish between ("bad") old regulation and ("good") new regulation is the extent to which even the more modern, seemingly consumer-oriented regulatory measures tend in practice to favor the entrenched. Shortly before becoming President Reagan's first chief economic adviser, Murray L. Weidenbaum, who made his reputation as a specialist on the impact of business regulation, co-authored a paper that argued persuasively that "one of the most serious consequences of Federal regulation is the threat to the continued existence of the small firm." Weidenbaum pointed out that "Federal regulation affects small business in a very selective and disproportionate manner." It was "a matter of simple arithmetic": if you divide the cost of meeting a Federal regulation by the number of units produced, a small manufacturer winds up paying more per unit than a large one; but since he lacks similar power to raise his prices, he finds it harder and harder to get the banks to lend him the money he needs to stay in business. This imbalance, in truth, can continue right up to the loftiest levels: it was easier for General Motors to meet the Naderesque array of new automotive regulatory requirements than Chrysler.

One well-documented example of the adverse impact of Federal regulation on small business, cited by Weidenbaum, is the foundry industry, more than 80 percent of whose 4,000 concerns employ fewer than a hundred workers. In the late Nineteen Sixties, the industry began to lose small plants because of a combination of recession and new edicts from the Environmental Protection Agency: a follow-up study found that more than a third of the firms responding cited EPA regulations as partly or totally to blame for their closings. Similarly, a more recent well-intentioned, and largely misguided, piece of regulation, the Employee Retirement Income Security Act, has contributed significantly (according to one survey, more than three times out of four) to the abandonment of tens of thousands of small-company pension plans, and saddled those that remained with needless paperwork and frequently counterproductive instructions on how they must invest. Yet when the Reagan Administration tentatively suggested that it might be nice to weigh the claimed effectiveness of any regulation against the actual costs it imposes on the economy, this was taken by the self-designated consumer "crusaders" as a wildly unacceptable heresy. Since then, as noted, the Administration itself has scarcely covered itself with glory in the area of deregulation. (It has yet to do anything as dramatic as what may be the Carter Administration's lone abiding economic achievement: the deregulation of the airlines.) After all, deregulation is risky, and whatever benefits may eventually accrue to the consumer, some of your friends and supporters may get hurt. Why strive to change the enormously costly Clean Air Act when the present system serves to protect established Eastern manufacturers and their Appalachian and Midwestern coal suppliers? Why repeal the Occupational Safety and Health Act—an example of nitpicking governmental interference that was lambasted frequently by candidate Ronald Reagan—when the large and powerful find it relatively painless to comply (no matter how unbearable the price for their smaller potential competitors) and when, as Lester Lave of the Brookings Institution observed, "If the big employer is accused of running an unsafe workplace, he's helped by being able to say, 'We have met every OSHA standard, and a few more besides.' "* Such slackening of

---

* In a similar vein, Marilyn A. Goldsmith, editor of the *National Tax Shelter Digest,* found that the real effect of Securities and Exchange Commission regulations in her field was "not to protect the investor from the sponsor, but to protect the sponsor from the investor." For example, when an oil program fails to return even the original investment, the investor has no recourse "because the SEC-required prospectus or offering memorandum (which he probably did not

Reagan's deregulatory zeal led *Fortune*'s Walter Guzzardi, Jr., to conclude that "the charge that the Administration is merely pro-business rather than pro-reform is not easy to dismiss." More precise, I would suggest, is that the Administration is characterized less by whether it is perceived as pro- or anti-"business" than by its continuance of a governmental regulatory apparatus whose ultimate effect is to guard the interests of those who entered the industries yesterday against those who might come in tomorrow with better products and lower prices. Is it any wonder that the great breakthroughs of the last generation have come overwhelmingly in those industries the Government has not yet figured out how to regulate?

HOW TO GET OUT OF THIS MESS

Interestingly, recognition of what to do in this area is more widespread than the will to achieve it. Serious students of widely varying initial mind-sets conclude after study that our present regulatory Goliath serves predominantly to increase prices, discourage competition and separate people and businesses from the costs of their own activities—as opposed, for instance, to simply making businesses pay for the pollution they produce. To continue to pretend that any of this truly serves "the consumer" (who happens to be, at one time or another, all of us) is merely to refuse to notice that the emperor is naked—and we're paying for his ride. In the name of regulating the economy, assuring "fairness," protecting consumers or serving some other presumed social good, we have established a network of regulations and Government interventions that has begun to strangle us, and that saps our ability to keep up with the times.

President Reagan's 1982 Economic Report correctly reported that the recent growth in the number and size of regulatory agencies has been greater than that which took place during the New Deal period, and that "the direct costs of Federal regulatory activities to the taxpayers are large"—having gone up by 50 percent,

---

read or understand) warned him that there was a significant risk that he would lose his money."

not counting inflation, just between 1974 and 1981. This was not a novel, or partisan, analysis. Barry P. Bosworth, director of the Carter Administration's (wildly ill-named) Council on Wage and Price Stability, acknowledged to me in a 1978 television chat that "Government has been causing inflation through its regulatory actions." But there is a general perception that we've all been brainwashed by Ralph Nader, and cannot take the truth. For example, even so ambivalent an observer of the free market as Paul A. Samuelson seemed to recognize during the so-called energy crisis of the late Nineteen Seventies that deregulation and decontrol were essential steps to any true solution. But he nonetheless said of Jimmy Carter's refusal to take these steps: "Given the political realities, he had no other choice. . . . Asking for repeal of all price controls on energy . . . had no chance of acceptance by Congress and the American people." Surely, it is time by now for those who would aspire to be leaders of American thought to stop talking "political realities" and start talking economic sense. And that means a wholehearted program for re-examining, and largely dismantling, those European-style governmental interventions that are demonstrably not the cheapest or most effective way of improving the health, safety, security and prosperity of the American people. We need to examine the carrot rather than the stick, and we need to get back to the ideas that generated our national economic success, rather than those that are eroding it.

A RARE KIND OF VICE

Two final thoughts on our real interests in the area of Government regulations and interventions—and then a cautionary glance at what may well be the next bad idea heading ominously down the pike:

(1) One of the most compelling reasons for weeding out the thicket of governmental regulations is that they serve, in practice, not to safeguard the (theoretically venerated) "little guy," but to restrict his free choice. When corporations, unions, farmers and other groups able to collect due bills in Washington obtain regulatory favors, the negative impact on the consumer can be fairly obvious. But he or she is damaged as well when, for example, a

zealot like Ralph Nader forces the Corvair off the road and out of the showrooms—and we learn only much later, after an extensive series of performance tests by the Department of Transportation (reaffirmed by a panel of independent experts), that the much-maligned car was, in fact, "at least as good as the other vehicles tested." The consumer is hurt when manufacturers are compelled to overload their cars with an expensive array of so-called (yet often highly dubious) safety devices—whose actual effect on any auto-safety statistics, as *Barron's* Robert M. Bleiberg aptly pointed out, "is scarcely visible to the naked eye." The consumer is victimized when gung-ho bureaucrats at the Food and Drug Administration, acting on ridiculously inconclusive laboratory evidence, attempt to rush to judgment against saccharin. (How sweet it wasn't.)

Indeed, the relatively powerless have reason to fear excessive statist regulation both as consumers (where they find their choices limited by the imposition of elitist and frequently faddish tastes) and as potential producers. Walter Williams, continuing his crusade to make his fellow blacks aware of the value to them of a free market, and the danger in their present overwhelming support for those who would curb it, likes to cite the difference between operating a taxicab in Washington and in New York. In Washington, anybody who can come up with the $5,000 or so to buy a taxicab and insure it can become a taxi driver. Result: two out of three District of Columbia cabs are black-owned. In most other cities, however, taxis are heavily regulated—"in the public interest," of course—with an array of ceilings, special permits and other devices. In New York, the going rate for one of the legally restricted number of taxi licenses was up to $60,000 in the early Nineteen Eighties. (There were times in the previous decade when it cost more to buy a license to drive a taxi in New York City than to buy a seat on the New York Stock Exchange.) Result: blacks and other new entrants are discouraged and/or forced into illegal "gypsy cab" operations. The system tells these people they cannot lawfully aspire to be entrepreneurs in their chosen profession. The system, plainly, is nuts.

(2) It is getting to be time for those who seek a happier American economic future to stop paying so much attention to Ralph Nader. The self-designated consumer activist was an engaging figure when

he first appeared on the national scene, and General Motors transformed him from a pest into a hero when it overreacted so spectacularly to his dubious charges against the Corvair. But by now Nader has become a dangerous "special interest" himself: operating a network of lobbies with a seven-figure annual budget, associating himself when convenient with the radical left, and producing an endless stream of hyperventilated would-be exposés, significant portions of which turn out, on examination, to be unfactual at any speed.

As the U.S. public that once admired him so extravagantly and uncritically has begun to voice doubts about the value and cost-effectiveness of many of the burdens he pressed on the American economy, Nader has become ever more shrill—and ever more foolish. In 1978, for example, while pushing one of his innumerable pet proposals (to end the right of states to make their own laws on corporate chartering), Nader exceeded even some of his own previous records for going off the deep end. U.S. corporations, he announced, are not just beyond "the rule of law" (a revelation that may come as a surprise to firms that spend an immense sum each year simply to comply with Federal paperwork) but actually "determine the direction of our economy. While the country heaps all the burdens of our economy on the White House, the real power is in the hands of the corporations."

What a marvelous discovery! Obviously, it was IBM, not Lyndon Johnson, that decided to wage simultaneous war on North Vietnam and poverty, without paying for it, and thereby sent the country on an inflationary binge. Obviously, it was Xerox, not Richard Nixon, that insisted on wage and price controls in 1971, and thereby contributed to a decade-long erosion of real corporate profits. Obviously, it was AT&T, not Congress, that made such unfavorable changes in the capital-gains laws in 1969, and U.S. Steel that secretly engineered a decline in its share price from $104 in 1959 to less than a quarter that amount two decades later. They did it all on purpose, because they are the ones who really run the economy. What a brilliant exposé!

Such inanities would be beneath serious comment were not Nader's basic (and still overly publicized) approach so harmful to the very people he professes to defend. Dr. Robert Hessen of the Hoover Institution, author of *In Defense of the Corporation*, pointed out trenchantly that Nader not only was off-base factually an astounding part of the time, but was misleading at his core: "Nader seeks to create a massive coalition on behalf of his programs, but what he intends to deliver to the rank and file is really the opposite of what they want or imagine they will get. The rank and file want more power, more self-determination and a larger voice in the institutions that affect their lives. Instead, Nader's blueprint is for a social system in which all decisions are to be made in the public sector, that is, in the political arena, and therefore one in which private spheres of action and opportunity are sharply restricted or totally obliterated. Instead of being sovereign self-owners of themselves and their property, individuals would be at the mercy of majority rule, with no entitlement to anything which the majority did not vote to allocate to them."

There are those who would always prefer to have their paranoia fed than confront reality, and for such addicts of self-delusion there will, I suppose, always be people like Ralph Nader to tell them they are right, and that it's the nasty, evil corporations who are the enemies of a better life. But that is no reason for the rest of us, who recognize that Government itself produces nothing other than red tape, to continue to whoop him on—or tacitly to allow others to do so unrebutted. Nader's increasingly stale demagoguery could be dismissed as laughable if it didn't come at a time when anti-business rhetoric and legislation are so plainly hobbling the economy, and helping to keep us from attaining the progress and prosperity that once seemed America's inevitable destiny. The central economic fact of the last two decades is that firing successive torpedoes at businessmen—however popular a sport it seemed at the time—not only has failed to elevate poorer Americans but has cruelly caught them in the wreckage.

(3) The bad idea that I fear we may have to worry about in the near future is one that has been around before, done us harm, but never seems to go away for good. This sleeping snake in the American economic garden is wage and price controls. Polls periodically indicate an ominous amount of underlying support for them, despite their unbroken record of miserable failure, including, as recently as the Nineteen Seventies, in the United States and in Canada. Controls always seem such a simple remedy: Prices are going up. We want to control them. Ergo, eureka! Let's have wage and price controls.

By now, this wacky notion of "power to the bureaucrats"

should prevail only in a nation afflicted with terminal amnesia. But what troubles me is that ours is a nation not conspicuously endowed either with a sense of history or with the virtue of patience. We do not like inflation, but we also do not like paying the price of containing it, especially when the price, as lately, has been so severe (and, as we have seen, more severe than necessary). Given that background, the sirens singing of a magical panacea may yet emerge once more.

As anyone who has taken even the most superficial look at two or three millennia of economic history (from the Emperor Diocletian to Richard Nixon) should be painfully aware, wage and price controls are a seductive fraud. They have two main flaws, either one of which should disqualify them from use in any country except one you're consciously trying to wreck. The first is that they don't work. They never have worked for long—not in any country, in any century—and no matter how fierce the enforcement machinery. (Diocletian had a very severe penalty for violating his Roman wage and price controls: he killed you. But even his controls couldn't survive his government's continued debasement of the coinage.) In peacetime, with no great sense of national emergency or purpose, they would be likely in the U.S. to work even less well, and less long, than usual. Perhaps just long enough to create serious distortions, dislocations and shortages. The second major flaw of wage and price controls is that they distract attention from the true causes of inflation to the mere symptoms. This, incidentally, is why they are such perennial favorites of politicians and their big-government apologists in academe. Instead of letting the public's wrath settle where it belongs, on the Government that actually creates and prolongs the inflation, through irresponsible fiscal and monetary policy, controls focus on the victims: on those private citizens, business and labor, who are trying to adjust their lives to the Government's inflation. When Nixon turned so melodramatically to controls in 1971 (one of his most admired acts as President, and one that was hailed initially, if shortsightedly, by many businessmen who appeared to regard it as a governmental gift to cost controllers everywhere), the rate of inflation in the uncontrolled economy had been running at an annual rate of less than 4 percent. Three years later, after the public had been successfully distracted by a long series of controls "phases," the inflation rate had tripled. Controls don't really stop inflation; they just stop us from thinking about it for a while, and that may be their greatest danger of all.

Ironically, some of those who presided over the Nixon controls, and their inevitable breakdown, have been the most alert to the dangers of reimposing them. Hence, while the "liberal" W. W. Rostow was arguing in 1982 that "the time has come for a wage-price freeze," Paul W. McCracken, who had been Nixon's chief economic adviser, was confessing that "the clear lesson" of the Nixon controls had been that they had "delayed the return to reasonable price stability and imposed distortions on the economy that weakened its subsequent ability to deliver gains in real income." There was a period when Walter W. Heller, who had been chief economist for Presidents Kennedy and Johnson, seemed to flirt with the idea of controls—a wavering that brought cries of joy from the anti-market fanatics clustered around Senator Edward Kennedy, and pleas that Heller "cross the Rubicon" and advocate controls. But when I questioned Heller directly about it on television in 1980, he dissociated himself from Kennedy on this issue ("I don't happen to go along with him on wage-price contols") and said: "Wage-price controls involve huge costs. They suspend economic freedom, they involve a huge bureaucracy, they involve misallocation of resources, they lead to cheating and chicanery, and they don't hit . . . well, let's call it 'God, Volcker and OPEC' —not necessarily in that order. They don't, they can't control OPEC prices, they can't control the weather and they can't control interest rates. So for that reason I'm against them." Heller is frequently an uncomfortable hero for the economic left, with its Galbraithian-regal instinct for substituting Government fiat for the obstreperous marketplace. He has surprised his customary ideological allies on other occasions, for example by opposing the grandiose Humphrey-Hawkins scheme to legislate "full employment" while actually making it more elusive by adding to the underlying inflation problem.

Controls, in reality, aren't liberal or conservative; they're just silly. They function in the real world like a brick at the mouth of a steam kettle. For a little while they do seem to be reducing the inflationary steam (that's when all those network news commentators—economic "experts" to a man—deliver their stentorian messages about what a good, if overdue, idea controls were). But what truly matters, as any amateur cook can tell you, is what's going on underneath the kettle. And when the heat continues there, as it did so painfully in the U.S. during our last dalliance with controls, the underlying pressure from fiscal and monetary policy will eventually fill the entire room with steam—whether or not you try to keep the brick in place. So controls, however seductive they may occasionally appear in a period of economic frustration, are a thoroughly bad idea: tried and untrue. They impede freedom without in the long run impeding inflation. As with so many seemingly appealing calls for even further governmental intervention into our economy, they work against us, in our name.

There is also another, deeper danger in this yearning for controls (for Daddy to make everything all right). Mere talk about the possibility of someday turning to controls can itself be damaging, for it encourages businesses and unions to raise prices and wages more than they otherwise would, to reach the highest levels possible before the freeze. Since this fear of future controls can cause prices and wages to rise faster than they otherwise would, imposing wage and price controls is a rare kind of vice: nearly as damaging when you just talk about it as when you have the fun of going out and doing it.

IX

Getting Up the Energy

If you know any young person who would like to live well but has no conspicuous brains or talent, tell him or her to become a professional economic pessimist. It's not a bit necessary for the person to know any economics (indeed, that may well be an active hindrance), but there will always be a handsome living to be made. Over the years, watching manifold economic forecasters ply their occult trade, I have noticed repeatedly that if someone makes a wrong optimistic prediction, the audience will neither forgive nor forget; but if someone makes a wrong pessimistic prediction, hordes of people will be ready to forgive him or her at the drop of a semicolon. ("Well, maybe not *yet*" will be the prevailing attitude. And: "Well, things aren't *that* great, *are* they?") There are well-known professional gloomsters who, in my personal experience, have yet to stumble on an accurate forecast for anything more challenging than what day of the week comes after Thursday, but whose annual incomes would comfort a maharajah. I used to wonder why this should be so, but now I think I know: Most people are scared to death about money. First, they think they will never get any; if they somehow manage to acquire some, they are convinced it will all be gone tomorrow. And so, when somebody comes along and tells them that the economic situation is even worse than they had feared, the visceral tendency is to believe that one is hearing the (darkly suspected) inside poop at last. Maybe that's why horror movies are so much more popular than documentaries.

215

But if we are to make sense out of an issue with as high a quotient of hysterical befuddlement as energy, we would do well to begin by recognizing this national addiction and starting to deal with it. The United States is a nation of optimists forever being awed by pessimists. The same instinct that caused Americans to pay large lecture fees to Oscar Wilde in the Nineteenth Century so he could tell them how irredeemably uncouth they were leads us in the late Twentieth Century to make best-selling authors of virtually anyone who flays the system and forecasts its imminent collapse. It's as if Americans all felt a little guilty about their success—and were unwilling to believe their good luck.

Hence it became fashionable in recent years to assert that the U.S. not only could not continue to grow economically, but that it should not even make the attempt. The buzzwords were "limits to growth," and the argument was that Americans already used such a large chunk of the world's resources in proportion to their population that it was an antisocial act even to aspire to live better. In a society whose propensity for self-flagellation is awesome, this argument quickly gained almost unquestioning acceptance in imposing sections of academic and political thought. No matter that Malthus is long gone, and America's food production is prodigious. No matter that anti-automation theorists have been discredited, and the machine is clearly seen to be a creator of jobs (as, surely, the computer and the robot eventually will be seen, too). We still want to believe the worst at every turn, and there will never be a shortage of moralists eager to tell it to us. It may not be cheerful, but it sure is profitable.

Now that there is growing public recognition that we were sold a grotesquely overpessimistic set of forecasts on the outlook for energy, however, it seems fitting to pay some attention to those nonconformists who had the nerve right along to rebut the "limits to growth" crowd—with its smug certainty that the world was about to run out of resources, and that we dastardly Americans were to blame. Dr. Carl H. Madden, for example, saw things more clearly than was stylish back in 1976, when he wound up a distinguished thirteen-year stint as chief economist for the U.S. Chamber of Commerce, and argued that the very phrase "limits to growth" was considerably less self-explanatory than it seemed.

"First," he said, "it is wrong in implying that growth means producing more and more of what industrial societies have been producing at an obscene rate. The history of human life on earth shows that social evolution always drives human activities into new pathways. Indeed, each major human age produces its own materials. Resources have never been as 'natural' as textbooks suggest. They come from raw materials that have value only when human knowledge shines on them and separates them from the earth to serve human purposes. Examples are everywhere." In other words, in a market environment, oil may conceivably run out someday—but human ingenuity won't. In a valedictory article for *Nation's Business* magazine, Madden pointed out that neither average real incomes, nor energy sources, nor traveling capacities, nor life expectancies changed much between the time of Jesus and the time of George Washington, but all have exploded since, vastly improving the typical standard of living and refuting the notion that profit-induced prosperity enriches only the wealthy. "Growth —in the sense of the evolutionary advance of applied knowledge to satisfy freely expressed wants—is the only way to feed the world's hungry and improve the quality of life," Madden declared. "The poor, here and abroad, need no doctorates to understand that growth is better than no-growth." A similar note was sounded by that formidable futurist Herman Kahn, who maintained in his book *The Next 200 Years* that the world had the capacity to move toward unheard-of affluence while conquering pollution, starvation, pestilence and war. "Americans are going to be enormously wealthy," Kahn predicted, "so they must learn how to spend their wealth without becoming satiated, disappointed or fashionably anti-materialistic." Taking aim at the faddish 1972 Club of Rome doctrine that demanded sharp restraints on economic growth, Kahn said anti-growth elitists "already have a high standard of living and do not see any real future gain for themselves if others improve their economic standards—although they may not recognize these as their true feelings." It's interesting to see such voices arising, though they plainly do not yet prevail. The U.S. undeniably has the potential for proving the optimists as wrong in the future as the pessimists consistently have been in the past, but the historical record in the market of ideas suggests that it is still premature to sell America short.

DOOMSDAY WILL BE A LITTLE LATE THIS YEAR

It should now be clear even to the slowest learners in our political and academic midst that energy conservation *is* working in the United States, and very much better than we had been led to believe it would: that, year after year, higher energy prices have led to lower energy consumption—apparently to the total amazement of all those "energy experts" who had been making such a lovely living for themselves over the course of a decade by going around the country scaring the pants off all the audiences they addressed, telling us that we were about to run out of energy within the next thirty days, and that we Americans were going to have to put on our hair shirts and live much worse in the future (and that this would be good for us, because we were so wasteful and immoral and profligate in the first place). Their predictions have been so awful that it's surprising some of them stayed out of government. (Maybe next year we should make them available as unity advisers to OPEC.)

There is nothing novel about such dreadful forecasting on energy. More than six decades ago, authoritative petroleum "experts" let it be known that the U.S. would run out of fuel within five years. Similar doomsday projections have surfaced periodically ever since. As with such related examples of predictive folly as the routinely erroneous forecasts on tax receipts and budget deficits, these calculations are correct only if you assume that the world stands still, that everything remains as it was when you first punched the data into your computer. In real life, incentives and price play critical roles in fostering change. A tax cut can actually increase receipts and reduce deficits; a boost in the cost of oil can limit the utilization of petroleum and encourage the search for alternatives. Yet when the U.S. encountered an "energy crisis" in the Nineteen Seventies, the dominant view was that this was something entirely different: that the rules of common-sense economics had somehow been repealed, and that we needed massive governmental interference lest we "freeze in the dark" because of our selfish, doomed ways.

For years, the biggest untold story about the U.S. economy has been the remarkable and continuing success of American industry in reducing energy consumption. I know—because I kept trying to tell it. The story remained muted throughout the Nineteen Seventies because it did not fit the rhetoric or the policy of Washington —or of OPEC. Abroad, oil exporters went on trying to justify exorbitant price increases on the ground that they must make the wasteful Americans behave; at home, our alleged private failure to conserve made a convenient whipping boy for Washington's failure to implement a coherent energy-production policy. But what truly was occurring differed dramatically from the popular portrait of an inflexible America fated to have permanently lower living standards because of an inability to adjust to changing conditions on energy.

Consider: it was widely predicted that the annual increase in U.S. energy demand would continue to balloon in the late Nineteen Seventies and thereafter, with the long-term average never falling below 3 to 4 percent at best. Reality: though the figures were treated in Washington with all the enthusiasm that a politician normally bestows on an unfavorable poll report (and remain largely unpublicized to this day), energy demand dipped sharply below overall national economic growth years before our latest recession crippled industrial production. In 1977, for example, overall economic growth was a husky 4.8 percent; it was "authoritatively forecast" that the growth in energy consumption would be dangerously swifter than that. In fact, the energy figure came in at only 2.6 percent. For a year this development was described—if it was talked about at all in the prevailing alarmist circles—as a fluke. Friends in Washington told me that they were surprised at me for publishing this information: my facts were right, but it was a "one-year aberration" due to "special circumstances," energy demand would explode the following year and wouldn't I look silly then? Well, I listened respectfully—I'm always anxious to be educated in economics by my leaders in Washington—but by golly, somehow the rate of increase in energy consumption the following year was even lower (2.4 percent) than it had been in 1977. "Dangerously simplistic" and "just another temporary aberration in the long-term upward trend" were two of the more polite comments tossed at me when I duly reported that one. But, lo and behold, in 1979 (though the overall economy was still undergoing the longest peacetime expansion in American history) U.S. energy consumption not only slowed further but actually declined by a tenth of a percentage point. It soon turned out that there had been no "aberration" at all: overall U.S. energy use dropped by fully 3.2 percent in 1980, beginning a Nineteen Eighties fall so steep that by now the trend is discernible even to Congressmen.

One of the few economists who were on the beam right along was Robert L. Marks, of Siff Oakley Marks, whose views were considered eccentrically optimistic when I first gave them exposure in my newspaper column and speeches. Interestingly, Marks changed over the years only in reducing ever further his estimates of how much energy the U.S. would be using in the course of the next decade. As he put it, "We really have made meaningful progress with energy conservation. The U.S. is using less energy per dollar of real gross national product than at any time since World War II (and that's as far back as we've been able to find good data). The adjustments haven't been painless, of course. . . . But, as you've observed, such discomforts now are primarily the consequences of earlier Government efforts to protect us (via price controls). More important, however, and minimally noticed outside of industrial trade journals, are the tremendous strides that the nation's manufacturers have taken to reduce energy consumption. In 1979, total factory output was about 17 percent above the 1973 level, while total energy demands in the industrial sector were only 1 percent higher." In summary, long before the slowdown associated with economic recession, U.S. industry was making a historic transition to lower energy use. The implications of this for America's future are powerfully bullish. Factories are not going to revert to oil-gulping machines; airlines are not about to put their new fuel-efficient jets into mothballs and replace them with old-fashioned gas-guzzlers—nor, for that matter, is the individual American family likely to rip out its home insulation or implore Detroit once more to give it cars with 1957-style miles per gallon.

OPEC OF TROUBLE

In the economic world, of course, nobody ever urges you to relax. For years, it was drilled into Americans that rising oil prices were responsible for stalling the world's economies and rendering hopeless the fight against inflation. Such talk was flagrantly exaggerated from the start by scapegoat-seeking politicians. A dispassionate panel of economists calculated that the 1979 OPEC increase would in fact add no more than about a percentage point to our already-soaring double-digit domestic inflation and would retard our real economic growth even less noticeably. By any reasonable measure, OPEC's shenanigans were not good news for America's economy, which had been structured on the past reality (and future hope) of continuing low-cost energy. You might think, then, that the recent revelation of OPEC as a paper camel with dwindling influence, and dwindling prices, would be taken as marvelous news for the U.S. economy. Not a chance!

With the headlines full of talk about an oil "glut," with gasoline prices coming down around the country and some attendants actually saying "please" and "thank you" again, you could be forgiven for believing that it was time for some of the doomsday theorists to take off their ideological blindfolds. Instead, we heard talk about how dreadful the prospect of falling oil prices would be: it would hurt the oil companies, the coal companies and the search for synthetic fuels; it would hurt the banks; it would hurt the Mexicans and the British; it could set off an international financial cataclysm that the U.S. would have to step in to prevent. Where once we heard from eminent academicians and politicians that the free market, left to its own rapacious devices, would never bring down oil prices—that they would, indeed, increase geometrically from here to eternity—now we heard calls for bureaucratic intervention to keep prices up.

Instead of succumbing to such seesaw hysteria, let's get some perspective on how the world oil price has been rigged through the years. On October 5, 1973, the posted price of Mideast oil was $3.65 a barrel. That was probably only about half what a free market would have decreed, but the monopoly buying powers of the big oil companies kept the price artificially cheap. The following day, Egypt and Syria invaded Israel, and in an attempt to wield the "oil weapon" against U.S. support for the Israelis, the dominant Arab petroleum producers forced through a quintupling of the world oil price. From way too cheap, the price jumped to way too expensive, with no intervening stop at reality. The second major upward jolt also was political in origin: OPEC's second-strongest member, Iran, was ravaged by revolution, war and the onset of a medieval Ayatollah (who turned out to be the best argument in two centuries for the separation of church and state). The country's oil output was cut by 50 percent. The Yom Kippur and Khomeini shocks each led to enormous transfers of wealth from the world's many oil consumers to its few oil exporters: an estimated 2 to 3 percent of the globe's gross national product each time. Not too surprisingly, the *nouveaux riches* in the Organization of Petroleum Exporting Countries soon fell to bickering; as production controls reduced OPEC's output from nearly 32 million barrels a day in 1979 to little more than 17 million barrels a day in early 1983, the main burden fell on the feudal aristocracies of Saudi Arabia and the Gulf sheiks, which had the lowest-cost oil. As London's *Economist* observed, "In its last years OPEC has been a device for intensifying the inflationary slump in the West, while in the Middle East it has been shifting economic and political influence away from the Saudis (who obeyed official cartel arrangements that priced their oil out of the market) and toward Khomeini's Iran and Qaddafi's Libya (who signed the cartel agreement but have constantly undercut it)." In other words, the invincible monolith of OPEC mythology was increasingly being exposed as a squabbling pack of petty thieves. It couldn't have happened to a nicer bunch of guys.

Economically, OPEC's fate seemed foredoomed. Peter F. Drucker, writing in the *Wall Street Journal,* contended that the decline of OPEC's production to 60 percent of its pre-1973 levels and the likelihood of continuing downward pressure on prices both fitted neatly into the rules of cartel theory formulated in 1905 by the German economist Robert Liefmann "and validated by all subsequent experience": (1) a cartel is always a product of weakness ("Growing industries don't form cartels; only declining ones do" —industrial dependence on petroleum was falling even before the price hikes began); (2) if a cartel succeeds in raising the price of a commodity, it will depress the prices for all other commodities of the same general class (not only have the prices of all other primary commodities—agricultural products, metals and minerals—been falling since 1974, but "the share of disposable income that developed countries spend on all primary products, including oil, is lower today than in 1973"); (3) a cartel will begin to unravel as soon as its largest and lowest-cost producer has to cut production by 40 percent to support the weaker members (the day was delayed by the devastation in Iran, but Saudi Arabia lately has had to cut by more than 40 percent to prevent the cartel price from collapsing); (4) any cartel undermines the market shares of its members within ten years or so (OPEC, whose share of the industrialized nations' oil imports fell from nearly 60 percent in 1973 to about 45 percent in 1982, found itself losing market position to outside newcomers such as Mexico, the North Sea and Gabon); and (5) in the end a cartel permanently impairs the position of its product, unless it cuts prices steadily and systematically (experience suggests that "for a long time to come, petroleum will lose markets fast when it becomes more expensive but will not regain markets by becoming cheaper"). In short: Don't fool with Mother Market.

So OPEC's decline is neither astonishing nor undesirable. Everett Ehrlich of the Congressional Budget Office was surely right in pronouncing himself "flabbergasted" that "after years of thinking higher prices were a bad thing, we could now think that lower prices are a bad thing." He noted that "lower oil prices are the only source of new purchasing power that doesn't come off the back of the budget." In the end, a more rational, market-attuned oil price would help any number of groups: from such energy-dependent industries as airlines and steel to those vast debtor nations, such as Brazil, among the world's oil importers. As for the banks, their long-range interest surely lies where the country's does: in a healthier, more rapidly growing, less inflationary economy; a more prosperous America will not lack for prime lending opportunities.

Some people think we should hasten OPEC's demise by imposing a new tax on imported oil. Professor M. A. Adelman of the Massachusetts Institute of Technology told me on "Wall $treet Week" in 1979 that he was convinced that the way to stop OPEC was for the consuming nations "to levy a sliding-scale ad valorem and tariff on crude oil—which means, in simpler language, that every time the producing nations raise their price, we raise the tariff on it even more. And that means that the consumer reaction is faster than it would otherwise be—that [the oil exporters] lose a great deal more business than they otherwise would." With such a tax, as S. Fred Singer of the Heritage Foundation has observed, the U.S. would be "stealing it from OPEC and putting it in the Treasury." The idea is to shore up the domestic market and ultimately decrease the nation's dependence on imported oil.

But while it is tempting to deliver the final uppercut to a reeling OPEC, I confess I am inherently wary about alleged solutions to our economic problems that somehow always seem to involve a new tax and a new governmental intervention into the marketplace. (I have a suspicion that I know who usually winds up paying such taxes in the end.) More important, it seems to me, is to move sensibly and courageously at last toward encouraging, rather than thwarting, America's own domestic production of energy—in other words, to get the Government's oily fingers not further in but further out.

THE REAL ANSWER ON ENERGY

Playing with the tariffs can be fun, but its benefits will at best be short-lived. Conservation is plainly a near-term necessity and is itself a vital form of national energy production. But I submit that the real answer on energy eventually must come from a more rational and concerted effort to increase our domestic energy supplies. I believe this country is going to have to turn in the Nineteen Eighties to something akin to the Manhattan Project that produced the atomic bomb in the Nineteen Forties or to the space program that sent men to the moon in the Nineteen Sixties—not, I hasten to add, in terms of one more massive new Government spending program (heaven knows we don't need another one of those, and that crowd couldn't do the job anyhow), but in terms of having the incumbent President do what none of his predecessors has been able or willing to do in the decade since the Arabs first socked us on the chin with their embargo: and that is to go on national television and say in simple, firm English that, from that night forward, the overriding, Number One priority of U.S. energy policy will be to take those steps, and make those compromises, that will enable us to increase our own domestic American energy resources.

Not only is this the only way that will ever truly work economically, but (far more important) it is the only way we can assure our grandchildren and their grandchildren that they will not be exposed every decade to some hideous new version of the Ayatollah Khomeini—but will, in contrast, henceforth be able to avoid the threat of international blackmail of the United States of America, whether that threat comes in the future from the Arabs, or from the Iranians, or from anybody else on this globe.

There was a time when it seemed reasonable to sit back and listen tolerantly to the ongoing U.S. parlor debate over whether we ought to produce any more energy of any kind: it all seemed dirty, unsafe, unpleasant or otherwise unacceptable to Jane Fonda. But reality has intruded rather nastily in recent years. A religious fanatic seizes power between the Caspian Sea and the Persian Gulf, impudently oversees the holding of American hostages and threatens the security of our energy supplies. In Saudi Arabia, which we are told is our truest, bestest friend in all the oil-producing world, the pricing policy of a periodically endangered, potentially fragile family dictatorship is promulgated from an ultra-plush Geneva hotel suite by the urbane Sheik Ahmad Zaki Yamani, aptly described by oil industry analyst Dan Lundberg as "one of the greatest opportunists on the planet." How foolish it is to assume that a temporary period of petroleum oversupply is a time for neglecting the task of building up U.S. resources for the Twenty-first Century. Those precarious countries bordering the Persian Gulf—Saudi Arabia, Iran and Iraq—are expected to account for more than half OPEC's production in the Nineteen Nineties, and it has been calculated that a mere 5 percent rise in energy demand in the U.S could mean a 50 percent increase in demand for Persian Gulf oil. It does not require even a mildly apocalyptic scenario to suggest that this does not represent an ideal long-term fallback position for the American economy.

If we are to move, for a compelling combination of geopolitical, economic and national-security reasons, to a greater degree of energy independence, it means first and foremost that we're going to have to make much better use of the best tool we have in this area: improving the market incentives for domestic energy production. That will involve, for example, fully removing at last what may be the single most stupid and counterproductive piece of legislation of the last decade—the so-called, and badly misnamed, windfall profits tax. (It was never actually a profits tax; it was always an excise tax: what Adelman correctly called "continued price control at a higher level.") No TV sitcom writer could come up with a more hilariously inappropriate series of alleged remedies than those we have attempted to apply at the Government level on energy. For a generation, Congressmen boasted of how their "compassionate" regulations were holding down the price of natural gas: they then expressed outright amazement, mixed with sinister suspicion, when the country ran short of natural gas. The first major fiscal response by the United States Congress to the "energy crisis" of the Nineteen Seventies was to reduce the oil-depletion allowance—which had been placed in the tax code decades earlier to encourage domestic production of energy. You figure it out. Or better still, accept this one-word answer: politics. A nation cheered Washington's Senator Henry M. Jackson, touted (absurdly) as an "energy expert," who decried the "obscene profits" of those awful old oil companies. There were no such rousing speeches when those same companies began suffering (what nobody called) "obscene profit declines." Even Ronald Reagan, who knew—and often said—how irrational the so-called windfall profits tax was, made it his dirty little secret to keep the tax alive because of the revenues his advisers promised it would produce.

A positive energy-production policy means, in addition to more sensible and less punitive taxes on potential producers of oil and other fuel alternatives, a national change of attitude toward the bottom line of all such efforts. It means that our President must lead us entirely away from the bizarre—indeed, the zany—economic theory that was repeatedly introduced into the country's energy debate by Associate Professor Carter: that the worst thing that could happen to the U.S., as we moved belatedly to solve our energy problems for the next century, would be if, along the way to that much-longed-for solution, some dirty rat made a very big profit. (I just wish somebody had sat him down once before he left the Oval Office and whispered in his ear: "Jimmy, that's the way we do business in America. That's the way we've done business for two hundred years. That's how we built the standard of living that was the envy of the entire world.")

Let me tell you another secret that has not yet surfaced in the Nineteen Eighties. This secret will emerge as we come to recognize that neither "gluts" nor "crises" are forever, and that the need for varied and reliable sources of U.S. energy may temporarily recede but will never disappear. For if a more rational energy policy does begin to produce better long-term results, if we do move significantly toward solving our massive energy problems for the century ahead—as I believe we can, and hope and pray we will —along the way to that deeply desired solution (and here comes the big secret), a lot of dirty rats are going to make a lot of very big profits. And let me confide something else. For myself, I hope their profits are not just obscene; I hope they're downright porno-graphic. Because that will mean that we are truly producing the energy America will need—and truly moving to solve our problem at last.

WHAT THE GOVERNMENT COULD TRY

Somebody said to me not long ago: "Lou, tell the truth. You've followed these affairs as closely as anyone in recent years; you've had Reagan's top economists on your program, and Carter's, and so on for a couple of Administrations before that. Do you, in your heart, really believe that this Government—or any Government— *can* solve our American energy problems?" And I replied: "No, I sure don't think they can. But the latest crew *could* try something that none of the others ever quite got around to. They could try getting out of our way—and letting *us* solve America's energy problems for a change."

Why, I think it's a miracle we ever got over the whale-oil crisis without the help of the Department of Energy.

OF MEN AND CARIBOU

Fools rush in where politicians fear to tread, so let's not leave this subject without touching on one more area where we have been fed sententiousness instead of sense. The kind of energy policy that would truly encourage national forward motion clearly would require, as well, a firmer hand in cutting through the current cha-otic and competitive Government regulations, whose principal ef-fects have been to boost costs, inhibit productive experimentation and substitute bureaucratic fiat for the natural testing of the marketplace. (This year, switch to coal; next year, oil. Forget nuclear for the moment: nobody likes it, so we're not going to concern ourselves with its possible safe development just now. Who cares that we led the world in war in this area, and lagged in peace? Let our grandchildren worry about that tomorrow: by then, we may be ordering the factories to install windmills.) It would mean, too, a little less pusillanimity and hypocrisy in trying to clarify our national thinking about the environment.

Ecology is not, as some polemicists have tried to make it, a classic liberal-conservative issue. Theodore Roosevelt was a brilliant architect of conservation; Alf Landon in 1936 spoke trenchantly of the need for what he called "long-range land-use planning," and he was scarcely a hippie by anyone's definition. In the Nineteen Sixties, though, many Americans trendily went overboard in one direction—acting as if we could and should immediately remove every impurity from our planet, with no regard whatsoever to how (or who's) to pay for it. The attitude seemed to be that where matters of the ecology were concerned, there were only two sides: the ecologists and the bad guys. (Pollution, understandably, had mighty few spokesmen.) But then, as the Seventies progressed and it became apparent that we had been stymied even in satisfactorily tapping our marvelous, internationally unique reservoirs of coal, a sort of counterrevolution began brewing—in which concern for the environment (and its "killer trees") was almost by definition a confession of flimsy thinking. The subject is too important for such routine demagoguery from either side. As the father of three daughters—a fact that may influence my views on some other subjects as well—I certainly share the environmentalists' concern for the future of the air we breathe and the water we drink. Who but a fool would not? This does not mean, however, that we must not weigh the reasonable costs of eliminating the last 1 or 2 percent of pollution, or consider whether the trade-off is worth the price, a price that sometimes must be paid in fewer jobs and lower living standards, as well as higher bills. The answer in the real world lies neither in callous tough talk nor in naive demands for ecological perfection now; the country has made immense progress in this area already, to all our benefits, and no matter how you slice it, the remaining decisions will require intelligent compromises that are both tough and sensitive—in all our interests.

If I had not already known the degree to which heated emotion had supplanted any semblance of cool reason on this subject, an incident back in 1973 would have branded it into my consciousness forever. The economist Pierre Rinfret—who has been called "flamboyant" so often that many people are convinced it must be his first name—appeared as my guest on "Wall $treet Week" and complained, in a casual aside, that the Alaskan oil pipeline had been foolishly delayed because of concern over, as he put it, "whether the caribou can jump over the pipeline." Well, you should have seen the angry public reaction. We're used to getting a lot of mail on "Wall $treet Week"—even then, we were averaging well over 1,000 pieces a week—but nothing in our previous experience could hold a candle to this one.

Some viewers, as you might expect, castigated Rinfret for his political advice (he had, after all, come on the program a year earlier, as the designated "principal economic spokesman" for the Nixon campaign, to assure us that high inflation and high interest rates would soon be things of the past, if we would only re-elect the President). Others criticized Rinfret's gloomy assessment of America's future and his advice to his own children to seek their fortunes elsewhere. But all that was as nothing compared to the groundswell for the caribou. In fact, the issue wasn't settled until we devoted a three-minute segment of a subsequent program to airing both sides of this grave national controversy; in addition to my reading excerpts from a few of the letters, we showed some film of a caribou at the National Zoo (not jumping at all, as it happens), and I displayed my own nonpartisanship by inviting the caribou to appear on "Wall $treet Week" whenever he felt like it, to discuss Pierre Rinfret.

X

My Bounty Lies Over the Ocean

We Americans are nothing if not fair: having hobbled our domestic economic policy with an array of ill-conceived governmental interventions, we have been more than willing to do the same to our foreign economic policy as well. Nobody can accuse us of a selfish desire to contain our foolishness here at home—or of acting to damage ourselves in only a limited or partial fashion. Modern American economic policy has been a tale of two follies: Folly Number One was the notion that if we spread our largesse abroad with a generosity unprecedented in human history the world would come to love and follow us. Folly Number Two—a reaction to the failure of Number One, but actually just the opposite side of the same counterfeit coin—was the belligerent belief that if the world wouldn't play by our rules, the answer was to erect a retaliatory economic wall around the U.S. That this happens to be the same philosophy known in simpler times as cutting off your nose to spite your face does not in any way inhibit those eminent statesmen who continue to garner applause by advocating it as if it were the all-purpose remedy for unemployment, faltering U.S. competitiveness and the decline of the buggy-whip industry. What these two follies have in common is their instinctive reliance on well-intentioned Government actions as a substitute for economic reality. Such gimmicks can be marvelously appealing, but they share one minor flaw: they don't work.

In this chapter, we'll try to find out why. We will also probe for an approach that might genuinely deliver an economic payoff for the U.S. in the final years of the Twentieth Century. An appropriate starting point toward greater rationality in this area would be a vow to conduct our foreign policy with a deeper and more abiding sense of how it is really going to affect our own American interests. This means that we ought to recognize that we have in recent years too often been playing ourselves for suckers. I can assure you that we have not fooled a single other nation on the face of this earth: we have merely deluded ourselves when we pursued a foreign policy that appeared to have as a principal aim a largely fruitless effort to make friends of our enemies—while we succeeded, all too brilliantly, in making enemies of our friends.

Part of the problem has been a self-defeating disregard for the economic implications of our overseas policies. Too often, they have been devised by theorists who appeared to believe that nothing so mundane as crass economics should be allowed to interfere with the higher calling of diplomacy. This was a continuing blunder that might have been more excusable if it had not been so uniquely American; as it was, it just tended to set us up repeatedly as good old Uncle Sucker. Indeed, amid all the portentous speculation about the international implications of the 1982 shift from Alexander Haig to George Shultz, perhaps the most enduring significance—and not just on the diplomatic scene—lay in the fact that the U.S. at long last had a Secretary of State with a solid background in economics. It seemed that if Shultz would only remember to dance with the skills that brung him, this could turn out to have been far more important than the passing headline concerns about whether Israel (or Europe) had been abandoned, whether Al Haig's temper should have been the subject of the next nuclear disarmament talks, or whether the Bechtel Group had suddenly become the prep school for the Reagan cabinet. For the uncomfortable truth is that in a world increasingly dominated by questions of basic economics, this country has been inadequately served at Foggy Bottom through a succession of Presidencies. Haig, despite his brief stint at United Technologies, was essentially a military man with interlacings of Government administration. His predecessors in the Carter era spent much of their terms pursuing quixotic policies that sometimes seemed deliberately to ignore national economic interests. As for Henry Kissinger, he once confessed to me (or was he boasting?) that "I know nothing about economics"—an acknowledgment that never in any way inhibited him from discoursing confidently on a wide range of critical issues whose heart lay in economics.

It was not just that Shultz had an academic background in economics (he was a former dean of the University of Chicago business school); that, as we have had sad occasion to discover, is not necessarily a guarantee of lasting common sense in the Washington jungle. The reason for having a modicum of hope that an overdue turning point in foreign economic policy might finally be arriving lay in a more practical consideration: in Government itself as well as in the private business world, Shultz had learned the hard way that politicians disregard market logic only at the nation's peril. I knew Shultz well during his years as Labor Secretary, budget director and Secretary of the Treasury, and I think the only time I ever embarrassed him was when I grilled him on national television about the actual efficacy and genuine consequences of imposing wage and price controls, a program that was, ironically, the single most popular economic act of the Nixon Administration; even foolish businessmen had joined the approving chorus, greeting controls as a lovely way to hold down the payroll. My question, from a distinctly different perspective, came as something of a surprise—and Shultz, who had his own private reservations about the easy consensus on this issue, visibly squirmed.

A significant part of Shultz's success as Secretary of State may ultimately be determined by the extent to which he and his boss are willing to apply Shultz's unusual degree of practical economic sense—and refortified toughness about market economics—to those foreign-policy questions that, in the end, reverberate in the nation's pocketbook. It means, for example, not bowing to those perennial advocates of sweet new economic deals for Moscow or Peking, or being swayed by career diplomats who still think we should curry favor in the "Third World" by subsidizing error and apologizing for profit. On an imposing array of other economics-related issues, one could at least hope that Shultz's badly needed expertise, grounded in economic realism, would contribute toward a noticeable difference—and one that would be positive for the domestic business scene. In that respect, this quiet man had a rare opportunity to leave a legacy that conspicuously escaped his more flamboyant predecessors.

Shultz, characteristically, started slowly. His softspoken, deliberate approach seemed colorless after the hyperthyroid dramas starring the likes of Kissinger and Haig. But there was evidence that he was beginning to bring at least some economic realism to Foggy Bottom. He was instrumental, for example, in disentangling the Reagan Administration from the hasty economic sanctions it had imposed against the Soviet natural-gas pipeline to Western Europe. Behind the scenes, he appeared to be working to dissuade Administration zealots from protectionist solutions to U.S. trade problems. It was disturbing, for those who hoped for more from him, that before he had been in office a year, Shultz seemed to have become one more target for the political practitioners of White House infighting. Anonymous Administration aides complained that, while efficient and likable, he was insufficiently "forceful"; others said Shultz had lost "the upper hand" in foreign policy to William Clark, then the President's national-security adviser. One could hope that Shultz, ever renowned as a team player, would survive such bickering and leave a more lasting imprint on U.S. foreign economic policy. Of lawyers, generals and diplomats, our foreign policy has had aplenty. It was nice to think of the changes that might at least be possible now that the country actually had a Secretary of State who could add.

A POLICY, NOT A RETREAT

If a more sensible foreign economic policy would be more hard-headed, this does not mean that it should involve a retreat into a hard turtle shell. The appropriate change would certainly not entail a return to old-fashioned isolationism, however much many Americans on both the left and the right patently yearn for such an escape. This troubled planet badly needs American leadership, even though it is fashionable nearly everywhere to doubt that these days, and it needs that leadership to be a good deal more relaxed and self-confident than it has tended to be in recent years. As one who, as noted, spent more than ten years living abroad—as a foreign correspondent in Europe, in Asia, all over the globe—I fervently believe that it is very much in the world's economic interest that our country finally begin consulting its own economic interests a little more intelligently and a little more consistently.

It means, for example, that we can no longer afford, in the pursuit of plainly spurious "détentes," ever again to be caught offering preferential trade terms to those who would bury us. It means that we should make maximum use of what we have—notably including the truly unique productive genius of America's farmers. (I once told a group in Des Moines that I thought the other 96 percent of us ought to be down on our knees every night giving thanks to the 4 percent of Americans who were farmers—for having done so magnificently, despite Government help.) But surely it is time now to start using our resources like tough, intelligent Yankee traders, not like candidates every year for the title of Saps and Suckers of the Universe. And it means, as we grope for a more effective relationship with our friends and with those who despise us, that American trade and foreign economic policy for the next decade cannot be made for us by kidnappers in Tehran, or blackmailers in Riyadh or Algiers; cannot be made in Moscow or Peking; cannot be made at the United Nations General Assembly—and surely should never again be made by such entirely misguided American missiles as Ramsey Clark and Andrew Young.

FOLLY NUMBER ONE: "PLEASE KICK"

Whatever the ultimate results of America's foreign economic policy in the Nineteen Eighties, and whoever its ultimate guiding personalities may be, let's hope we do not revert to the excesses of Folly Number One—when it became almost a badge of honor to beat on the United States, and when a number of our diplomatic policymakers seemed to be engaging in competitive self-abasement. The way to our pocketbook, much of the world came to believe, lay through our hyperactive national guilt mechanism. Indeed, sometimes it seemed as if the American people's attitude had changed, after two centuries, from "Don't tread on me" to "Please kick." Evidences of this strange bent for masochism surfaced at meetings such as that in 1977 in Paris, when we suffered through another round of abuse at an international economic conference on aid to "developing" countries. Apparently nobody found it insulting that the nineteen so-called Third World nations attending unanimously condemned the U.S. and seven other Western nations for not having made our checks larger. This country, whose worldwide assistance to others in the last generation is truly without precedent in human history, was flayed unmercifully—just as we have been at every similar conference since the earth's least successful peoples discovered they were a "bloc."

As long ago as 1964, when I was in Cairo for the major summit meeting of "nonaligned" nations, it was clear that their only true common policy consisted of loud—and generally unanswered—attacks on the United States. (Just as their only discernible common interest lay in raiding the coffers of the West.) This was a perversion even of the flimsy doctrine of "nonalignment" first promulgated by India's Prime Minister Jawaharlal Nehru. I interviewed Nehru at length in 1963 in his simple sunlit office in the sandstone Parliament Building in New Delhi, and talked to him on several other occasions before his death the following year. He always ritualistically repeated India's devotion to the three principles of "socialism, secularism and nonalignment"—but he was adamant that the last of these tenets was not an excuse for forming the world's poorer nations into what he disparagingly called a "third bloc." Indeed, the Indian leader had been intensely skeptical about the first "nonaligned summit meeting," at Belgrade in 1961, because he believed that "nonalignment" meant what it said —that it bestowed the freedom for each nation to steer its own course through the shoals of the nuclear age. He went along with the conference, however, using it partly as an opportunity to warn his colleagues against attempting to become a "third bloc" and thus sacrificing the very independence they were supposed to have chosen. Nehru, placing his emphasis on world peace, symbolized the brief golden age of nonalignment. In the postwar confrontation between the Goliaths of the United States and the Soviet Union, many nations—particularly those newly attaining independence— felt baffled and afraid, worried lest a nuclear holocaust destroy their dreams of material progress. They had in Nehru a guiding figure of towering eminence. While his influence might not always have been as great as they assumed (and while his theory was rooted in fundamental error: Moscow and Washington were not, in fact, equal threats to other nations), he was clearly admired in both East and West, as well as among the neutralists themselves.

Not one of his would-be successors as "leader of the nonaligned world," from Gamal Abdel Nasser on, could match him in this respect; and without the prestige of a Nehru, the nonaligned nations have been increasingly unable to hide the death of their policy. A "nonaligned" bloc that includes the likes of Cuba's Fidel Castro is an organization to be taken seriously only by State Department careerists.

Yet the hypocrisy of the "Third World" countries continues unabated. Consider the effrontery of Venezuela's minister for international economic relations, who regaled that 1977 meeting in Paris by denouncing Western offers of aid as "not commensurate with the magnitude of the great problems which the developing countries face" and "far below our expectations." This from the representative of a nation that is itself an enthusiastic participating member of the OPEC oil cartel: the group whose arrant selfishness and abusive use of economic power has damaged standards of living all over the world—notably including those in the poorest nations. For us to listen docilely to this kind of empty demagoguery on any occasion is to encourage its continuance, and to discourage the searching self-appraisals that might truly bring economic progress to these countries.

A more sensible U.S. policy toward the "developing" countries —in their interest as well as ours—would emphasize these four points:

(1) There really is no "Third World." Nations vary greatly, both in what is considered the industrialized West and in what is considered the underdeveloped world. The latter includes a range from oil-rich sheikdoms to the poverty-stricken marshes of Bangladesh. (Nor is it helpful, as some inventive diehards lately have attempted, to maintain the fiction of facile group definitions by creating new categories subdividing the "Third World" into "Fourth," "Fifth"—and ultimately, perhaps, "Eighteenth"— worlds. Leave the fifty-seven varieties to Heinz, which knows when to can them.) In the real—one—world, just as resources and problems may differ tremendously from country to country (and region to region), so do the techniques for dealing with them. Economic success or failure is not always foreordained by accidents of birth, either for nations or for individuals. See Taiwan vs. China, South Korea vs. North Korea and a string of other vivid

contrasts that make a mockery of any easy "North-South" delineation.

(2) We can help less successful nations, but we cannot do the job for them. The simplistic notion, popular whenever the representatives of the relative have-not nations gather in some posh hotel, is that the problems of poorer countries would be solved if only nations like ours would hand over a higher percentage of our gross national product. Two things are certain: it wouldn't work, and the percentage would never be high enough to satisfy the theorists of redistribution. I lived for more than two years in India, a country that, in terms of strictly economic aid, has been the most consistent drain on the American purse. Sadly, I am convinced that the Indian people would be better off today if we had withheld nearly all those billions of dollars. Too much went to the wrong places: to propping up a corrupt bureaucracy and to financing losing experiments in socialism. We were good of heart but weak of head. (One Indian observer suggested plaintively that things might have gone better if only the New Delhi Government had also been "nonaligned" between public and private enterprises.)

(3) The fast-fading colonial experience cannot be the perennial excuse for economic failure. Not only is the U.S. relatively guiltless in this regard, but in fact the economic infrastructure left by the colonial powers remains a key asset in many "developing" countries. Even more to the point, alibis for continuous failure—however theoretically valid—are no substitute for diligently pursuing economic progress now. It is also high time we stopped listening sympathetically to fiery accusations of "neo-colonialism" against multinational corporations, which in real life often represent the best hope of poorer nations to surmount national and historical barriers, and enter a more prosperous Twenty-first Century. If we do not speak up for such innovative, and hope-stirring, capitalism, who will?

(4) While we have no intention of pushing other nations around (and are willing to permit economic failure in those that insist on it), we do have some experience by now in what actually does work in economics—from Toledo to Taipei—and we intend to concentrate our future help on those who show good sense in making use of it. Devoted though many Americans are to wallowing endlessly in their own supposed guilt, the obvious economic

reality is that we will do better for others if we assert a little more respect for ourselves.

TOO GOOD A FRIEND AT CHASE MANHATTAN?

Two major changes have taken place recently in the ongoing battle over U.S. assistance to countries that often simultaneously savage our economic system and beg for a greater share of its benefits. The first, characteristically, is in nomenclature. Since "poor" apparently was considered an insulting designation, the original postwar euphemism was "underdeveloped" countries. The phrase purported to tell you more than it did (the way I figured it, one of the biggest underdeveloped countries in the world was the U.S.), but even it began to chafe after a while. And so, in determinedly upbeat fashion, the favored appellation became "developing." This was so flagrantly inaccurate in the case of some of these supplicants, however, that the new vogue phrase has become "less developed" countries—or, in the lingo of the trade, "LDCs." If a tenth of the time spent on devising euphemisms had been devoted to intelligently soliciting foreign private investment, and promoting a domestic incentive system, many of these countries would be worrying a lot less today about exactly what we called them.

A second major change has been in switching emphasis from outright aid to so-called loans—loans that, as the U.S. public increasingly has been discovering of late, in many cases quite likely will never be repaid. Hence we have been bombarded recently with alarms about the big American banks that, for some inexplicable reason, appear to have made so many weird overseas loans. To understand this phenomenon, you have to begin with a recognition that our liberal establishmentarians were having awful trouble getting those balky Congressmen to allocate enough money for every socialist experiment on the planet. The American taxpayer has never been exactly crazy about foreign aid, and as the realization grew that value for money was often considerably less than advertised, the notion became widespread that perhaps we ought to tend to our own frazzled economic knitting first. And so, as Tom Bethell pointed out in *National Review,* "In real terms, U.S. foreign aid—$7.7 billion in 1982—is half what it was in 1955." To the rescue of the giveaway specialists came the banks, who cheerfully went along with the concept of "recycling" hundreds of billions of dollars of OPEC money to "Third World" and avowedly Communist countries, on the pretense that these vast sums would someday be repaid. (The permissive lingo of the bankers was remarkably akin to that of many earlier aid officials; returning from Marxist Angola, David Rockefeller said an international bank like Chase Manhattan ought not "set itself up as a judge of what kind of government a country wishes *[sic]* to have.")

Before they knew it, these free-lending bankers—breezily acting in the belief that, as Citibank's Walter Wriston misleadingly put it, "countries don't go bust"—found that they were in a sea of bad debts far higher than their well-intentioned little heads. Indeed, a report by the House Banking Committee disclosed that the nine largest U.S. banks (Bank of America, Citibank, Chase, Manufacturers Hanover, Morgan Guaranty, Continental Illinois, Chemical, Bankers Trust and First Chicago) had outstanding loans to "LDCs" and Communist nations equal to about three and a half times their combined equity capital. The pressure was on for the Government to bail out the banks by increasing the U.S. subscription to the International Monetary Fund, without which the IMF might have to come up empty when a flotilla of debt-strapped nations came a-calling all at once.

Clearly, there should be a tight limit imposed on the extent to which the beleaguered taxpayer will be tapped to bail out imprudent bankers. The brunt of the financial penalty should fall where it belongs. (How ironic it is to see the same bankers who sternly rebuke you and me when we stray from the financial straight and narrow feverishly arguing that a competitive profit-and-loss system is marvelous for everybody except, of course, the bankers.) It is time we all, bankers and civilians alike, began to distinguish more critically among foreign petitioners for our cash. Mexico, for example, has a special call on our good will because of its geographical proximity, its economic significance (only Canada and Japan import more U.S. goods) and its legitimate prospects (not just oil but an industrious work force, particularly along the U.S. border, and a remarkable long-term real growth rate of 6.5 percent); but it is being damaged now by reckless nationalization and socialization, and if we do not attach reasonable conditions to any bailout, we will seem in retrospect actually to have been very poor neighbors indeed. But why in the world did we get in so deep with a country like Tanzania, whose Marxist leader Julius Nyerere won $1.5 billion in external loans—and the applause of countless world leftists for his "militancy"—while defaulting on debts to the U.S. and the World Bank, routinely disregarding conditions set by the International Monetary Fund, and transforming a bountiful land that had been one of Africa's breadbaskets into a ruined and bankrupt nation? And where did we get the idea that loans to Poland had to be safe because we could always count on the Soviet Union to bail them out (Moscow, in fact, turning predictably tough when its ally got in a jam)? The latest is that China, having already discovered how docile the U.S. can be when you give it an occasional smile between slaps, is itself beginning to eye the "soft" (i.e., frankly below-market) loan window at the World Bank—whose funds are largely extracted from U.S. capital markets and taxpayers. As the *Wall Street Journal* observed: "We have to ask ourselves soon how long we can afford to keep pouring capital into stagnant Communist economies." Surely, too, as the U.S. moves to tighten its belt on the lavish domestic-spending programs that are at the heart of the nation's historic budget problem, it is time to come in a few notches as well on what we have dispensed, with so much more generosity than wisdom, in lands far away from our own.

FOLLY NUMBER TWO: PUT UP A WALL

Folly Number Two in our foreign economic policy—the call for a higher trade wall to protect U.S. industry—is perhaps even more dangerous to us right now because of its obvious appeal to politicians seeking to capitalize on fears about the future of American jobs. Hence we see that eminent economic analyst and world statesman Teddy Kennedy telling steelworkers that "we must take whatever steps we must to see that Americans in the Nineteen Eighties and Nineteen Nineties will be buying American products made with American steel." Not to be outdone, that erstwhile high-minded liberal Walter Mondale announces: "We've been running up the white flag when we should be running up the American flag. . . . What do we want our kids to do? Sweep up around Japanese computers?" There is nothing narrowly partisan about such cant, however; Missouri's Republican Senator John Danforth informs us that "the problem that we have gotten into now is that the United States is practicing free trade, period—we are the exclusive practitioner of this ideal."

Okay, guys, you've won your rousing applause: now could you just back off for a moment and let us see what's actually going on in this area. There we find—surprise!—neither that the situation is as they have described it, nor that the remedies they demand would in truth do anything but net damage.

To begin with, such trade protectionism ignores history. Half a century ago, as virtually all serious historians now agree, nations that similarly tried to erect higher import barriers against other countries' products wound up shrinking trade and deepening the Depression. After World War II, realizing this, nations (now more than eighty of them) began gathering under the banner of the awkwardly named General Agreement on Tariffs and Trade (GATT), with the intention of learning from the protectionist errors of the Nineteen Thirties. The new organization worked admirably, not least for the United States. The export share of U.S. gross national product has more than doubled over the last three decades, to the benefit of American workers, businesses and farmers. I lived abroad during a period of maximum strength for the U.S. dollar and economy, and listened to a succession of American diplomats, business executives and union leaders preaching the glories of ever freer trade, of the free and unimpeded flow of goods and capital; in recent years, when the shoe moved slightly toward the other foot, I have found it a trifle difficult to reverse my own thinking quite so fast as, say, the steel industry or major segments of organized labor. Yet what we hear today is that talk about free trade is theoretical and "naive"; what we need now, we're told, is something different: "fair" trade. The assumption is that a country that encourages imports is making a sacrifice—which should be "reciprocated." But as the GATT secretariat correctly pointed out in a recent report, "The protecting country harms its own country first of all, and . . . any action which restricts its imports will also restrict its exports."

Let's see how this works: Protectionism raises the prices of the products protected, which no longer have to compete with the world market prices. This raises costs for consumers and businesses that use those goods. An import restriction like steel "trigger prices," for example, raised the cost of the steel used in appliances and other products U.S. companies were trying to export. Those products became harder to sell abroad. So by trying to prop up employment in the steel industry, the Government arbitrarily killed off potential jobs in these other, more marketable areas. The GATT report noted that an analysis of actual experience in a number of countries indicated that two thirds of an import duty is passed on to the export sector in the form of a "tax," while contributing to a lower level of national economic efficiency—and national income. In other words, even before you consider the possibility of foreign "retaliation" against U.S. exports, we hurt ourselves each time we race to "protect" ourselves. The astute Lindley H. Clark, Jr., calling this "shooting ourselves in the foot," observed incisively that "there can be no protection for the economy as a whole; someone has to pay for anything that one sector of the economy gains." It seems foolish enough to let big-government theorists "plan" our national investment in what they arrogantly claim to be able to recognize as the correct future growth areas for U.S. industry; how much more foolish it is to listen acceptingly to demagogues telling us that our future must lie in defending, at enormous national cost, the industries of our past.

"Aha," I can hear somebody saying right about now, "that's all very well in general—but we have a special problem with the Japanese. They have run up an enormous trade surplus with us over the last decade, yet they maintain noxious barriers to imports from the U.S. It just isn't fair, and we darned well better had retaliate." Well, I wish the Japanese would lower those barriers—in their own economic interest, as well as ours—and I favor strong, precisely targeted negotiation to convince them of where their interest lies. But our trying to pay them back in kind with across-the-board protectionism will wind up only slicing off a piece of our American nose. Consider, first, our own position. Are we really, as Senator Danforth exasperatedly insisted, that overly noble "exclusive practitioner" of free trade? Not on your import quota. As it happens, the U.S. has run up a trade surplus with the European Common Market over the last decade roughly the same size as Japan's surplus with us. (We don't hear so much about that, do we?) "Yes, but we do that honorably," the protest will come back. "We don't erect obstacles to imports into the U.S." Oh, yeah? How about, just for starters: "Buy American" statutes giving preference to domestic producers in Government procurement; the Jones Act prohibiting foreign ships from engaging in commerce between American ports; and an array of statutes limiting imports of agricultural and industrial products? Moreover, as Murray Weidenbaum pointed out after quitting the Reagan Administration, we can start the healthy process of reducing trade barriers by eliminating "our own obstacles to our own exports"—such as existing controls on exports ranging from oil and timber to horses sent by sea —and by encouraging our trading partners to open their markets "without using mechanisms that harm the international trading system or start a spiral of retaliation." Weidenbaum also had an apt remedy for the export problem created by the dollar's sharp rise in value against other currencies, a shift that made U.S. goods seem more expensive to foreign buyers: get down the interest rates that keep the dollar so high, by getting those wretched Government deficits under control at last. (Cheers! *Santé!* And *banzai!*)

Interestingly, trade protectionism is another area where (contrary to the folk wisdom that they never agree on anything) the nation's economists are almost totally in concurrence. Indeed, that former economics student Ronald Reagan (possibly reflecting the salubrious influence of his new Secretary of State) resisted the protectionist clamor in his 1983 Economic Report and asserted firmly: "While the United States may be forced to respond to the trade-distorting practices of foreign governments through the use of strategic measures, such practices do not warrant indiscriminate protectionist actions, such as domestic content rules for automobiles sold in the United States. Widespread protectionist policies would hurt American consumers by raising prices of the products they buy, and by removing some of the pressures for cost control and quality improvement that result from international competition." One could hope that Reagan would adhere to his own words in this case; nothing could be more loony than the local (also known as "loco") content bill that would require major world automakers to manufacture domestically 90 percent of the value of their cars by 1986—thereby offending everybody from Canada to

Japan, and costing the U.S. itself investments, jobs and exports. (When I lived in India and drove something called a Hindustan Ambassador, a similar regulation required a larger share of domestic parts in each year's model; the predictable result was that a fairly old Hindustan Ambassador wasn't such a bad little car, while the new models were overpriced and underperforming.)

You would think U.S. automakers—themselves victimized by the artificially rigged price of their major ingredient, steel—would begin to learn some of these lessons. You might wonder, too, why an issue on which economists find little to argue about should continue to attract hordes of eager politicians to the opposite side. For that matter, you might wonder why President Reagan, so trenchant in 1983, went the opposite way when it came to limiting Japanese auto imports in 1981.* So if any of this still seems a mite theoretical, let's now examine that "voluntary" quota on Japanese cars, and see why such things still happen—and whom they actually help and hurt.

Those who believe they are helped by limitations on Japanese autos are relatively small in number but enormously organized and identifiable. They include the U.S. auto companies, the United Auto Workers and the communities whose economies rely heavily on domestic auto production. On the other hand, those who are hurt by such actions are far more numerous and far more significant economically—but far less cohesive. (Guess which side has more political clout.) They include anyone who would have liked to buy a Japanese car but couldn't; they include anyone who wanted to buy an American car anyhow, but who now found it more expensive than it would have been if foreign competition had been unrestrained; they include many others who weren't even in the car market, or thinking much about this subject—such as

---

* Reagan repeated the error later in 1983 when he imposed stiff extra duties on Japanese-made heavy motorcycles. This protectionist move, like its predecessor, was clearly political. The U.S. motorcycle industry consists of only one company, Harley-Davidson, and affects only 2,500 workers. But officials had expressed fears that the Administration would be "vulnerable" if it allowed Harley-Davidson to go under. Ironically, the imposition of higher tariffs might turn out to benefit two Japanese companies, Honda and Kawasaki, which had established production facilities in the U.S.—and would now be further shielded from foreign competition. Let the bad economics roll!

workers in export industries, who found sales of their products lower than they might have been, and others who weren't hired because these market-efficient industries were not expanding as they might have. Thus, to justify this kind of restrictive anti-growth protectionism as a "jobs" measure is to look no further than a week from Tuesday—or just plain to engage in a political lie. The quotas did not enable Detroit to reopen plants; they merely raised prices, limited choices and encouraged Japanese automakers to fill their allotments with higher-priced models that competed more directly with our sagging "Big Three." Once, while he was still Ronald Reagan's chief economic adviser, Murray Weidenbaum slyly asked me if I knew who was going to win the next Nobel Prize in economics. "No, Murray," I straight-manned, "tell me who is going to win the next Nobel Prize in economics." The Government's top economist grinned boyishly. "Whoever can figure out," he replied, "how limitations on Japanese auto imports fit into supply-side economics."

HOW TO DEAL WITH FRIENDS—AND ENEMIES

Just as we are wrong to let xenophobic emotions interfere with rational self-interest in dealing with our friends (after all, as Prime Minister Yasuhiro Nakasone has pointed out, Japan is already the biggest market for American agricultural products, taking 58 percent of our beef exports and 39 percent of our citrus; besides which, if the Japanese learn the international economic lessons as fast as they've learned the domestic since World War II, they'll be crumbling their remaining trade restrictions faster than you might think), so we are wrong to attempt to ignore the realities of economics in dealing with our adversaries.

Consider first what happened when we handed the Soviet Union that infamous wheat deal at President Nixon's Moscow summit in May 1972. Two months later, Soviet buyers entered the U.S. market and bought up all our emergency wheat reserves at the going price of about $1.31 a bushel. "The Soviets had an excellent crop and really didn't need U.S. wheat," recalled Professor Beverly Kitching of Chicago State University. "They sold and resold their American wheat contracts in commodity exchanges around the world, boosting wheat prices from about $1.31 to $6 a bushel in eighteen months." Moreover, at the time the Soviets increased prices for the American housewife and stole profits from American farmers, the loan terms approved by Nixon were 6 percent and up to three years to pay; an even more generous new law assures that in any future such deal the Soviets might have up to ten years to discharge their debt. It should not, I think, require too much argumentation to convince us that this is a route we should tread more warily in the future.

The other side—trade acts as punishment—carries just as many flaws as the notion of trade acts for rewards. Trade sanctions, like import restrictions, exude a sort of visceral appeal to those to whom foreigners are, at best, an annoyance—and, at worst, the reason for all our woes. The trouble, again, is that the sanctions just don't work. Even the moral point becomes ambiguous when it can be clearly seen that, for example, embargoes stiffen the supporters of apartheid in South Africa—and fail totally to dislodge the Soviets from Afghanistan. The final bill tends to wind up on our own shores; American creditors bore the brunt of Jimmy Carter's freeze of Iranian assets, and American farmers were the true victims of his grain embargo. Ronald Reagan, under Western European pressure, finally had to back off from his adamant opposition to the Soviet gas pipeline. (In this, he was guided, wisely, by Shultz, who had pointed out incisively before taking office that trade sanctions are a messy weapon that often misses the target and floors the one who fires.) The point is that we should neither cater to nor moralistically shun those whose systems oppose ours: we should do the business that is good for America. The last President to serve two terms in the U.S. would have understood this better than some of his successors. "We should sell the Russians," Dwight Eisenhower once said, "anything that they can't shoot back."

XI

Oui, the People!

The most beautiful part of being a typically irresponsible, free-spending, high-taxing American politician is that in the end, when your actions produce entirely predictable economic chaos, you can turn right around and blame it on your constituents. Best of all, they probably will buy it. In the University of U.S. Thought, the perennially popular courses include Guilt 301, Mea Culpa 202 and Hit Me Again I'm American 407. It's not just in the obvious sense that we are the fools who voted for these fellows, and hence are arguably getting the Government we deserve. (The average politician, if told that 52 percent of his constituents were leaning toward virgin sacrifice as a cure for inflation, would promptly have a word or two to say in favor of propitiating the wrathful gods. On a quota system, presumably.) But even worse: after these politicians are installed amid the extraordinary appurtenances of Washington political power, they lose no time in explaining that what is good in our lives comes benevolently from their hands, while what is bad is the unfortunate but inevitable result of our own unseemly avarice. That they should make this attempt is perhaps understandable (re-election being the grand prize in their lives, if not necessarily in ours); that we should let them get away with it is less forgivable. Yet we Americans seem ever ready to accept arguments that exaggerate Government's role as a problem solver and understate its role as a problem creator and exacerbator.

We have seen how this worked in areas such as energy, where

Americans listened docilely to accounts of our own culpability (by a President shivering in a cardigan), hastened to implement 55-mile-an-hour speed limits and lower thermostat settings—and allowed the establishment of an even grander Government bureaucracy as our only hope for salvation. How baffling, then, that when we finally moved not to increase but to remove Federal controls, the problem at which those impediments supposedly were directed magically seemed to solve itself. That "permanent" shortage, that enduring and frightening "crisis," simply vanished. Could there really be a free—and working—market out there in this world, after all? Similarly, we were bombarded for years with campaigns designed to deflect blame for inflation. ("It's not just Government," a cowboy humorist informed us in one major advertising campaign—a worthy successor to the chestnut that tries to sell U.S. Savings Bonds by urging us to "take stock in America": a total confusion between debt and equity that would lead to the suspension of a first-year stockbroker.) Then it turned out that when the Government stopped printing money at a multiple of the rate that even this economy could reasonably handle, inflation (abracadabra!) came tumbling down faster than anyone in Federal City had contemplated. And just before the 1983 economic recovery became so unmistakable that even politicians and economists had to notice, that unreconstructed apostle of Government-the-savior, John Kenneth Galbraith, let it be known in a television interview that there was no hope of economic revival because we had not taken the interventionist steps he advocated—but were foolishly trusting in that messy private marketplace to do the job for us. Once again, it would seem, the wrong people were taking the course in Mea Culpa.

This does not mean, however, that the last of our ten areas, the Individual, is any less critical than the first nine (Education, the Budget and Taxes, Monetary Policy, Banking and Credit, Labor, Business, Regulations and Restrictions, Energy and Foreign Policy). For in the end, each of us is left with the abiding question: What the devil can we do until we get leadership that will not just talk pretty at election time, but will actually get in there and do what needs to be done? As we live in hope that Ronald Reagan eventually will come through more fully—and put our money where his mouth is—I suggest that you keep some powder dry. In your own affairs, I think it's essential that you seek such protection against a possible resurgence of inflation as you possibly can —for yourself and for your family. That's not unpatriotic, as self-righteous politicians periodically imply; it may ultimately be the most profound and enduring form of patriotism, providing islands of private solidity in a sea of public mismanagement.

But how can you do it, once you have determined on this course? Well, for example, by saving and investing as best, and as intelligently, as you can, in a difficult, frustrating and ever-changing environment. And don't let anyone ever tell you that it's easy, or that there's one magic investment that always goes up, or that there's one infallible human being who can always "get you in at the bottom and out at the top." As we have recently had occasion to discover once again, such a person has not yet been born—even in the state of Florida. That's why we at "Wall $treet Week" can't just put on the same guest every week, why we try always to give you the widest possible range of expertise and opinions on the widest possible range of investments—even though we know this leaves to you the difficult and painful task of individual thought and decision. The one consolation I can offer is that if you actually indulge in that process, you're likely to find that you not only come out ahead of most other individual investors, but you're probably going to beat 95 percent of those august institutional investors as well. (Just as one should not believe everything he or she hears in Washington, so one should not believe everything heard in Wall Street, either. That is a haven for the biggest bunch of nervous Nellies in the United States of America. Those fellows are forever panicking one way or the other. Paul Samuelson once calculated that the stock market had predicted eleven of the last four recessions.) Those dominant institutional investors—the pension and mutual funds, the banks and insurance companies—now account for more than two thirds of the trading on the New York Stock Exchange, and this extensive dollar activity is sometimes confused with wisdom. Don't you believe it. The typical institutional investors have all the characteristics they (incorrectly) ascribe to the individual investor: they tend to be stampeded by each passing emotion, they tend always to be buying at the same time, always to be selling at the same time—and always to be buying and selling the very same issues. (Once, while addressing a meeting of institutional investors, I apologized for the harshness of some of my appraisals, but said I was speaking to them under an unfortunate circumstance: I was familiar with their actual investment records.) The individual who can remain cool amid this institutional hysteria often does remarkably well. Besides, he has a couple of special advantages: the size of his transactions is not large enough to disrupt the normal price course of a particular security (which means that he can get in and get out economically, without raising the price when he buys and lowering it when he sells), and he doesn't have to report his quarterly results to anybody (which means that if he's smart and doesn't get hung up with cocktail-party boasts about how well he's doing, he is able to maintain a time perspective somewhat longer than a week from Tuesday).

The smart individual, then, will find ways to set a few bucks aside, even when everybody else around him (and his own desires for instant material satisfactions) tells him that this is "impossible": that all his earnings must be spent. He will take advantage of the slim inducements provided by the Government to encourage savings and investment, such as Individual Retirement Accounts. He will be distrustful of would-be gurus who announce that they have called the last twenty-three turns of the investment markets (yet always seem to strike out just when you begin to follow them). He will remain flexible and keep some balance in his investments. (I have, for example, long disappointed gold bugs and gold haters alike by suggesting that perhaps 5 to 15 percent of a person's long-term investments ought to be gold or gold-related. I doubt that this will be the best-performing part of the portfolio over the next decade, but it is a useful hedge, and enables many people to sleep better at night—which is certainly an acceptable use of their money. Over the years, gold's price tends to be affected by such factors as the U.S. inflation rate, the degree of perceived world instability and the prevailing price for crude oil. To guarantee that all these will remain low for the next decade is further than I personally would be willing to go.)

Well-selected real estate will continue to have a useful investment role, too, despite the despair of much of the early Nineteen Eighties. (I once wrote a newspaper column that, inadvertently, almost precisely called the turn on the break in California real estate prices. I said I was no special expert in this area, but had been disturbed to notice three guests within two weeks on TV talk shows confidently advising their viewers that they could not lose money on California real estate; one lady announced that an increase of 2 percent a month was guaranteed. I observed that my experience with markets suggested that whenever somebody told you you couldn't lose money on a particular investment, or that some apparently dazzling return was guaranteed, it was time to button your wallet pocket and look elsewhere.) The tax system encourages real estate ownership through special deductibility and depreciation provisions, and land that meets the classic real estate test of "location, location, location" is itself a useful hedge at a time when permanent control of inflation remains elusive. That illustrious investment adviser Will Rogers advised Americans a couple of generations back to "buy land—they ain't making any more of it." He also counseled that making money in the stock market was easy: "You buy a stock that goes up, and when it goes up you sell it. And if it don't go up, you don't buy it." For most Americans, though, the Nineteen Eighties should be a mite different from the Nineteen Seventies where real estate is concerned; members of the typical family probably will think of their home more as the place where they choose to live—the role it has occupied through most of American history—rather than as the shrewdest investment they could possibly make.

While counseling flexibility and individual thought (which, when prescient, is marvelous for the ego as well as the pocketbook), I will not duck the question of where I think the bulk of the average family's investment portfolio should be placed. I have long believed that the Nineteen Eighties would be the decade of common stocks. I said so frequently during the late Nineteen Seventies, and a national magazine used this apparently eccentric assertion as its headline on a cover story about me in 1980. As regular viewers of "Wall $treet Week" know, I have no special interest in peddling stocks, or anything else; if we could find a guest who would tell our viewers how to make more money by trading rare speckled goldfish, we would put him on in a flash. (We're no strangers to fishy markets of any kind.) But I was convinced that a historic turn was coming in the stock market. My avowal of this view did not always make me popular. When I told one interviewer in the spring of 1982 that the secret of investment success was merely to buy low and sell high—and she, predictably, laughed as if I hadn't said anything worthwhile—I added that the advice was easier given than taken: stocks were low right then, I told her, but you couldn't get the average person to buy them. (Common stocks are the only commodity in America that reverses normal market behavior: when you cut their price in half, nobody wants to buy them; but if you double the price of IBM, it's suddenly considered a terrifically desirable acquisition.) After the historically dramatic and sustained run-up in stock prices that began in August of that year, it became less unfashionable to speak well of prospects for the stock market. On the theory that what you really want to know, though, is what I've done for you lately, let me give you my updated long-term view. It is, as it happens, exactly the same: we have barely begun this decade of common stocks.

I have three main reasons for reaching this judgment. They are political, economic and psychological. Politically, as I have tried to suggest throughout this book, the media preoccupations with such misleadingly compact slogans as "Reaganomics" or "supply-side economics" have been a classic case of ignoring the next generation's forest while focusing on this week's tree. Ronald Reagan is interesting historically because, unlike most modern U.S. political leaders, he did not move toward the country, but waited for the country to move toward him. In this important respect—a phenomenon that often has been misunderstood even by his own accommodation-minded White House advisers—the Reagan election triumph in 1980 can be seen as a product of a continuing national tide, and not just as some highly personalized aberration. In short, then, this change of national mood is not tied exclusively to a single President (or a single party), and cannot be altered by a single election's results, favorable or unfavorable.

Imagine that this book had appeared at the start of 1978, and that I had written something like the following: "This year, this (Democratically controlled) Congress, with Jimmy Carter continuing to sit in the White House, is going to come up with a tax bill that will surprise you. It will not be anything like the one you're reading about in the Washington press reports, or hearing about on the evening television news. It will not have anything to do with 'the three-martini lunch,' and similar excursions into demagogic irrelevancy. It will not raise the capital-gains tax, as the President insists it should. It will, in fact, lower the capital-gains tax, and it will lower personal income taxes and it will lower the corporation income tax as well.'' Surely, most readers, in the climate prevailing then, would have turned to a companion and said: "Who is this loon, and what world is he living in?" In fact, though, every one of those things happened in the 1978 tax bill. Congress may not have gone as far as some of us would have wished, but it unmistakably reversed the anti-savings, anti-investment trend that had evidenced itself so devastatingly in the tax bills of 1969 and 1976. Congress went dramatically further down this new pro-savings, pro-investment path in 1981, despite its regrettable backward step a year later. Now, why did Congress embark on this significant new course in 1978? Why did it reverse the trend of a decade of national tax legislation? Why did a Democratic Congress deliver an unprecedented humiliation to the tax program of a Democratic President? As I observed in the earlier discussion of the budget and taxes, I'm inclined to doubt that this was because our noble legislators had undergone a spiritual conversion that year on the road to the District of Columbia. On the contrary, I suspect that, as usual, their damp fingers were reaching for the wind, and that they detected a somewhat different breeze from their constituents. I believe that this breeze is flowing still, with varying vigor but unmistakable persistence. What powers it is disillusionment with endlessly expanding Government; it carries less hostility to business, less repugnance toward profits, a greater respect for economic growth and freely operating markets. All that eventually must be good for business, good for the economy, good for the country—and good for the stock market. The changing political climate should be a decided long-range plus for investors in equities.

Economically, there is a pair of factors pointing eventually to much greater stock-market gains. The first is that by any of a long string of historical economic measurements, stocks remain cheaply priced—though obviously not so cheaply as before they began their massive advance in 1982–83. To make money in investments, it is never necessary to be able to pick the exact bottom and the exact top: indeed, that capacity still eludes every human I have encountered. All you really have to decide is whether a particular investment is closer to the basement than the clouds. And most stocks are still a long way from any fundamental overpricing; indeed, when the Dow Jones Industrial Average was charging to new nominal records in early 1983, it was still—adjusted for inflation—only about a third as high as it had been in 1966. In other words, the market would have had to triple in order to set an authentic new all-time record. And that encouraging reality leads us to the second economic factor: comparative performance. The trouble with most investment advisers, I have found, is that they give their counsel by looking through a rearview mirror. They tell you what you should have done. This is not a terribly difficult, or challenging, task. Thus the vendors of gold heavily advertised, at the start of the Nineteen Eighties, how beautifully gold had done in the Nineteen Seventies. Similarly, a decade earlier, the mutual-fund industry kept showing us what a winner it had been in the Nineteen Sixties. On neither occasion was the boastful campaign as useful a guide to the future as to the past. Heck, *I* can tell you what you *should* have done; you should have taken all your money at the start of the Nineteen Seventies and put it into Chinese ceramics, selling them at the peak of the "collectibles" craze a decade later. I hope you were that brilliant: I wasn't. I have to do my investment thinking by looking not through the rearview mirror but through the (always foggier) front windshield. And my suspicion is that the greatest room for explosive growth in the next decade lies in those investments that have not already increased geometrically in the last. Given that markets generally race to excess in both directions, I think there are economic arguments for sticking predominantly with those investments that seem to be on a vigorous comeback trail rather than those whose admirers are lost in nostalgia about the glories of yesterday.*

* Attractive groups within the stock market are numerous. The technology area, while given to periodic bursts of overenthusiasm, clearly will play an increasing role in America's future. The demographic changes referred to earlier will bring investment opportunities, too. A maturing population may want fewer jeans and more business clothes. The growing group of affluent retirees will be in the market for travel, leisure-time activities and health care, including pharmaceuticals and hospitals. The rapidly changing financial-services industry provides numerous avenues for successful investment. Energy companies will return to favor as "oil glut," like "oil shortage," proves temporary. Particularly desirable over the longer term may be companies that stress domestic energy production and com-

Finally, there is the psychological reason for making this assessment of the stock market. Despite the remarkable improvement in stock prices tracing not just to the spectacular 1982 turnaround but as far back as the market lows of 1974 (since which time, hundreds of stocks have strongly outpaced the Dow Jones Industrial Average), despite the unimpeachable fact that millions of investors have made a great deal of money in the stock market during those years, the average American seems neither to know nor believe it. (Nor was such skepticism limited to the admittedly uninitiated; right through the big market advance, I received telegrams and phone messages every week from professional advisers who wanted me to be the first to know that they had, that day, called the exact top of the market—except of course, as it soon turned out, they hadn't.)

Go out into the streets of the average American community, stop the first twenty people you meet and ask them about the stock market; the typical response will be something like this: "Look, I may not be the smartest person in this town, but at least I am smart enough not to take my hard-earned money and put it in the stock market." And history suggests that whenever this is the overwhelmingly typical response, that time has, in fact, been a pretty good time to take your hard-earned money and put it in the stock market. (In contrast, when the dominant mood is unrestrained euphoria concerning the stock market, when every party you attend is full of talk about how you can't lose in Wall Street, and how the local brokerage has just acquired a miraculous twenty-three-year-old gunslinger who will triple your money by Saint Swithin's Day, history suggests that that will be a very good day to start taking your profits and looking elsewhere.) My father tells of encountering his old friend Bernard Baruch around the time the Dow Jones Industrial Average was hitting its Twentieth-Century low in the summer of 1932 (the closing bottom was 41.22, in case

---

panies that provide oil services and equipment; the oil business remains chancy, and it's comforting to have some of your chips on the firms that will do business no matter who hits the gushers. While "cyclical" companies, those whose fortunes tend to match the overall economy, will come in and out of favor, longer-term investors should emphasize "growth" companies: those that can persistently increase their earnings at a rate faster than that at which the general economy is expanding.

you like to collect macabre statistics). Baruch, to my father's surprise, was looking extremely chipper. And when my father observed that it had been a "tough day at the market," Baruch smiled, shook his head and allowed a faint glint to enter his shrewd old eyes. "Not for the buyers," he replied.

Now, none of this should be taken as short-term get-rich-quick advice. (I am as wary of those financial best-sellers that purport to tell you how to achieve affluence by next Tuesday as I am of those that inform you the world will end a week from Thursday.) I would never advise anyone to take all the money he or she could beg, borrow or steal and put it in the stock market, or anything else. To begin with, sensible financial planning requires starting with liquid assets: cash and those equivalents that can be quickly, dependably turned into cash at moments of personal or family emergency. (Distress sales of more speculative assets tend to be disappointing sales.) It also makes sense to take care of insurance needs and to be buying (or saving to buy) a home before embarking on possibly more ambitious investment adventures. Even at that point, it is well to keep in mind that markets move in both directions; some of the best advice ever given about the stock market was that of J. P. Morgan: "It will fluctuate." This means that volatility is a market characteristic you will want to factor into your own investment planning, which suggests equally avoiding panicky selling and overly effusive buying. A wise program for many investors is what is called "dollar-cost averaging": make up a list of some of the fastest-growing, financially sound corporations in America— the ones you yourself are convinced will be catering most efficiently to the nation's changing needs, desires and life styles in the Nineteen Nineties—and then put a set amount of money into each of those stocks at set intervals. Unless and until you find a fundamental reason to change that list, then, you will be investing that set amount of money every month, or three months, or six months, or whatever you can afford—without regard to where the price of the stock is that day (i.e., how many shares of the particular stock you are acquiring each time), or where the Dow Jones Industrial Average is that day, or what the merchants of hysteria are selling out on Page One that day. If you pursue that kind of intelligent, sustained investment program with diligence over the next decade, I suspect that you will be a good deal happier and richer when it is completed. The only thing that could prove me wrong (and I don't expect to be wrong) would be an economic catastrophe of such dimensions that you really would not have saved yourself by putting all your funds instead into gold bullion, or Southern California real estate, or those fabled rare speckled goldfish. My advice, I hasten to add, is not based on any conspicuous belief in the quality of our political leaders; it is based, instead, on a belief in the basic, and recently revivified, strengths of the American people. It's my view that, despite all evidence to the contrary, our country will somehow muddle through to greater prosperity over the next decade—and if it does, the stock market should participate handsomely.

I wish it to us all.

YOU CAN BE A CAPITALIST, TOO

Saving and investing for the future no more makes you a part of "Wall Street" than learning to drive makes you an official of the Department of Motor Vehicles. But those who would convince us that all economic benefits must flow from a benevolent (if bankrupt) Government often try to create a class-war distinction between those who do such investing and those who, as they see it, are simply too deprived. This is nonsense far more often than the average person realizes. More than 30 million Americans are direct stockholders and more than half the nation is involved indirectly through such stock-owning affiliations as pension funds and insurance companies. Indeed, that economic philosopher Peter Drucker has argued that the true economic condition of the country is becoming "pension-fund socialism," as ownership of the means of production is transferred to the workers themselves through their massive retirement funds. The genuine fat cat, then (though neither he nor anyone else probably would recognize him as such), may be wearing not a silk topper but a hard hat. But you need not indulge in such theoretical speculation to see your own self-interest in this area. We humans are by nature gifted rationalizers, and it is easy to conclude that we simply can't afford to do any saving or investing this year. Resist the impulse. Those who do well in this area are by no means universally born to affluence or the recipients of enormous current incomes; my mail at "Wall $treet Week" regularly contains dazzling success stories from "ordinary" workers who, starting small but continuing regularly, have amassed investment portfolios that would shame the average lawyer or corporate executive in their town. Character can be as important as capital in this area.

There is, incidentally, no discernible connection between personal self-advancement and political-economic views professed for others: everyone, I have found, can rationalize his own search for a more comfortable life style. When it comes to one's own home and family, there is nothing "conservative" or "liberal" about wanting to live better—and being absolutely convinced that you deserve it. I once interviewed a multimillionaire advocacy lawyer and asked him whether it was true that he called himself a socialist. "Absolutely," he replied with the pride of the truly self-righteous. "Well," I said, "you live in a lavish apartment on Park Avenue, you travel around New York City in a chauffeured limousine, you live a life that to 99.9 percent of the American people would seem a life of impossible luxury. Do you see any contradiction between the way you live and the values you profess?" "None whatsoever," he declared without a moment's doubt or hesitation. "I wish our society were structured differently—but, since it isn't, I will live in it as best I can." So, when people ask whether capitalism is not an economic system built on "greed," it would be well to keep in mind that all economic systems are built on "greed": our own in fact may give the average guy the best chance of satisfying his own legitimate desires without some bureaucrat telling him he is a criminal for wanting to live as well as the commissars.

The problem of capital formation is not unique to capitalist societies; every country, no matter how it organizes itself, must face this basic problem of how it is going to amass the money it needs to grow. Rather than apologize for the traditional American answer to this problem, we should hail and treasure it, for it gives to the average wage slave the chance to build his own estate, and to provide a measure of financial security for himself and his family that is unattainable in more class-ridden societies. In an era when self-reliance has gone out of favor in many intellectual quarters, we should honor and encourage those who pursue it, and not denounce or impede the worker who wants to own his own taxi, send his kid to a better college or provide more generously for his own retirement. To be sure, the typical small investor is not going to attain the riches of Croesus (or even Rockefeller), but he is a far more solid citizen than those demagogues who would cut him off at the pass.

THE INTELLIGENT ECONOMIC CONSUMER

Unfortunately, most conventional advice to individuals seeking better ways of coping with our national economic troubles has been of the most superficial "personal finance" variety: e.g., how to beat inflation by buying your air conditioners in January and your skis in July. The view in this corner is that the individual's most important role in this area is to become a more skeptical consumer of political pap about the structure and functioning of the U.S. economy. He or she should be wary of those who prate about "compassion" and then wind up "compassionately" laming the golden goose of American production. When the discredited answers of endless income redistribution are promulgated as a "compassionate" substitute for the working methods of private incentives and investments, the wise individual will be smart enough to recognize this as demagogic gruel—and punish at the polls those who reflexively confect it. Jack Kemp was surely right when he commented on "Wall $treet Week" in 1983 that we could not genuinely "help America's poor by making America poor."

The intelligent economic consumer will also reject those at either end of the ideological spectrum who attempt to frighten us by exaggerating America's weaknesses. He will remember that, difficult though the problem of assimilating a "baby boom" of new workers has been, the U.S. actually created 24 million new jobs in the Nineteen Seventies while Europe gained only 2 million. (And the unemployed remained in that condition far longer over there: 30 to 50 percent of each Western European nation's jobless stayed that way for six months to a year, while the median duration in the U.S. was about eight weeks.) He will be suspicious of those who maintain that we have fallen hopelessly behind in comparative living standards. As Walter W. Heller perceptively pointed out, "When exchange-rate distortions are stripped away to reveal the actual flow of goods and services per person in different countries, the U.S. still leads the pack. With U.S. per-capita output as the benchmark, the closest competitors are Germany, France and Japan, at 90, 80 and 70 percent of our living standard.''

Similarly, the more astute consumer will reject the faddish view that we are no longer masters of our own economic destiny: that economic problems have become so international in their complexity that no one country can hope to solve them. This was part of the implicit rationale for much of the hand-wringing that characterized the Carter years. In truth, though, the U.S. remains by far the strongest entity in world economics. For years this enabled us to export our own inflation to the rest of the world. But it has worked just as unmistakably on the positive side; when the U.S. moved to a less inflationary policy in the early Nineteen Eighties, the results were awesome and almost breathtakingly swift: by early 1983, the U.S. inflation rate was the lowest of all major industrialized nations. Clearly, as this book frequently has contended, ours is an interdependent world in which no nation is an island unto itself, but there is still one nation capable of firm and impressive leadership—in either direction. In case anyone has forgotten, it's the occasionally self-doubting giant that nestles between Ontario and the Rio Grande. As Walter Hoadley, the discerning former chief economist for the Bank of America, observed, ''A new surge in American home-grown confidence, based on a more realistic appraisal of our capability and resources relative to all others, could touch off a wave of new expansion of enormous value to our people. Almost certainly it would be followed by a similar wave in other parts of the world, helping to ease many political and economic tensions. . . . In stark reality, actual or perceived weakness of the U.S. now constitutes one of the most destabilizing forces across continents as well as within our national boundaries. In contrast, any new global perception and conviction of more U.S. will and power to compete internationally will constitute an exceedingly strong force to accelerate national and global economic growth, as well as contribute to peace for ourselves and others.''

The wise consumer, then, will be dubious of those who run down our national potential, or tell us that our growth is behind us, or seek to pit us against our neighbors by insisting that one man's prosperity must now depend on another man's loss, or in general tell us that the vast potential of human economic freedom must now be subordinated to imperial economic fiat from Washington. He will be, perhaps, most suspicious of all of those who perpetuate statist mythology in the Orwellian misconception that it is truly in the interests of—of all people—"the consumer." He will laugh at those Congressmen who inform us that we must continue to control natural-gas prices "to help the consumer"—who presumably is assisted most by Government-induced shortages, artificial production limitations and bureaucratic resource misallocations (and who presumably has slept right through the recent experience in which the free market brought down the price of oil where all the "planners" had failed). He will scorn those "consumer crusaders" whose loudly professed concern for our individual interests (for which they immodestly claim the unique right to speak) always seems to translate ritualistically into distrust of private enterprise and reverence for the enlargement of Government. In short, the next time a "humane" apostle of even bigger Government tells him that some new proposed aggrandizement of Washington's interventions into America's liberties is necessary and desirable to keep the rude private economy from doing damage to "the consumer," our intellectually armed consumer will know the precisely correct response. It is the cheer that was born in the Bronx.

WHAT MORE WE CAN DO

What else can the prudent individual do, besides trying to arm himself intellectually and financially? He can vow to make his own contribution to improving the quality of America's economic output. Fully 63 percent of 508 U.S. manufacturers surveyed by the Conference Board in 1983 reported that they were using some foreign-made machinery in their American factories not because of "unfair trade practices" or "slave labor" or any of the customarily trumpeted rationales but simply because they found that the equipment made abroad was higher in quality. Several years ago, when the Japanese incursions into the U.S. automobile market were first becoming dramatic, I asked the reigning Number One auto analyst in Wall Street, Ronald Glantz, what were the principal reasons for this phenomenon. "Well, first of all," he replied, "they make better cars." Each of us can make an internal pledge, in his own as well as the national interest, to work a little harder and care a little more about the product that emerges at the end of each day's work. We may even find that in this search for excellence we have improved not just the quality of our work but the quality of our lives.

In a more defensive sense, I think it would be sensible for the average individual to seek to borrow the techniques of cost-of-living clauses in his or her own personal arrangements of all kinds. Instead of merely decrying the fact that others got there first and have made possibly excessive use of this tool, I would recognize that in one form or another it will be here to stay until we do a much better job of permanently controlling inflation. This means that those who have neglected these techniques ought now to think creatively of how they might intelligently put them to use, to their own advantage, wherever possible. Some defense against future inflation ought legitimately to be part of every long-term contract you sign, whether on the income side as an employee or on the yield side as a lender or investor. Indeed, if the Government itself is sincere about finally getting its financial house in order, it might simultaneously reduce the carrying costs of the national debt and offer new protection to thrice-burned lenders by issuing Government bonds whose return would be indexed to future rates of inflation. Understandably skeptical bond buyers, who recently have demanded historically high risk premiums against the prospect of future inflation, might indeed settle for a lower current return if they were contractually assured such protection by the issuing Government itself. Such a change would help every taxpayer, too, by trimming the inescapable interest expenditures in the Federal budget.

What else can the well-armed citizen do to protect his other interests? Here's one I think is tremendously important: I think you ought to alert your representatives in Congress that you are going to be watching them closely, and insisting that they keep their word (on which many are clearly so anxious to renege) to continue indexing the Federal income-tax system to inflation.

Here is the perfect litmus test for responsibility in handling the people's money. Yet many in Washington have been trying ever since this vital provision found its way into the tax code in 1981 to welch on what threatened to be the best tax benefit you never got. That benefit is so-called tax indexing, a fancy name for a simple idea: the Government should have to ask for a tax increase when it wants one, and not be able to let inflation do its dirty work for it. Written into the 1981 tax bill during its passage through the Senate was a provision that, starting in 1985, three key items—tax brackets, personal exemptions and the standard deduction—would be adjusted each year, in the taxpayer's favor, to reflect the inflation rate. While the indexing provision (for which some of us had been arguing for many years) got considerably less attention than President Reagan's plan for three-year across-the-board tax cuts, indexing was potentially of much greater value to the typical taxpayer— particularly those in lower- and middle-income groups. Lowest-income taxpayers would benefit most from indexing of the $1,000 personal exemption and the $3,400 "zero bracket amount," or standard deduction. And since the tax brackets change more rapidly at lower levels, so-called bracket creep—being pushed into a higher percentage bracket solely by inflation, rather than by any real economic gain—was more severe among those of moderate incomes. (The Government once calculated that repealing indexing would raise the taxes of those with incomes under $10,000 by more than 9 percent—but those with incomes over $100,000 by less than 2 percent.) Moreover, indexing promised, at all economic levels, that the income-tax system would, for once in our lives, be on the level: ending the traditional system under which Government's own inflation annually pushed its citizens into higher tax brackets, but left them with less buying power.

Given these undeniable benefits both in economics and in equity, you might wonder why indexing has been so controversial. The answer, unfortunately, is simple and familiar: politics. Signs had been mounting ever since the provision was enacted that it might be an early victim of Washington's preoccupation with budget balancing through tax increases rather than spending cuts. For all its more recent fervor, the Reagan Administration itself scarcely earned unrestrained plaudits on this subject. Indeed, Treasury Secretary Donald Regan volunteered in 1982 that "indexing we'd discuss," adding pointedly that it "wasn't part of the President's original package"—and neglecting to mention that Reagan proudly took credit for the indexing provision. (In case you're baffled by Reagan's initial failure to propose indexing, I asked a top member of his staff in early 1981 why he had not done so—and was told that the reason was simple: the idea of indexing had "no sex appeal." And you think *I'm* tough on these politicians?)

Congress's reluctance to adhere to indexing is even easier to explain. As things stand, the tax writers of Congress are immensely important personages in our society. (To see allegedly all-powerful businessmen fawning over a key committee chairman has been one of the lesser pleasures of my convention travels.) If you maintain indexing, you are taking away from these fellows an important part of their ongoing prerogatives: not just the ability to tinker aimlessly with the rules of the game, but the ability to deliver—with seeming magnanimity—periodic highly popular tax "cuts" that are, in reality, only partial and erratic adjustments to the intervening inflation. No wonder, then, that House Ways and Means Chairman Dan Rostenkowski—whose powers would be among those most significantly curtailed—derisively tried to castigate indexing as "simply throwing a lifejacket against inflation." (His Senate counterpart, Finance Committee Chairman Bob Dole, deserves more credit for favoring indexing "as a simple matter of equity" and arguing that "no issue is more important to the working man or woman.") Over the years, when I have privately discussed indexing with key national legislators, the typical response has been wounded astonishment that I would take away their present ability to enjoy annual "inflation dividends": without indexing, you see, inflation pushes people into higher percentage tax brackets each year, and thus (though their real incomes have not risen, and may indeed have fallen) the Government's share of their paychecks is enlarged, and Federal revenues increase even faster than wages and prices. This hidden, unlegislated tax boost for U.S. workers was patently unfair—particularly for the "little guy" and the "ordinary middle-class American" for whom politicians always show such solicitude at election time. It was a system that in an era of continuing inflation allowed high-percentage tax brackets originally aimed at "the rich" to scoop deeply into the incomes of the average American family, whose true economic condition was anything but affluent. Best of all, nobody had to vote for the additional tax. And all the power to alleviate this annual injustice even slightly lay in the hands of the guilty recipients: those spending-happy Congressmen who shared such a large responsibility for the inflation itself, and whose periodic tax "remedies" were (predictably) far more likely to delve into electorally packaged income-redistribution schemes than into anything resembling the restoration of simple equity. Yet when brash folks like myself have had the temerity to propose a change to automatic indexing (or to insist now that it be fully implemented), the characteristic reaction on Capitol Hill has been a sense of injury that we would impede the ever-expanding money machine that Congressmen have depended on to finance all their exciting new spending. "What do you want us to have to do," they would ask me indignantly, "actually pass a bill explicitly raising taxes every time the Government needs more money?" "That's exactly what I want you to have to do," I have replied, "and, you know, I don't think that under those conditions you will do it as often or raise taxes as much."

The counterargument tends to dress itself in apparently pragmatic clothes: indexing is a splendid ideal, and might indeed be a more equitable way to run a tax system in the best of all possible worlds, but we simply can't afford it right now—just look at the size of those deficits. The Congressmen who talk this way are reminiscent of the fellow in the old story who murdered both his mother and his father and then pleaded in court for clemency on the ground that he was an orphan. Who in the world do they think is responsible for the present sorry state of the budget—and what conceivable evidence is there that giving them even more tax revenue would get them to behave more carefully with the people's money in the future? The Treasury estimates that the repeal of indexing would raise tax revenue by $17 billion in 1986, $30 billion in 1987, $44 billion in 1988 and even more in later years; by 1988 this would mean that the repeal of indexing, all by itself, had raised taxes by more than 10 percent. What's more, this is based on the Administration's possibly optimistic long-range inflation forecasts (even after a decade of inflation at only 4 percent, taxes without indexing would be 25 percent higher); it could well be worse: a 6.5 percent inflation rate would mean a tax increase, without indexing, of $80 billion (instead of $44 billion) by 1988 alone, while a replay of the escalating inflation rates of the Carter years would increase nonindexed tax receipts in 1988 by a whopping $120 billion. Do we really want to encourage the habitual spendthrifts in Congress to look forward to this additional grand theft from the people? As Martin Feldstein, then the chief Reagan economic adviser, persuasively argued in a *Wall Street Journal* article in 1983, the repeal of indexing would give Congress a strong incentive to pursue inflationary policies: "With indexing gone, spiraling inflation would generate a surge of tax revenues that could finance greater Government spending while permitting Congress the political luxury of voting occasional 'tax cuts' that actually failed to offset inflation but provided a framework for income redistribution." No wonder, then, that Feldstein concluded that "the long-term success or failure of Ronald Reagan's economic program is likely to hinge more on retaining tax indexing than on any other piece of legislation." Is that an interesting enough idea for you—or would you rather have the White House preoccupy itself with "sex appeal"?

Ironically, those noneconomic Reagan advisers whose notions of smart politics always seemed to involve repudiating portions of the program on which he was elected had been characteristically slow to grasp the potential popular strengths of indexing. It would benefit everybody, essentially, because the tax system would be fairer and more honest (legislators would have to call a tax increase a tax increase—and not take it under the table as an automatic inflation bonus). But, most of all, indexing would help lower-income people; as noted, inflation-induced "bracket creep" was more common with them because tax brackets are closer together at the bottom end of the scale, and personal exemptions are proportionately more important. With all the talk, largely fraudulent though it may have been, about how most of the 1981 tax changes amounted to "welfare for the rich," you might think there would have been more outcry from the White House—and, for that matter, from the "compassion"-attuned media—about the continuing threat to default on full tax indexing (which, according to a 1980 study by the Advisory Commission on Intergovernmental Relations, would have twice as much impact on taxpayers making $10,000 as on those making $50,000). But, unless the public wakes up in time, an almost-unnoticed throat-cutting still could occur.

Long before the Congressional assault on indexing began making the front pages, I talked about this with one of the country's top experts on the prospective change, and was disturbed to find that he shared my concern that the average taxpayer was about to be betrayed without ever fully understanding what was being done to him. Francis M. Gaffney, national tax director of the Main Hurdman accounting firm and a member of the indexation task force of the American Institute of Certified Public Accountants, told me that although he was "firmly convinced" that the present system "can be inequitable and repressive on low- and middle-income taxpayers," it would be "difficult" to keep the promised relief, "since indexing will stop making available to our Federal Government the continuation of increasing amounts of tax revenue without the necessity of passing specific laws to raise that revenue." The future change pledged in 1981, and grudgingly begun in 1985, "will only be maintained," Gaffney warned, "if there is a greater understanding on the part of the American voters of indexing and the impact it will have on the tax burden borne by them."

The question, then, becomes: Are you mad enough to let your Congressman know that you, at least, are aware of what indexing could mean in restoring equity and sanity to the nation's tax code—and are determined to preserve it, as promised? I'm convinced that one of the most useful steps an intelligent individual can take in his or her own interest in the immediate future is to demand that this Government (which, for all its perennial finger-pointing at everybody else in our society, remains itself the one true source of most of this nation's inflation—which started the inflation, and which annually prolongs it through its own fiscal and monetary irresponsibility—at least no longer be allowed to punish us each year by letting *its* inflation boost *us* into ever higher tax brackets, with ever lower buying power. As the bare minimum for progress there, for decency and equity and honesty, we ought to insist without equivocation that the Government be compelled to come through on its highly belated promise, and continue fully indexing *its* tax system to what is, after all, *its* inflation. We will thus stop letting the Government itself, through the Internal Revenue Service, become each year the biggest single beneficiary of the Government's own inflationary villainy.

Indexing won't solve all our tax problems, but it will go a long way toward improving and clarifying the rules of the game. And (as I hinted earlier) any economic idea that gets that many conventional, entrenched, power-nourished Congressmen that exercised cannot, I suspect, be all bad for the rest of us. The power to tax was correctly defined by Chief Justice John Marshall as involving the power to destroy; legislatively lessening the destructive power of fickle Congressmen over our individual economic lives should not, I venture, be viewed as unfortunate by anyone who lives more than three miles beyond the Potomac.

The Challenge and the Chance

If our noble public servants were to make just one resolution for themselves in the years immediately ahead, please let it be this: don't let America's pain have been in vain again. Yet while the U.S. economy moved in the mid-Nineteen Eighties from the anguish of deep recession to three years of unfamiliar expansion, the fundamental problems outlined in this book unhappily moved little closer to enduring solution. The menace of exploding debt not only failed to disappear, but changed into ever larger and more hideous numbers. As budget deficits persisted and grew even during the prosperous portion of the economic cycle, those in command grew ever vaguer and less optimistic about transforming red ink into black. By 1985, a re-elected Ronald Reagan was admitting that his target for the U.S. deficit by the end of his second term had expanded to an incredible $144 billion—which meant, given the notorious unreliability of anything resembling a long-term forecast in Washington, that there was no longer any genuine target at all. Ironically, the country seemed readier than ever for the new direction it was conspicuously failing to get: Walter Mondale, preaching in 1984 the old-fashioned follies of income redistribution, had been rejected in forty-nine states. He had been the personal choice not only of the AFL-CIO bosses, whose influence waned ever more conspicuously, but of the media-revered "liberal" Congressional apparatus headed by Tip O'Neill. All in the end turned out to be paper pussycats. Mondale's celebrated (but conventionally leftist) running mate, Geraldine Ferraro, made the cover of *Ms.* but in the end could not deliver even her own Congressional district—or a majority of Italian-American women. America's voters seemed to be speaking as loudly as they could.

And how did the re-elected Reagan Administration respond? By having its then Secretary of the Treasury, Donald Regan, propose a tax "simplification" plan that looked like a rewrite of Jimmy Carter's lost hopes—right down to increasing, rather than lowering, the tax on capital gains (and even abolishing the dreaded, and ever more mythical, three-martini lunch)—while the President himself allowed himself to be cornered into promising to abandon any thought of reining in future Social Security benefits. Regan, before swapping jobs with White House Chief of Staff James A. Baker 3d, blandly produced a tax plan so attuned to routine fiscal demagoguery, and so remote from any genuine concern for encouraging savings and investment, that it wound up being denounced by the Administration's best and wisest friends in American business—while being praised to the skies by the likes of George McGovern and Ralph Nader. A more sensitive operation might have been given pause by this reaction, but White House staffers preferred, as usual, to give it a purely political twist: what fun it would be to stand with "the people" against "the special interests," and never mind that Ron had devoted a quarter century to campaigning against just such sophistry.

Ironically, though his popularity had never been greater as his second term began, Reagan also had never been further away from the ideas by which he first made his way to Washington. Consider: the original Reagan program had four main planks.

Spending was to be cut. It wasn't; the Government's slice of the nation's income expanded to new record proportions. By 1985, the dreams of dramatic spending reductions had gone mockingly awry, often with the President's own foolish assistance. And the old promise of a balanced budget by 1983 had long since been consigned to the junk heap of historic bad jokes.

Taxes were to be cut. The much-vaunted 1981 reduction didn't deliver any net tax relief at all until 1983 and 1984—when, not at all coincidentally, the long-awaited economic recovery finally arrived. But Congress chipped away, year by year, at the limited benefits it had permitted, meanwhile rendering the tax code ever more complicated even while it talked glibly about "simplification." The 1985 edition of *J. K. Lasser's Your Income Tax* commented that the

1984 Tax Act—the fourth annual outbreak of massive tax tinkering in the Eighties, with more assuredly to come—was "the most complex tax measure passed in thirty years," had "no one objective or theme," but managed "to make an already complicated tax law much more complex and onerous." For the executive and legislative architects of this monstrosity then to moralize about the tax code, as they cheerfully did in 1985, was nervy even by Washington's expansive standards.

We were to have a steady monetary policy. We didn't; the only thing consistent about Federal Reserve policy has been its wild inconsistency. To be sure, the overall effort was, correctly, to moderate the inflationary growth of money. Moreover, despite all the empty talk about an alleged failure of "monetarism," this plainly worked; we achieved with remarkable rapidity what the gloomsters—and the Keynesians—had called "impossible": a dramatic slowdown of price increases. Nineteen eighty-four was the third straight year in which consumer prices increased at a rate of 4 percent or less. But the erratic month-to-month and quarter-to-quarter implementation of this monetary policy served both to keep interest rates higher than they should have been—nervous lenders simply didn't know which way the Fed was going to veer next—and to worsen and prolong the economic slowdown. Even when recovery came, this uncertainty continued to frustrate any serious private efforts at long-range planning. It's important, then, to distinguish between the beneficial effects of an overall multiyear thrust and the damaging effects of having failed to pursue it more steadily. Seen in this light, both of the "surprising" results were predictable: inflation did indeed come down, but the recession was needlessly exacerbated. As noted in Chapter IV, some decline of economic activity invariably accompanies any effort to check a serious inflation, and those snake-oil salesmen who glibly promise otherwise have read no history. But the ill effects can be mitigated and shortened by clarity of policy and consistency of execution. We needed significantly more of both. As for the Reagan Administration view of monetary policy—to the extent it existed at all—it appeared to have evolved by the mid-Eighties into calling constantly for easier money out of one side of the mouth, while taking full credit for Paul Volcker's successful inflation control out of the other.

Finally, a major policy of deregulation was to be carried out. As we've seen, you'd need a highly partisan microscope to discern any momentous progress on that one.

But concern about the long run has never been a major preoccupation in our nation's capital, and the short-run economic news was undeniably good: real growth in 1984, at 6.9 percent, was the best since 1951, while the annual increase in the GNP deflator, a broad measure of price increases, was the lowest since Lyndon Johnson's Presidency. Could it be that a rosy new era had dawned, and all those nagging old problems we'd been worrying about should be consigned to the ideological ash can? Alas, no. Clark Gable once suggested as his own epitaph: "He was lucky, and he knew it." We as a nation were lucky on inflation, and didn't know it. As OPEC's death throes continued apace, world commodity prices stayed dramatically under control. U.S. workers, chastened by a savage recession, were notably slow to escalate their wage demands amid a recovery marked by sustained joblessness. Plant capacity was so ample as to avert any immediate concern about "overheating." And, best of all for a nation that continued to run up deficits as if there need never be an accounting, foreigners looked so approvingly at the vigorous U.S. recovery, and at our renewed status as a haven of stability and relative sense, that they poured marks, francs, yen and pounds into the American economy and into American securities—thereby making the dollar historically strong (to the distaste of American exporters and the joy of American tourists) while providing the wherewithal to fund our deficits without triggering immediate inflation. But only an ostrich, or a politician, would assume that we had truly eradicated the business cycle—or abolished arithmetic.

With all the hyperthyroid media attention that focused first on the passing symptoms of recession, then on the "miracle" of recovery, we were in danger of forgetting why we undergo this periodic agony. The fundamental problem was, and is, inflation. It was ominous that, while politicians prematurely celebrated "permanent victory" over inflation in the mid-Eighties, the rate of price increases actually was higher than it had been as recently as 1971, at which time we found that inflation level so intolerable that we turned in desperation to wage and price controls. The recent relaxation of any concern about the continuing threat of inflation's resurgence is dangerous—and familiar. Three times in the Nineteen Seventies, when the inflation rate temporarily receded and unemployment rose, we announced that the former problem was licked and the latter demanded our full attention. Three times we were wrong. In truth, as we should have learned by now, but apparently haven't, these problems are inextricably entwined. Each time we abandon all pretense of fighting inflation, the cycle begins anew. The inflation bogey comes back at even higher levels than in the last go-round. Distortions and imbalances are created throughout the economy, trust in our currency deteriorates both abroad and at home, and interest rates—the price of money—go even higher, as lenders reckon they need ever-greater protection against this cheapening of their assets. Ultimately, as the country threatens to go into the inflationary tank that has drowned so many other nations over the centuries, the politicians and monetary authorities move belatedly to slow things down. The worse the inflation, the more severe the necessary cure. When deep thinkers on the public payroll tell us that promises to balance the federal budget were just a $200 billion misunderstanding, when they pretend that unrestrained spending as usual is terrifically "compassionate," when they act as if inflation won't return no matter how foolishly we behave, it's time to take economic swimming lessons once again.

The good news lately has been that the economy picked up steam spectacularly after a multiyear period of sluggishness that spanned two formal recessions, under two Presidents. The bad news, however, is that the conventional economic thinkers of Washington seem to be picking up steam, too. Just when we have a shot at the first noninflationary recovery in two decades, the unreconstructed political hacks on both sides of the aisle appear determined to wreck it by charging ahead on the same tax-and-spend track that brought us to economic collision in the first place. It's time for somebody to throw the switch on them.

Cause and effect are the vital missing ingredients in most current discussions of economy. Sweeping judgments are made about the program of whoever happens to be sitting in the White House at the time, but more often than not this is just barroom rhetoric. Ronald Reagan was no more solely responsible for the dreadful recession of 1981–82 than he was solely responsible for the roaring recovery that ensued. At first, when we were undergoing a wrenching downturn, the idea built up that the President's economic program could safely be denounced as a failure, suitable for interment—when a more accurate analysis would be that the program was a set of promising ideas that nobody actually ever bothered to try.

While a large part of the blame for failure to translate the eminently sensible (and scarcely revolutionary) original Reagan goals into economic reality lies with the political opposition, the President's putative allies in Congress were far from innocent. The erratic Bob Dole whooped through a ludicrously counterproductive tax increase in 1982 that, within a matter of months, could be seen to be slowing the economy and widening the deficits it was designed to reduce. And it turned out that Howard Baker was really interested in cutting domestic spending only when you didn't happen to be talking about, say, the Clinch River breeder reactor or the Tennessee Tombigbee canal. (Congress, overall, would have to improve its record to qualify as mediocre. For all the occasional talk about recognizing past errors, Congress basically continues on a spend-and-spend, tax-and-tax binge that frightens those whose investments could create jobs and winds up increasing suffering among those whom the legislators say they are protecting and defending. As a minimal resolution for itself, Congress should pledge, with or without White House assistance, to stop posturing about keeping Social Security inviolate—or reaching only for tax-paid Band-Aids such as those advanced in 1983—and start passing some sensible long-range changes that would truly keep the system solvent.)

Then there's President Reagan himself—a tax cutter in 1981, a tax raiser in 1982; a budget balancer in 1980, a creator of record deficits in 1985. He, too, has scarcely earned an unblemished report card in economics. His initial assault on Federal spending was overly timid, with fully three quarters of the budget exempted from any cuts at all. More recently, he has failed notably to accompany his insistence on heightened defense spending with any meaningful plan for reversing the expansion in so-called entitlements: those runaway domestic-spending programs that have laid such an insupportable, and universally damaging, tax on those who do the nation's work.

The President, in truth, has never been the "stubborn ideologue" (or, indeed, the "ultraconservative") who has been regularly depicted in so many of our news media: the facile creation of some of my journalistic colleagues to whom, I suppose, anyone to the right of the latest Harvard University faculty consensus is a reactionary—and Fidel Castro, presumably (as I suggested earlier), is an economic moderate. The authentic Ronald Reagan is a flexible politician who was not above doing a little easy scapegoating of Wall Street in 1981, or indulging in the ridiculous demagoguery of "jawboning" the banks to lower interest rates in 1983. (It doesn't take a graduate degree in political science to understand that the banks, like Wall Street, are always readily available for any vote seeker who wants to demonstrate "populist" credentials by taking cheap shots at expensive places. To the extent that this may be emotionally therapeutic to the politician involved, I suppose it does no permanent harm. But, in the real world, blaming the banks for interest rates is about as rational as blaming the thermometer for the temperature it shows.) When, in 1985, he refused to propose either a credible way out of the entitlements dilemma or even a clearly overdue new procurement and management regime at the Pentagon, the real Ronald Reagan may actually have been standing up again.

It would be nice if, before leaving the White House, the President would return to basics: submitting not a holier-than-thou Balanced Budget Amendment but a braver-and-smarter-than-thou Balanced Budget. He was surely right when he said the proper route to such an elusive balance is not through further tax increases, however disguised, but by reducing the share of national income taken away from private growth and sent to Washington. To reach this vital destination, though, he will have to tame those of his political counselors who have been guilty successively of overpromising and overcompromising. With each new Administration in recent years, I have been asked to analyze the men chosen as Presidential advisers in economics, and I have dutifully, publicly done so. By now, though, I have become convinced that this is a meaningless academic exercise: the issue is not what these learned economists are going to tell the President, but to whom he is really going to listen—and what he, personally, is then likely to do. If Jimmy Carter pays heed to Ham Jordan rather than Mike Blumenthal, if Ronald Reagan is swayed more by Mike Deaver than Marty Feldstein, then the apparent distinction between political and economic advisers becomes a chimera. In the end, most modern Presidents have gotten their operative economic advice from their political advisers. In Reagan's case, his inner political circle's initial nonsense about painless overnight success through the magic new remedy of "supply side" economics was as foolish as were the opposition's heated retaliatory denunciations of "Reaganomics." The actual Reagan program was less startling—and less coherent—than either side claimed. Later, the White House geniuses began urging the President to "moderate" his "extremism" and cooperate instead on a "bipartisan" economic program with such models of governmental frugality as Tip O'Neill. Why be "stubborn" about genuinely curbing spending or encouraging savings and investment when the polls say the public now has other things on its mind? Didn't the President amiably win overwhelming re-election, even if he did neglect to mention until embarrassingly late in the campaign that it might be nice to have a supportive Congress, too?

Well, sorry, but—"centrists" to the contrary—if one person says two and two make four, and someone else insists that two and two make five, the best possible answer does not automatically lie in compromising on four and a half. And the test for all our lawmakers will not be how well they rate in each week's passing poll (or fickle media assessment), or how much they publicly bleed for the unfortunate, but how well they avoid recklessly reinflating—and thus creating even worse joblessness the next time around. The real cruelty would be to commit all the same inflationary mistakes once again. If the politicians cannot extend their own memory spans a bit, the electorate will surely have to begin to extend its. After a long stall clearly traceable to previous unchecked Government spending, the private economy is struggling at last to recover and set out toward a better era; the last thing it needs now is one more blast of inflation—from a speeding train of reckless spenders, powered by the winds of Washington.

WHY I'M STILL AN OPTIMIST

Where, then, does that leave us? Often those who happen to agree with my less than reverent assessments of our political leaders ask me how, given these deficiencies in Washington, I can continue to emerge as an optimist. The answer is simple: the nation is immeasurably stronger than its politicians. We can continue to hope for a President who will not just embark on a better economic track but will turn out to be a true long-distance runner (and not just a flashy sprinter, shifting from lane to lane with each new report from Dr. Gallup); we can continue to try to redirect the breezes that influence the wet fingers of Capitol Hill. But our ultimate power, and our brighter future, must come from inside. If you have stayed with me this long, you know I don't believe that we can just sit back and be rescued by a knight on a white horse—even one presented by the President of Mexico, with jelly beans in its saddle bags. The American President's role is undeniably important: both by action and by regularly talking economic common sense, he can alter the focus of too many recent Administrations on "luck" and "circumstances," and overcome that feeling of being buffeted by irresistible gales that make failure and frustration inevitable, of having to endure fatalistically (if "fairly" and "compassionately") while our national condition inexorably deteriorates. (As a strong foreign leader named Napoleon Bonaparte once put it, "Circumstances? I *make* circumstances.") But while sound leadership can help us to survive on a planet that will never be without risk, the genuine source of my still-guarded optimism lies elsewhere. It lies in you and me.

Out of the disillusionment that is so evident in our society, something truly hopeful has begun to sprout. Don't look now, but there are, indeed, some deeply encouraging signs—signs going beyond a single year, or a single economic cycle, or a single party, or a single President—some signs that, believe it or not, from one coast of this country clear across to the other, capitalism may just be coming back into style in the United States of America.

And if it makes it (and don't think it will not face a titanic struggle from the rear-guard forces of state control), that's going to be the biggest real economic story not just of the Nineteen Eighties but of the entire American generation ahead.

There are things going on in our country that, though slimly reported, are historically important. I get around the country practically every week of the year, not just speaking but listening, too, and what I heard during our latest economic cycle was quite different from what I had heard during other recent periods of

economic decline and recovery. By the time conditions got anywhere near the bottom in the past, the woods had been full of
people demanding that the Government step in and "control"
distasteful elements in the wayward economy. This last time, the
woods seemed full instead of people saying, in effect: "The heck
with having the politicians control the economy. This time, can't
somebody control the politicians—who keep lousing up the economy."

I submit that a nation whose thought patterns are evolving in
that way is not necessarily a nation heading for inevitable doom.
What's more, there has even been some unmistakable impact on
the denizens of the Washington jungle. Where until recently the big
issue in economics had been who could be more "fair" and
"comprehensive" in taking even more of the people's money away
from them, we began to be treated to such occasional spectacles as
the one observed earlier: the United States Congress, of all people,
accusing Ronald Reagan of fiscal irresponsibility—and insisting
that he pay more attention to getting rid of the deficits in the
Federal budget. Now, some people, to be sure, have been a trifle
cynical about this sudden interest of the long-term arsonists in
heading the national fire brigade. They have doubts about this
marvelous new competition in fiscal responsibility. They detect—
would you believe it—a whiff of insincerity, a hypocrisy along the
Potomac. For myself, though, I am (as you may know) a naive and
trusting soul. When our political leaders talk this way, I applaud
unreservedly. As far as I'm concerned, let this brand-new battle to
see who can deal most responsibly with the people's money rage
on unabated for at least the next 150 years.

Even when the interest is not wholly authentic (which is, alas,
about 99.3 percent of the time), it is at least symptomatic of a great,
and I believe, hopeful new truth about America: a truth that was
written pretty clearly on the continental wall, for those not too
ideologically blinkered to see it, long before Ronald Reagan sent
Jimmy Carter and Fritz Mondale back home to their word proces-
sors. For the politicians have begun—however feebly, however
imperfectly, however inconsistently—to get at least some of the
message that so many of the people have been trying for so long to
send them. (As Willard C. Butcher, chairman of the Chase Manhattan Bank, aptly put it, "A different realization is sinking in. Whole

societies are rediscovering that governments cannot create wealth. They can only divide, subdivide, allocate and consume wealth. And the bigger they are, the more national wealth they consume. Entire populations are rediscovering that productivity cannot be regulated into existence—but is all too easily regulated *out* of existence.") And that's why I am not, in the end—in any sense— one of these highly fashionable (but soon, I believe, again to be proved highly wrong) prophets of extreme, inevitable and unrelenting gloom and doom for the American economy of the next decade. Despite all the doubters, and the would-be governmental stewards of our alleged infirmity, we have within ourselves the potential for a future prosperity of a strength beyond anything even these blessed shores have ever seen.

IT'S UP TO US NOW

Finally, then, it really is up to us. I don't want you to think that I have written this book as your friendly neighborhood Pollyanna. I don't believe that we're about to solve all our major American economic problems (we may *never* get them *all* solved), but I believe earnestly that, contrary to too much of what we continue to hear and read these days, we do, most definitely, have a chance.

For the first time in my lifetime—for the first time in half a century—the mood of the American people plainly *is* changing. After half a century in which every one of us was brought up to believe that whenever a social or economic problem could be detected anywhere in our society, the proper way to deal with that problem was somehow to expand the role and authority of the Federal Government, Americans of all descriptions and every economic group have been discovering, one by one, that that alleged panacea turned out to be a bit of a phony: that it didn't work the way it was advertised to work, and that we had better be looking for a better way to solve our problems in America in the next half-century.

I believe that there is such a better way, and that that better way would be a way that emphasized individual freedom, personal responsibility, human incentives and opportunities—and those vast and unfathomable natural resources that still lie buried within each of the 240 million of us individually. But if those who believe as I do that that would be a better America, a freer America and a more prosperous America for every one of its citizens just sit back on our hands and let those who believe otherwise do all the talking, get all the headlines, make all the running, then I think we will be criminally liable to our children and to our grandchildren.

I hope we won't miss this historic opportunity truly to turn our country around. We cannot all be national leaders, but, more important, we can all be contributors to national thought. Sometimes people say to me, "What do you want me to do? Write my Congressman?" That alone can be helpful, and sometimes more meaningful than you think: you may not convert him, but chances are the fellow can count. Beyond that, there are myriad available arenas in which the concerned citizen can speak: letters-to-the-editor columns in publications, parent-teacher associations, chances to talk oneself to students and others about what the system actually has meant to you. We hear much of the traditional importance of voluntarism in America; I suggest you enroll yourself now as a permanent and enthusiastic volunteer for the American economic system. For if that crusade fails, many of the others will become irrelevant. I would hope that a year after reading this book, you would be able to look into yourself and say with sincerity: "Well, I did my part—and, you know, I honestly do believe that we are on our way at last." That may not give us final triumph in our quest for the still-possible dream, but at least it would give us occasion to hope that it would never be said of us, as it once was of the British, that the reason the sun never set on the British Empire was that God didn't trust the English in the dark.

Index

281